JOURNEYS

Reader's Notebook

Grade 5

Houghton Mifflin Harcourt

Contents

Unit 1

Lesson 1:   A Package for Mrs. Jewls   1

Lesson 2:   A Royal Mystery   13

Lesson 3:   Off and Running   25

Lesson 4:   Double Dutch: A Celebration of Jump Rope,
Rhyme, and Sisterhood   37

Lesson 5:   Elisa's Diary   49

Unit 2

Lesson 6:   Quest for the Tree Kangaroo   61

Lesson 7:   Old Yeller   73

Lesson 8:   Everglades Forever:
Restoring America's Great Wetland   85

Lesson 9:   Storm Warriors   97

Lesson 10:   Cougars   109

Reader's Guide: *Hound Dog True*   121

Unit 3

Lesson 11:   Dangerous Crossing   157

Lesson 12:   Can't You Make Them Behave, King George?   169

Lesson 13:   They Called Her Molly Pitcher   181

Lesson 14:   James Forten   193

Lesson 15:   We Were There, Too!   205

Unit 4

Lesson 16:   Lunch Money   217
Lesson 17:   LAFFF   229
Lesson 18:   The Dog Newspaper   241
Lesson 19:   Darnell Rock Reporting   253
Lesson 20:   The Black Stallion   265
Reader's Guide: *About Time: A First Look at Time and Clocks*   277

Unit 5

Lesson 21:   Tucket's Travels   301
Lesson 22:   The Birchbark House   313
Lesson 23:   Vaqueros: America's First Cowboys   325
Lesson 24:   Rachel's Journal: The Story of a Pioneer Girl   337
Lesson 25:   Lewis and Clark   349

Unit 6

Lesson 26:   Animals on the Move   361
Lesson 27:   Mysteries at Cliff Palace   372
Lesson 28:   Fossils: A Peek Into the Past   383
Lesson 29:   The Case of the Missing Deer   394
Lesson 30:   Get Lost! The Puzzle of Mazes   405

Reading and Writing Glossary   G1

Name _____ Date _____

Reader's Guide

A Package for Mrs. Jewls

What Was He Thinking?

When a story character tells a story, we only know what he or she is thinking and feeling. When a narrator tells a story, the readers get to know what all the characters are thinking and feeling, even if the other characters do not know it.

Read page 22. Look for information about what Louis is thinking or feeling. Write his thoughts in the thought bubble. Start with *I*, like you are Louis. Remember, other characters may not know what he is thinking!

Think about the information in the thought bubble. How does this information help you understand the plot of the story?

_____

_____

_____

Read page 25. What is Louis thinking or feeling now?
As Louis, write your thoughts in the thought bubble.

Think about the information in the thought bubble. How does this information
help you understand the plot of the story?

_____

_____

_____

_____

_____

_____

Name _____ Date _____

Lesson 1
READER'S NOTEBOOK

A Package for
Mrs. Jewls
Vocabulary Strategies:
Using Context

Using Context

The items below include two sentences. Choose a word from the box to fill in the blank so the second sentence restates the italicized idea in the first. Use context clues to help you choose the correct word.

> numb   deliver   stranger   package   label
> trick   courtesy   matter   surprise   unorthodox

1. Louis began to *lose the feeling* in his fingers. His hands became

   _____.

2. It was *a box wrapped in brown paper*. A _____ had

   come in the mail.

3. His visit was *not expected*. The students enjoyed the

   _____.

4. Safety was *a serious subject*. Our committee discussed the

   _____.

5. The *directions on the bottle* were "once a day." Medicines always

   come with a _____.

6. *Good manners* make life easier. It pays to practice

   _____.

7. An *unknown teenager* came to the park. The class avoided the

   _____.

8. The *practical joke* upset a few of the boys. A _____ is

   not always funny.

9. My aunt *brought* a present. She was excited to _____

   it to my sister.

10. The teacher had a *peculiar* system. Her instruction was

    _____.

Name _____ Date _____

Short Vowels

Basic Write the Basic Word that best completes each group.

1. a force, a pull, _____

2. cheap, miserly, _____

3. rock, teeter, _____

4. pledge, vow, _____

5. panicky, excited, _____

6. stack, batch, _____

7. unfeeling, deadened, _____

8. pep, power, _____

9. speedy, fast, _____

10. crumple, squash, _____

11. amusing, silly, _____

12. point, aim, _____

13. hard, strong, _____

14. climate, temperature, _____

15. clutch, grab, _____

Challenge 16–18. Imagine you are hiking up a mountain. Describe the experience. Use three of the Challenge Words.

_____

_____

_____

_____

_____

_____

Spelling Words

1. breath
2. wobble
3. blister
4. crush
5. direct
6. promise
7. grasp
8. numb
9. hymn
10. shovel
11. gravity
12. frantic
13. swift
14. feather
15. comic
16. bundle
17. solid
18. weather
19. energy
20. stingy

Challenge

instruct
distress
summit
massive
physical

Spelling Word Sort

Write each Basic Word beside the correct heading.

ă	Basic Words: Challenge Words: Possible Selection Words:
ĕ	Basic Words: Challenge Words: Possible Selection Words:
ĭ	Basic Words: Challenge Words: Possible Selection Words:
ŏ	Basic Words: Possible Selection Words:
ŭ	Basic Words: Challenge Words: Possible Selection Words:

Spelling Words

1. breath
2. wobble
3. blister
4. crush
5. direct
6. promise
7. grasp
8. numb
9. hymn
10. shovel
11. gravity
12. frantic
13. swift
14. feather
15. comic
16. bundle
17. solid
18. weather
19. energy
20. stingy

Challenge
instruct
distress
summit
massive
physical

Challenge   Add the Challenge Words to your Word Sort.

Connect to Reading   Look through *A Package for Mrs. Jewls*. Find words that have short vowel sounds. Add them to your Word Sort.

5

Name _____ Date _____

Proofreading for Spelling

Find the misspelled words and circle them. Write them correctly on the lines below.

Today I planted a hundred apple seeds. The wether is fine and dandy. This morning, it was so cool that I saw my breth. A little chickadee followed me along today. His short himm to the sun made my work as light as a fether. I wish I were as fast as that tiny bundel of energie. My shovle rubbed a blyster on my hand. This evening it is numm. By day's end, my bag of seeds was getting heavy. But as long as I can wobbel along, I will not be stinjy with my seeds. Boys and girls need apples to krush into apple cider. They love apple butter and apple pie, too!

1. _____   7. _____

2. _____   8. _____

3. _____   9. _____

4. _____   10. _____

5. _____   11. _____

6. _____   12. _____

Spelling Words

1. breath
2. wobble
3. blister
4. crush
5. direct
6. promise
7. grasp
8. numb
9. hymn
10. shovel
11. gravity
12. frantic
13. swift
14. feather
15. comic
16. bundle
17. solid
18. weather
19. energy
20. stingy

Challenge
instruct
distress
summit
massive
physical

Simple Subjects and Simple Predicates

A sentence is a group of words that expresses a complete thought. Every sentence has two parts: a subject and a predicate. The **simple subject** is the main word that tells whom or what the sentence is about. The **simple predicate** is the main word that tells what the subject is or does. When a sentence is a command, the subject is understood but not stated.

simple subject   simple predicate
The school <u>staff</u> (awaited) the delivery of the package.

[<u>You</u>]   (Hold) the door open, please.

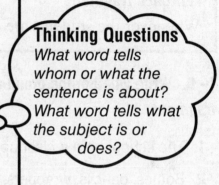

Thinking Questions
What word tells whom or what the sentence is about? What word tells what the subject is or does?

1–4. Read the complete sentences below. Underline the simple subject and circle the simple predicate.

1. Frank delivered packages and mail to the school every day.

2. The package in the brown box was by far the heaviest.

3. The contents of the box weighed over 50 pounds!

4. Luckily he spotted Louis in the doorway.

5–7. Read the complete sentences below. Write the simple subject and circle the simple predicate.

5. The early morning is a busy time for the school principal. _____

6. Wait by the classroom door. _____

7. The teacher wrote the directions on the board. _____

Sentence Fragments

A sentence is a group of words that expresses a complete thought. A **sentence fragment** is a group of words that does not express a complete thought.

sentence fragment
Whenever the students are outside.

Thinking Question
Does this group of words tell whom or what and also what is or what happens?

1–6. Write whether the group of words is a *sentence* or a *sentence fragment*.

1. The school held a cleanup day. _____

2. Bottles, pencils, wrappers, and other trash. _____

3. Whoever picks up the most garbage. _____

4. There will be prizes for the students. _____

5. Students need to keep the schoolyard clean. _____

6. The overflowing garbage barrels. _____

7–10. Read the sentence fragments below. Write whether the sentence fragment needs a subject or a predicate in order to be a complete sentence.

7. trash like bottles, paper, and cans _____

8. recycling these materials here _____

9. picked up garbage on the beach on Saturday _____

10. students from Mr. Martinez's class _____

8

Name _____ Date _____

Writing Complete Sentences

Every sentence has two parts: a subject and a predicate.
The subject tells whom or what the sentence is about.
The predicate tells what the subject is or does. The
complete sentence expresses a complete thought.

sentence fragment

The birds, frogs, and crickets at the lake (needs predicate)

complete sentence

The birds, frogs, and crickets at the lake fascinated the
visiting students.

Thinking Questions
*Does each group of
words tell whom or what
the sentence is about?
Does it tell what is or
what happens?*

**Activity Read the sentence fragments. Write a subject or predicate to
complete the sentence fragment and make a complete sentence.**

1. _____ was very helpful to Tanesha.

2. Jennifer's favorite class _____.

3. _____ gave a very interesting slide show about turtles.

4. The _____ were covered with diagrams.

5. Students who planned experiments _____.

6. _____ is about the rain forest and its animals.

7. Those clothes, books, and computer supplies _____.

8. Students from the fifth grade class _____

Possessive Nouns

Singular Noun	Singular Possessive Noun	Plural Noun	Plural Possessive Noun
Carla	Carla's hat	buckets	buckets' handles
book	book's chapters	people	people's ideas

1–4. Write the possessive form of the noun in parentheses.

1. (students) The _____ mouths were opened in shock.

2. (box) They could not believe the _____ contents.

3. (Today) _____ activity is examining plants.

4. (Sam) _____ stomach ached from laughing so hard.

5–8. Combine the sentences using possessive nouns. Write the new sentence on the line.

5. The classroom had glass doors. The glass doors were closed.

_____

6. The students were using computers. The computers belonged to the school.

_____

7. The coughing disturbed the students and their two teachers. The principal was coughing.

_____

_____

8. The robots rushed toward the door. The robots belonged to the teachers.

_____

Name _____ Date _____

Lesson 1
READER'S NOTEBOOK

A Package for
Mrs. Jewls
Grammar: Connect to Writing

Connect to Writing

You can fix a fragment by combining it with a complete sentence or another fragment.

Sentence and Fragment	Complete Sentence
Seth and his brothers all went to school. In the city.	Seth and his brothers all went to school in the city.
Fragments	**Complete Sentence**
The school in Dallas. Has lots of fun things to do.	The school in Dallas has lots of fun things to do.

1–8. Read each pair of sentence fragments. Fix the fragments to make a complete sentence. Write the new sentence on the line.

1. Abel's friend Sasha. Was absent from school today.

_____

2. Won the contest! The school's quiz team.

_____

3. Is old but good. My computer.

_____

4. Brett and Jemaine. Are lab partners in biology class.

_____

5. Will get a prize. The very first student.

_____

6. Thirty-seven blackbirds in the park. The students counted.

_____

7. Is the place an animal lives. A habitat.

_____

8. Rose in the test tube. The level of the liquid.

_____

Focus Trait: Purpose
Adding Vivid Words and Details

Without Details	With Details
Tamara found a box. She ran to the classroom.	In a cupboard in the library, Tamara found a mysterious box full of old essays. She ran to the classroom to show her teacher.

A. Read each sentence without details on the left. Then add words and details to fill in the blanks and show the events and your purpose more clearly.

Without Details (Unclear)	With Details (Clear)
1. Angela walked over to the gym. She saw her friend Misha there.	After _____, Angela _____ to the gym. She saw her friend Misha there _____.
2. We were reading when we heard a strange noise.	We were reading _____ when we heard a noise _____.

B. Read each sentence. Think about your purpose, then rewrite the sentence to make the events more understandable and meaningful. Add vivid words and details.

Pair/Share Work with a partner to brainstorm vivid words and details for your sentences.

Without Details	With Details
3. We had a long spelling bee.	
4. It started in the morning.	
5. Katia got stuck on a hard word.	

 Reader's Guide

A Royal Mystery

Think Like an Actor

Do you want to be an actor? You need to study the text. When you study a character's dialogue, or the words a character says, you will get a better idea of what the character is like. If you take notes, you can play the part even better!

Read page 52, Scene II. Look for dialogue that tells you about what each character is like. Write the line from the play and tell what it says about that character.

	Althea	Rena
Dialogue		
Her Character		

Read page 55, Scene V. Look for dialogue that tells you about what each character is like. Write the lines from the play and tell what they say about that character.

	Althea	Rena
Dialogue		
Her Character		

Name _____ Date _____

Lesson 2
READER'S NOTEBOOK

A Royal Mystery

Vocabulary Strategies:
Prefixes *non-, un-, dis-, mis-*

Prefixes *non-, un-, dis-, mis-*

The words in the box begin with a prefix. Choose a word to fill in the blank and complete each sentence. Use context clues and the prefix meanings that are shown to help you.

unfamiliar	uncertain	unlikely	nondairy
nonproductive	disagree	discomfort	discontented
misconduct	misled	misplace	misunderstand

"not"

1. The new chef is _____ with that recipe. She has not seen it before.

2. Poorly fitting shoes will cause the feet _____.

3. With regular study habits, failing the science test is

   _____.

4. Keep thinking about the good things in life to avoid feeling

   _____.

5. People who cannot drink milk use _____ products.

6. We are _____ of what time the guest speaker will arrive.

7. In most cases, it is _____ to worry about the past.

8. The two groups _____ about the best way to solve the problem.

"wrong"

9. An audience was _____ by the magician's illusion. They got the wrong idea.

10. The students' _____ was punished with a detention.

11. People often argue because they _____ each other.

12. If you _____ the key, you will not be able to get into the house.

Long *a* and Long *e*

Basic   Write the Basic Word that best fits each clue.

1. to swing back and forth _____

2. to welcome _____

3. the daughter of one's brother or sister

   _____

4. to wander away from a group _____

5. feeling shame or guilt _____

6. exhibit or put on view _____

7. to set free _____

8. to do again _____

9. wires and bands used for straightening teeth

   _____

10. approval or admiration _____

Challenge 11–14.   Write some sentences that friends might say to
each other during a game or contest. Use four of the Challenge Words.
Write on a separate sheet of paper.

Spelling Words
1. awake
2. feast
3. stray
4. greet
5. praise
6. disease
7. repeat
8. display
9. braces
10. thief
11. ashamed
12. sleeve
13. waist
14. beneath
15. sheepish
16. release
17. remain
18. sway
19. training
20. niece
Challenge
terrain
succeed
betray
motivate
upheaval

Spelling Word Sort

Write each Basic Word beside the correct heading.

/ā/ spelled *a*-consonant-*e*	Basic Words: Challenge Words: Possible Selection Words:
/ā/ spelled *ai*	Basic Words: Challenge Words: Possible Selection Words:
/ā/ spelled *ay*	Basic Words: Challenge Words: Possible Selection Words:
/ē/ spelled *ea*	Basic Words: Challenge Words: Possible Selection Words:
/ē/ spelled *ee*	Basic Words: Challenge Words: Possible Selection Words:
Other spellings for /ē/	Basic Words: Possible Selection Words:

Spelling Words

1. awake
2. feast
3. stray
4. greet
5. praise
6. disease
7. repeat
8. display
9. braces
10. thief
11. ashamed
12. sleeve
13. waist
14. beneath
15. sheepish
16. release
17. remain
18. sway
19. training
20. niece

Challenge
terrain
succeed
betray
motivate
upheaval

Challenge Add the Challenge Words to your Word Sort.

Connect to Reading Look through *A Royal Mystery*. Find words that have the /ā/ or /ē/ spelling patterns on this page. Add them to your Word Sort.

Name _____ Date _____

Proofreading for Spelling

Find the misspelled words and circle them. Write them correctly on the lines below.

Campers and counselors: Beware! Yesterday a food theif was caught hiding beneith a table in the camp cafeteria. He appeared sheeepish, ashamd, and sad, as if he had a desease of the heart. Luckily, one of our kitchen staff was especially alert and awaike while making our usual lunch fiest. I praize Ms. Woo for her fine skill in using the belt from her wayst to catch the furry thief. Her reward from this office is a big red heart to wear on her slieve. To repete: please remane alert for any other streigh visitors, especially four-legged ones who need further trainning before they can eat in the cafeteria. Please relaese any such visitors out-of-doors without delay.

1. _____   9. _____
2. _____   10. _____
3. _____   11. _____
4. _____   12. _____
5. _____   13. _____
6. _____   14. _____
7. _____   15. _____
8. _____

Spelling Words

1. awake
2. feast
3. stray
4. greet
5. praise
6. disease
7. repeat
8. display
9. braces
10. thief
11. ashamed
12. sleeve
13. waist
14. beneath
15. sheepish
16. release
17. remain
18. sway
19. training
20. niece

Challenge
terrain
succeed
betray
motivate
upheaval

A Royal Mystery

Grammar: Kinds of Sentences

Declarative and Interrogative Sentences

A **declarative sentence** tells something. It ends with a period.

It isn't easy to try out for a play.

An **interrogative sentence** asks something. It ends with a question mark.

Why are people nervous when they get on stage?

Thinking Question
Does this sentence tell something or ask something?

Activity   Write the sentence using correct end punctuation and capitalization. Then label the sentence *declarative* or *interrogative*.

1. the play needed eight different characters

   _____

   _____

2. have you ever been in a play or on stage

   _____

   _____

3. why is it easy for some people to talk on stage

   _____

   _____

4. some people are shy with people but good at acting

   _____

   _____

Name _____ Date _____

Imperative and Exclamatory Sentences

An **imperative sentence** gives an order. It ends with a period.

Hang up that sign for the play.

An **exclamatory sentence** expresses strong feeling. It ends with an exclamation point.

You did a great job on the sign!

Thinking Question
Does this sentence give an order or express strong feeling?

Activity Write the sentence using correct end punctuation and capitalization. Then label the sentence *imperative* or *exclamatory*.

1. wow, I love creating movie posters and signs

_____

_____

2. make a poster for the school play

_____

_____

3. hang it on the bulletin board in the hall

_____

_____

4. what a great variety of posters our class made

_____

_____

5. we've really improved since the beginning of the year

_____

_____

Kinds of Sentences

A **declarative sentence** tells something. An **imperative sentence** gives an order. They both end with a period.

An **interrogative sentence** asks a question. It ends with a question mark. An **exclamatory sentence** expresses strong feeling. It ends with an exclamation point.

Who can be an artist?

Thinking Question
Does this sentence tell something, ask something, give an order, or express strong feeling?

Activity Write the sentence using correct end punctuation and capitalization. Then label the sentence *declarative*, *imperative*, *interrogatory*, or *exclamatory*.

1. tell me all you know about being an artist

   _____

   _____

2. do most artists make a lot of money

   _____

   _____

3. some artists become very famous and rich

   _____

   _____

4. how exciting it must be when someone buys your work

   _____

   _____

Irregular Verbs

Present Tense	Past Tense
bring	brought
sing	sang
fly	flew
steal	stole

1–4.   Write the correct form of the verb in parentheses to complete the sentence.

1. (say) Whoever _____ acting was easy was joking.

2. (tell) The professional actor _____ us how many hours he works.

3. (come) The actor _____ to our class because he is Jesse's cousin.

4. (begin) The professional actor _____ his talk with some pictures of a movie set.

5–8.   Circle the four incorrect verbs in the paragraph. Then write the correct past-tense form of each verb on the lines below.

We practiced for the school play every night. What did we do? First, the director choosed people for certain parts. Then, we had to learn our lines. At first, I thinked I would never learn them. After we knowed our lines, we practiced how to move around on stage. Later, we maked our costumes and tried them on. Finally, we were ready for the big night!

_____

_____

Connect to Writing

No Sentence Variety	Varied Sentence Types
I would like you to read these paragraphs about making movies. Making movies used to be very different from the way it is today. I wonder what you know about making movies already.	Read these paragraphs about making movies. How different the process used to be from what it is today! What do you know about making movies already? Read on to find out more.

Activity Change each underlined declarative sentence to another kind of sentence. Write the new sentences on the lines below.

People have been making movies since the early 1900s. I wonder what making the earliest movies was like. I think watching a very old movie is exciting. You can find some of them on the Internet.

The earliest movies were not very complicated. I do not want you to think making those earliest movies was easy. The cameras were very big and hard to move around. They only recorded pictures in black and white. There was no sound either, so the actors couldn't speak. It is safe to say that people who made early movies had to work very hard.

1. (interrogative) _____

_____

2. (exclamatory) _____

_____

3. (imperative) _____

_____

4. (exclamatory) _____

_____

Focus Trait: Development
Adding Sensory Details to Show Feeling

Weak Voice	Strong Voice
The actors waited for the show to begin.	With butterflies in their stomachs, the actors waited nervously for the show to begin.

A. Read each weak sentence. Add sensory details and other vivid words to give the writing more feeling and make the voice interesting.

Weak Voice	Strong Voice
1. People had lined up early to get in.	The _____ stood outside in a line, _____.
2. Just before the doors opened, all the lights went out in the theater.	_____, the theater was _____.
3. The people began to move around because they didn't know what to do.	The crowd _____ and began to _____, _____ of what they should do.

B. Read each weak sentence. Then rewrite it to add sensory details and vivid words. Use words and details to develop the speaker's attitude or feelings.

Pair/Share Work with a partner to brainstorm words and details for your sentences.

Weak Voice	Strong Voice
4. Later, people went back to their cars.	
5. The actors were disappointed, and some didn't sleep well that night.	

Reader's Guide

Off and Running

Vote

Write a Speech

Read page 89. Miata wants her classmates to be interested in what she has to say. How could she make her speech even more appealing to her classmates? She might speak in a less formal way to connect with them. Look at Miata's original speech. Then, rewrite it to help her connect to the audience. What language or idioms would make her speech more engaging?

Miata's Original Speech

"We can put some really nice azaleas and pansies outside our windows. The walls will be all clean, not like they are now."

Miata's New Speech

_____

_____

_____

_____

_____

Name _____ Date _____

Read page 91. Imagine that Rudy has won the election. He is writing a letter to the principal to ask for more recess time. Think about his speech. Then change the language of his speech, using more formal language that will make his letter more serious in tone.

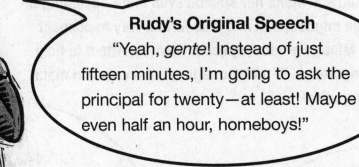

Rudy's Original Speech
"Yeah, *gente*! Instead of just fifteen minutes, I'm going to ask the principal for twenty—at least! Maybe even half an hour, homeboys!"

Name _____ Date _____

Lesson 3
READER'S NOTEBOOK

Off and Running
Vocabulary Strategies:
Using Context

Using Context

Read each sentence carefully. Then write the definition of the underlined word, using context clues to help you determine which meaning in the box is correct.

address   platform   post   ticket

address 1. location of a person or organization **2.** formal speech; **platform 1.** stage **2.** set of principles **3.** part of a shoe that gives height **4.** flat, high area of ground; **post 1.** wooden support **2.** military base **3.** political job; **ticket 1.** slip of paper that allows entry **2.** label for merchandise **3.** list of candidates

1. The party members wrote their <u>platform</u>, hoping that their ideas would appeal to voters. _____

2. If you lose the <u>ticket</u> from the shirt, the sales clerk won't know how much to charge us. _____

3. The soldiers were sent to a <u>post</u> in Alabama for additional training.

   _____

4. In a democracy, the people choose who fills the <u>post</u> of the presidency. _____

5. The two friends ran as president and vice president on the same <u>ticket</u>. _____

6. She gave her speech from a <u>platform</u> at the front of the room. _____

7. Miata wrote her <u>address</u> to the class and then practiced it for her father. _____

8. The teacher handed each student a <u>ticket</u> to the exhibit.

   _____

9. The package went to the wrong <u>address</u>. _____

10. We pounded the tent <u>post</u> into the ground as far as it would go.

    _____

Long *i* and Long *o*

Basic Write the Basic Words that best replace the underlined words in the sentences.

As my dad and I **(1)** <u>walk</u> around the Stars baseball stadium, I am amazed at the **(2)** <u>tallness</u> of the structure. While we **(3)** <u>near</u> the entrance, I smell the **(4)** <u>aroma</u> of sizzling hot dogs. The roaring crowd and huge park **(5)** <u>thrill</u> us. With the score tied in the ninth inning, one of the Stars players gets **(6)** <u>tossed</u> out at first base. The crowd and I **(7)** <u>express disapproval</u> at the umpire's call. But the Stars still have a **(8)** <u>small</u> chance to win when their **(9)** <u>strong</u> player, Joe Blast, comes up to bat. The crowd now turns **(10)** <u>quiet</u>. Then Joe smashes the ball for a home run and there is no way to **(11)** <u>restrain</u> the crowd. My dad asks me if I had fun and I **(12)** <u>say</u>, "It was the best day ever!"

1. _____	7. _____
2. _____	8. _____
3. _____	9. _____
4. _____	10. _____
5. _____	11. _____
6. _____	12. _____

Challenge 13–15.   Your team is playing its biggest rival in a baseball game. Write about what happens in the game. Use three of the Challenge Words. Write on a separate sheet of paper.

Spelling Words

1. sign
2. groan
3. reply
4. thrown
5. strike
6. mighty
7. stroll
8. compose
9. dough
10. height
11. excite
12. apply
13. slight
14. define
15. odor
16. spider
17. control
18. silent
19. brighten
20. approach

Challenge
require
reproach
defy
plight
opponent

Spelling Word Sort

Write each Basic Word beside the correct heading.

/ī/ spelled *i*-consonant-*e* or *i*	Basic Words: Challenge Words: Possible Selection Words:
/ī/ spelled *igh* or *y*	Basic Words: Challenge Words: Possible Selection Words:
/ō/ spelled *o*-consonant-*e* or *o*	Basic Words: Challenge Words: Possible Selection Words:
/ō/ spelled *oa* or *ow*	Basic Words: Challenge Words: Possible Selection Words:
Other spellings for /ī/ and /ō/	Basic Words:

Challenge   Add the Challenge Words to your Word Sort.

Connect to Reading   Look through *Off and Running*.
Find words that have the /ī/ and /ō/ spelling patterns on this page.
Add them to your Word Sort.

Spelling Words

1. sign
2. groan
3. reply
4. thrown
5. strike
6. mighty
7. stroll
8. compose
9. dough
10. height
11. excite
12. apply
13. slight
14. define
15. odor
16. spider
17. control
18. silent
19. brighten
20. approach

Challenge

require
reproach
defy
plight
opponent

Proofreading for Spelling

Find the misspelled words and circle them. Write them correctly on the lines below.

Maria and I decide to sell cookie dogh at the bake sale. We make a signe that reads "Last customer is a hairy spyder." Mom says to compoze another sign because this one may strick people as too negative. We both grone and say to defign *negative*. To replie, Mom rises up to her full 5-foot hieght and gives us her warning look. We aply our thinking caps and aprroach it from a different direction. We come up with a message that will briten the day of all cookie lovers who read it: "All you can eat, $3." Mom says, "That could be a mitey big problem." We controll ourselves and say nothing. We decide on this sign message: "Best offer takes all!" There is a slite risk that we won't sell anything, but all we need is one cookie lover who likes to smell cookies baking.

1. _____   9. _____

2. _____   10. _____

3. _____   11. _____

4. _____   12. _____

5. _____   13. _____

6. _____   14. _____

7. _____   15. _____

8. _____

Spelling Words

1. sign
2. groan
3. reply
4. thrown
5. strike
6. mighty
7. stroll
8. compose
9. dough
10. height
11. excite
12. apply
13. slight
14. define
15. odor
16. spider
17. control
18. silent
19. brighten
20. approach

Challenge
require
reproach
defy
plight
opponent

Complete Subjects and Predicates

Each sentence has a **complete subject** and a **complete predicate**.

A complete subject has all of the words that tell whom or what the sentence is about. A complete predicate has all of the words that tell what the subject is or does.

complete   complete
subject   predicate
We all recounted the votes.

Thinking Questions
What are the words that tell whom or what the sentence is about?
What are the words that tell what the subject is or does?

Activity   Circle the complete subject and underline the complete predicate in each sentence.

1. The girl with the blue ribbon was running for class president.

2. The poster with the sparkles was Reina's.

3. Reina's parents and friends helped write her speech.

4. The past class presidents always worked to improve the school.

5. All of the students cast their votes.

6. Someone in the lobby yelled that the votes were in.

Subject-Verb Agreement

The subject and verb of a sentence should agree.
Singular subjects need singular verbs. Plural subjects
need plural verbs.

plural subject and verb   **singular subject and verb**

We are recounting the votes, so everyone has to wait.

Thinking Questions
Is the sentence about more than one person, place, thing, or idea? If so, is the verb plural?

Activity Write the correct form of each verb.

1. Everyone (has, have) _____ already voted in the election.

   The students (is, are) _____ excited to hear the results.

2. The principal (was, were) _____ going to recount the votes

   by herself. The teachers (has, have) _____ offered to help.

3. All of the students (thinks, think) _____ Reina won. She

   (is, are) _____ not as certain.

4. Mr. Rushing (tell, tells) _____ the rowdy students to be

   patient. They (begin, begins) _____ to quiet down.

Commas in Compound Sentences

In a **compound sentence**, the shorter sentences are usually joined by a comma and the word *and*, *but*, *so*, or *or*.

Reina planned to write her speech alone, but her friends offered to help.

Thinking Questions
Which groups of words express a complete thought? What word joins the two complete thoughts?

Activity Add the correct punctuation to make each item a compound sentence. Then write the word that is used to join the shorter sentences.

1. Blue and red confetti fell from the ceiling _____ it covered the winner.

2. Music played in the auditorium _____ we thought it was too loud.

3. The winner wanted to give a speech _____ a teacher turned

   down the music.

4. Reina thanked everyone for voting _____ she promised to work

   hard for the school.

5. She wanted to raise funds by selling class T-shirts _____ the

   class could wash cars.

Punctuation

Declarative

Miata was nervous but excited too.

Interrogative

Will Miata run for office next year?

Exclamatory

I hope so!

Imperative

Vote for Miata.

Write the sentence using correct end punctuation and capitalization. Then label the sentence *declarative, imperative, interrogatory,* or *exclamatory*.

1. why did Ellen run for president and not Jose

_____

_____

2. being elected president takes a lot of time

_____

_____

3. stop daydreaming and listen to the speech

_____

_____

4. that was the best campaign speech I've ever heard

_____

_____

5. isn't it time to work on the posters

_____

_____

34

Connect to Writing

| and | but | or | so |

Activity   Each item contains two separate sentences. Join them together to write a compound sentence on the line below. Use a word from the box to complete each sentence. Remember to check your punctuation.

1. The losing candidate was sorry to lose. He accepted his defeat.

_____

_____

2. Everyone celebrated at Mia's house. They all cheered Reina.

_____

_____

3. Reina was glad she won. She was sorry Roy had to lose.

_____

_____

4. All of the students had school the next morning. They left early.

_____

_____

Focus Trait: Elaboration
Writing Dialogue for Characters

Weak Dialogue	Strong Dialogue
"I do not think I have enough time to prepare the speech. I have too many other things to do."	"I don't think I'll have time to get a speech ready. I'm way too busy!"

A. Read each example of weak dialogue. Using the sentence frames, elaborate on each one to make events and feelings clear.

Weak Dialogue	Strong Dialogue
1. "I am running for class president. Please vote for me."	"_____ I'm running for class president. _____ _____ vote for me!"
2. "Mother, you do not understand how much work I need to do before the election. I should not have to do the dishes tonight."	"Mom, I've _____ before the election! _____ the dishes tonight?"

B. Read each example of weak dialogue. Rewrite each one to show the speaker's personality.

Pair/Share   With a partner, brainstorm language that sounds natural for the speaker. Sentence fragments can be used.

Weak Dialogue	Strong Dialogue
3. "Please be quiet, class. It is too loud to hear the speaker."	
4. "I would be sad if I didn't win the election. I have worked very hard to get elected."	

36

Reader's Guide

Double Dutch

How Do You Start a Double-Dutch Team?

A coach from your school wants to start a double-Dutch team. The coach doesn't know anything about the sport. Based on information from "Double Dutch," what advice would you give him?

Read page 119. Think about the steps Coach Rockett used to start his team. Then write an e-mail to the coach explaining how you would start a double-Dutch team. Be sure to use transition words that make the sequence of steps clear.

New Message
To: Frank W. Baker
From:
Subject: Starting a Double-Dutch Team

_____

_____

_____

_____

_____

_____

Good luck,

Carla

Name _____ Date _____

The new coach e-mailed you back. He did everything you said, but the team is still struggling. What advice would you give next? Write another e-mail in reply. Use quotes from page 123 to help motivate the coach and get the team on track.

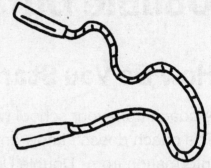

	New Message	
To:	Coach	
From:		
Subject:	Problems with the Double-Dutch Team	

_____

_____

_____

_____

_____

_____

_____

_____

_____

I hope this helps,

Carla

Suffixes *-ion, -tion*

The nouns in the box all end with a suffix. Choose a word from the box to fill in the blank and complete each sentence. Then write the base word.

competition   rotation   production   application   operation
organization   division   opposition   solution   protection

1. Those who have mastered double Dutch may want to try qualifying

   for a _____. _____

2. In any sport, it is important to wear the right gear for

   _____. _____

3. The cycle of day and night on Earth is caused by the planet's

   _____. _____

4. She completed a short _____ to attend the volleyball

   camp. _____

5. It is difficult to do long _____ without paper and a

   pencil. _____

6. Completing a large job requires teamwork and _____.

   _____

7. The school musical is a student _____ that takes

   several weeks to plan. _____

8. When you encounter a problem, it is fine to ask for help to find a

   _____. _____

9. When a person or group fights a new idea, they are called the

   _____. _____

10. When her dog was lost, she undertook a rescue _____

    to find it. _____

Vowel Sounds: /ōo/, /yōo/

Basic Write the Basic Word that best completes each group.

1. misplace, mislay, _____

2. street, boulevard, _____

3. soup, thick broth with vegetables, _____

4. charge, blame, _____

5. involve, contain, _____

6. suppose, think, _____

7. mystify, puzzle, _____

8. injury, wounds, _____

9. voyage, boat trip, _____

10. free, unattached, _____

Challenge 11–14. Write a paragraph that uses four of the Challenge Words.

_____

_____

_____

_____

_____

_____

_____

Spelling Words

1. glue
2. flute
3. youth
4. accuse
5. bruise
6. stew
7. choose
8. loose
9. lose
10. view
11. confuse
12. cruise
13. jewel
14. execute
15. route
16. cartoon
17. avenue
18. include
19. assume
20. souvenir

Challenge
conclude
pursuit
intrude
subdue
presume

Spelling Word Sort

Write each Basic Word beside the correct heading.

/o͞o/ spelled *u*-consonant-*e*	**Basic Words:** **Challenge Words:**
/o͞o/ spelled *ue*	**Basic Words:** **Challenge Words:**
/o͞o/ spelled *ou*	**Basic Words:** **Possible Selection Words:**
/o͞o/ spelled *ui*	**Basic Words:** **Challenge Words:** **Possible Selection Words:**
/o͞o/ spelled *ew*	**Basic Words:**
/o͞o/ spelled *oo*	**Basic Words:** **Possible Selection Words:**
/yo͞o/ spelled *u*-consonant-*e*	**Basic Words:**
Other spellings for /o͞o/ or /yo͞o/	**Basic Words:**

Spelling Words

1. glue
2. flute
3. youth
4. accuse
5. bruise
6. stew
7. choose
8. loose
9. lose
10. view
11. confuse
12. cruise
13. jewel
14. execute
15. route
16. cartoon
17. avenue
18. include
19. assume
20. souvenir

Challenge
conclude
pursuit
intrude
subdue
presume

Challenge   Add the Challenge Words to your Word Sort.

Connect to Reading   Look through *Double Dutch: A Celebration of Jump Rope, Rhyme, and Sisterhood.* Find words that have the /o͞o/ and /yo͞o/ sounds with the spelling patterns on this page. Add them to your Word Sort.

41

Name _____ Date _____

Proofreading for Spelling

Find the misspelled words and circle them. Write them correctly on the lines below.

My big brother Eric had to chuse between delivering newspapers and finishing an art project before school. I offered to help. "I will exacute delivery of your newspapers while you finish your project." He agreed, grabbing his bottle of glew, saying I was a fine yewth. I knew his paper roote because I had often helped him. During my bike cruze along the way, I met Wendy, who was playing her floot like a cartune musician. She agreed to help me so I wouldn't loos my perfect attendance record. I took one side of the avanue and Wendy took the other. We finished early and enjoyed a morning veiw of the autumn sun shining like a jewal. Eric tied up the loos ends of his project, and we all kept the feeling of accomplishment as a souvanir of our teamwork. Wendy invited me to dinner that night for a bowl of her mother's steew!

Spelling Words

1. glue
2. flute
3. youth
4. accuse
5. bruise
6. stew
7. choose
8. loose
9. lose
10. view
11. confuse
12. cruise
13. jewel
14. execute
15. route
16. cartoon
17. avenue
18. include
19. assume
20. souvenir

Challenge

conclude
pursuit
intrude
subdue
presume

1. _____   9. _____

2. _____   10. _____

3. _____   11. _____

4. _____   12. _____

5. _____   13. _____

6. _____   14. _____

7. _____   15. _____

8. _____

Recognizing Nouns

A **noun** is a word that names a person, a place, or a thing.
A **common noun** names any person, place, or thing. A
proper noun names a particular person, place, or thing.

proper noun	common noun
Reed Junior High School	*hosts the* *tournament.*

Thinking Questions
What word names a person, place, or thing? Is the word general or specific?

1–4. **Write the nouns and tell whether each is *common* or *proper*.**

1. Francesca watches the Radio City Rockettes perform.

_____

2. She learns dance steps from them.

_____

3. Her dance teacher, Roma, used to be a Rockette.

_____

4. Francesca's mother once performed at Radio City Music Hall.

_____

5–17. **Underline all the nouns in this paragraph.**

On weekends, Sarah played with the other girls on her block. The
children drew hopscotch squares on the sidewalk. They played jump
rope and chanted rhymes. On Tuesdays, she studied African dance and
hip-hop at Bert's Studio.

Capitalizing Proper Nouns

Proper nouns must be capitalized. If a proper noun is two words, capitalize both. If it is three or more words, capitalize each important word.

proper noun
New York City is full of talented performers.
Capitalize the first letter of abbreviations, such as *Mr.* or *Ms.*, and end with a period. Also capitalize initials, such as *C. S. Lewis*, and acronyms, such as *FBI*.

Thinking Questions
How many words make up the proper noun? Which words are important?

1–4. **Write the sentence on the line. Capitalize the proper nouns.**

1. The jump rope team from harlem is very talented.

_____

2. Their team name is the dazzling ropers.

_____

3. They performed at the thanksgiving day parade in new york.

_____

4. They became so popular that they were invited to the white house!

_____

5–7. **Write the sentence on the line. Capitalize abbreviations, initials, and acronyms.**

5. My mother jumped rope on the corner of 125th st and second ave in nyc.

_____

6. mr david a. walker developed double dutch into a world class sport.

_____

7. The *New York Times* featured the national double dutch finals.

_____

Capitalizing Proper Nouns

When a proper noun is the name of an organization, capitalize each important word. An acronym is a proper noun made up of initials, or the first letter of important words. Capitalize all of the letters in an acronym.

name of organization or acronym
University of North Texas or UNT

Thinking Questions
Do the words name a kind of group or one group in particular?

Activity Rewrite the sentence on the line. Capitalize the proper nouns.

1. ritchie and aleesha founded the middle school jump club.

_____

2. Would you like to see jumping rope as a sport in the olympics?

_____

3. The japanese team is one of the best in the international double dutch federation.

_____

_____

4. Our tournament hosted ohio's jammin' jumpers.

_____

5. talura reid invented her rope-turning machine at the university of michigan.

_____

6. The american double dutch league is also called addl.

_____

7. dddd stands for a group called dynamic diplomats of double dutch.

_____

Commas in Sentences

Commas	
after **introductory words** such as *yes, no,* and *well*	Yes, I will go to the game with you.
to set off a **noun in direct address**	Carla, will you come to the game with me?
in a **series**	The girls wear multicolored shirts, skirts, and shoes.
in **dates**	The championship game is on October 3, 2014.
in names of **places**	The game will be played in Chicago, Illinois.

1–5. Add commas where they are needed.

1. The team traveled to Chicago Boston and New York this year.

2. No the championships are not being held in Orlando Florida.

3. The team finals officially end on November 2 2013.

4. Helen do you think the team will win the grand prize?

5. The team works hard practices every day and competes well.

6–8. Combine the sentences to form a series.

6. Stacey bought leggings. Stacy bought a costume. Stacey bought dance shoes.

_____

7. You can buy drinks at the counter. You can buy food at the counter. You can buy tickets at the counter.

_____

8. Katya will give you food. She will give you napkins. She will give you a plate.

_____

Connect to Writing

When proofreading your writing, **capitalize** words that name the following:

people	places	organizations	titles

holidays	days of the week	months of the year

Also capitalize acronyms and abbreviations.

Activity   Underline letters that should be capitalized. Circle letters that should be lowercase.

Two years ago, my Dad left his job with major league baseball to work for Nippon professional baseball, which is like a Japanese mlb. My family moved to Tokyo in april, when The Japanese school year begins. I was worried about being the Newcomer at tokyo Girls' middle school. Then I found out that everyone loved to jump Rope during recess. Some girls, like etsuko and tomoko, can do stunts and tricks. I made friends by teaching new rhymes, and now we're making up rhymes with Japanese and English Words! My teacher, ms. tanaka, says that on friday we can teach a rhyme to the class.

Focus Trait: Purpose

Flashback and Flash Forward

Story Starter

Every winter, James waited for snow. He was a snowboarding fiend. When people saw him storming the slopes, they'd call out, "Yo, Jumpin' James!" because he was that good. And James knew he was good, too. He always answered with a spin, a blinding grin, and a spray of snow. This year, he wanted to practice a new trick. All he needed was snow.

Think about how you might use the devices of flashback and flash forward to make the story about James more interesting. Rewrite the Story Starter to include events in sequence and the devices of flashback and flash forward. Continue on another sheet of paper, if needed.

_____

_____

_____

_____

_____

_____

_____

_____

_____

Reader's Guide

Elisa's Diary

Write a Diary

Elisa's diary pages help us understand what Elisa is thinking and feeling. The pages support the theme of the story, too.

Read pages 147–148. Write another page from Elisa's diary.
As Elisa, describe your experience trying to speak in class.
What happens? How does Elisa feel about it?

Name _____ Date _____

Read page 151. Write another page from Elisa's diary that summarizes her conversation with José. Think about story details as you connect this experience with her previous day in class.

Suffixes *-ly, -ful*

The words in the box all end with a suffix. Choose a word from
the box to fill in the blank and complete the following sentences.

> officially   probably   actually   particularly   slightly
> successful   meaningful   plentiful   forceful   wasteful

"in a certain way"

1. Obey the rules and do not do anything you are not

   _____ allowed to do.

2. A newspaper reports the facts of a story the way they

   _____ happened.

3. The hem was uneven, with one side _____ longer than

   the other.

4. He often washed the dishes but was not _____ fond of

   drying them.

5. By the time she watered the lawn, it was _____ too late

   to save it.

"full of"

6. If you want to play team sports, the after-school leagues are

   _____.

7. The batter hit the baseball with a sudden, _____ swing.

8. Practice is an important part of a _____ juggling act.

9. It is _____ to throw bottles, cans, and paper in the

   trash bin.

10. A life that is lived to help others is a _____ life.

Vowel Sounds: /ou/, /ô/, and /oi/

Basic Complete the puzzle by writing the Basic Word for each clue.

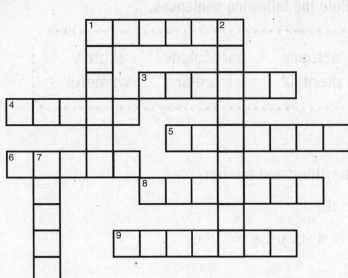

Across

1. to swoop and seize
3. a small, shallow dish
4. damp
5. behaving in a mischievous way
6. to scare or frighten
8. a public sale
9. to demolish

Down

1. a harmful substance
2. to meet
7. eighth month

Challenge 10–14. Suppose that a police officer talks to your class about crime prevention. Write some sentences about what you learned. Use four of the Challenge Words. Write on a separate sheet of paper.

Spelling Words

1. ounce
2. sprawl
3. launch
4. loyal
5. avoid
6. basketball
7. moist
8. haunt
9. scowl
10. naughty
11. destroy
12. saucer
13. pounce
14. poison
15. August
16. auction
17. royal
18. coward
19. awkward
20. encounter

Challenge

poise
loiter
exhaust
assault
alternate

Spelling Word Sort

Write each Basic Word beside the correct heading.

/ou/ spelled *ou* or *ow*	Basic Words:
	Possible Selection Words:
/ô/ spelled *aw, au, a*	Basic Words:
	Challenge Words:
	Possible Selection Words:
Other spellings for /ô/	Basic Words:
	Possible Selection Words:
/oi/ spelled *oy* or *oi*	Basic Words:
	Challenge Words:
	Possible Selection Words:

Spelling Words

1. ounce
2. sprawl
3. launch
4. loyal
5. avoid
6. basketball
7. moist
8. haunt
9. scowl
10. naughty
11. destroy
12. saucer
13. pounce
14. poison
15. August
16. auction
17. royal
18. coward
19. awkward
20. encounter

Challenge
poise
loiter
exhaust
assault
alternate

Challenge   Add the Challenge Words to your Word Sort.

Connect to Reading   Look through *Elisa's Diary*. Find words that have the /ou/, /ô/, and /oi/ sounds on this page. Add them to your Word Sort.

Proofreading for Spelling

Elisa's Diary
Spelling: Vowel Sounds:
/ou/, /ô/, /oi/

Find the misspelled words and circle them. Write them correctly on the lines below.

The big game is Thursday night after the varsity player auxtion. We'll be given a roiyal welcome as we warm up. I wonder if I can avoyd another akward fall this time and make my loyel fans happy. Also, I don't enjoy seeing the fans skowl when I mess up. Coach says that an ounze of prevention is worth a pound of cure. That means it pays to be careful. So, I have worked hard in all the drills to keep balance. I will set up the lonch of the ball so I don't sproll out on the court. I hope I can do as well in the game as I have in practice. Shooting a basketbal when the pressure is on is no job for a cowerd. I can't wait to get out there and desroye the competition!

Spelling Words

1. ounce
2. sprawl
3. launch
4. loyal
5. avoid
6. basketball
7. moist
8. haunt
9. scowl
10. naughty
11. destroy
12. saucer
13. pounce
14. poison
15. August
16. auction
17. royal
18. coward
19. awkward
20. encounter

Challenge
poise
loiter
exhaust
assault
alternate

1. _____   7. _____

2. _____   8. _____

3. _____   9. _____

4. _____   10. _____

5. _____   11. _____

6. _____   12. _____

Making Nouns Plural

A **singular noun** names one person, place, thing, or idea.
A **plural noun** names more than one person, place, thing,
or idea. Form the plural of most nouns by adding -*s* or
-*es*. Look at the ending of a singular noun to decide how
to form the plural.

Thinking Question
*What is the noun's
ending?*

plural noun

*We celebrated a lot of **holidays** in Mexico.*

Activity Write the plural form of the noun in parentheses.

1. During May we had (celebration) on Cinco de Mayo.

_____

2. It is the day the Mexican army defeated (soldier) from France.

_____

3. People in the government give (speech) and everyone plays (game).

_____

4. Many people have (party) during the day and eat Mexican (dish).

_____

5. People dance to Mexican (song) and wear Mexican (costume).

_____

6. Kids get to break (piñata) and pick up all the different (candy).

_____

55

More Plural Nouns

Many nouns are not made plural according to the regular rules. To form the plural of some nouns ending in *f* or *fe*, change the *f* to *v* and add *-es*. For others, add *-s*. To form the plural of nouns ending in *o*, add *-s* or *-es*. Some nouns have the same form whether singular or plural.

plural noun

*My grandfather has two **shelves** of books about our culture.*

Thinking Question
Does the noun require -s or -es to make it plural, or is the plural formed in another way?

Activity   Write the plural form of the noun in parentheses.

1. Preparing our family's Thanksgiving dinner takes two (day).

_____

2. Some of the (woman) search the woods for wild berries.

_____

3. Sometimes they see (goose) overhead while walking home.

_____

4. My father always divides the pumpkin pies in two (half).

_____

5. I eat so much ice cream for dessert that my (tooth) ache.

_____

6. Every year we say that it is the best meal of our (life).

_____

Collective Nouns

A **collective noun** names a group of people, animals, or things that act as a unit. Treat a collective noun like a singular noun, unless it names more than one group.

singular collective noun

Our <u>class</u> planned a celebration.

plural collective noun

All grade 5 <u>classes</u> are invited.

Thinking Questions
Which word names a group of people, places, things, or ideas? Which verb describes what the group does?

Activity Underline the collective noun in each sentence. Write whether each collective noun is singular or plural.

1. The teacher chose Elisa for the spelling team. _____

2. Elisa's family was happy when she won a spelling bee.

   _____

3. José spoke to a school audience about the traditions

   of Guatemala. _____

4. José's father is on several committees at the community

   center. _____

5. In the United States, a jury decides whether a person is

   innocent or guilty of a crime. _____

6. Both groups planned to perform a show together in August. _____

Making Comparisons and Using Negatives Correctly

Incorrect	They **won't never** cancel the game even if it snows.
Correct	They **won't** cancel the game even if it snows.

I've never seen such a **large** crowd.

The crowd at last week's game was **larger**.

The final game of the season attracts the **largest** crowd of all.

These are **good** athletic shoes.

Those are **better** athletic shoes than these.

His athletic shoes are the **best**.

Len got off to a **bad** start.

Heidi got off to a **worse** start than Len.

Philip got off to the **worst** start of all.

That player moves **naturally**.

He moves **more naturally** than I do.

He moves the **most naturally** of all the players.

1–5. **Write the word or words that correctly complete the sentence.**

1. (isn't, is) This game _____ nothing like our first game.

2. (more skillfully, most skillfully) Billy plays soccer _____ than Robert plays.

3. (better, best) The team has a _____ chance of winning this game.

4. (ever, never) The school hasn't _____ had a strong team.

5. (worse, worst) Last year's team had the _____ record in school history.

6–10. **Circle the five errors in this paragraph. Then correct the errors on the lines below.**

I didn't think nobody noticed how well I played in last night's game. Then today Coach Malone told me that I had played the better game of my basketball career. After talking to the coach, I walked home with the most widest grin on my face. He doesn't never say things like that. In fact, it was the most nicest thing he ever said to me!

_____

Connect to Writing

Using exact words can make your writing more interesting.

Less Exact Noun	More Exact Noun
She dropped us off at the place.	My mother dropped us off at the practice field.

Activity   Replace the underlined noun with an exact noun. Write the new sentence on the line.

1. The coach blew the thing to get our attention.

   _____

2. Billy needs new football stuff.

   _____

3. The man's words made the team laugh.

   _____

4. The player threw a touchdown pass at the buzzer.

   _____

5. The sounds in the stadium were loud.

   _____

6. At the end of the game, all the people stood up and cheered.

   _____

7. The coach took the team to a restaurant for food.

   _____

8. We ordered five pizzas with toppings.

   _____

Elisa's Diary
Writing: Narrative Writing

Focus Trait: Conventions
Creating Strong Dialogue and Descriptions

A strong voice shows a speaker's emotions, attitude, or point of view. It sounds
natural and reveals the speaker's personality. End punctuation adds expression.

Weak Voice	Strong Voice
"I didn't know we were playing today," Greg said.	"No way! Are you sure? I thought we said today was no good," Greg groaned.

A. Read the sentences. On the line below, explain why the second voice is stronger.

Weak Voice	Strong Voice
She pointed to the bike and said, "I like that one."	"Wait—that's the one," she gasped, jabbing her finger at the beauty in the corner. "That's my bike!"

1. _____

_____

Weak Voice	Strong Voice
"The view of the traffic from the top of the capitol is great."	"I love watching the tiny cars travel into tunnels, between buildings, and into the gaps in traffic."

2. _____

_____

**B. Read each weak sentence. Then rewrite it to create a voice. Use words and
details that show the speaker's thoughts, personality, and attitude.**

Pair/Share Work with a partner to brainstorm sentences. Remember to
use quotation marks and other punctuation marks.

Weak Voice	Strong Voice
3. Scott said that the ball was hit into the outfield.	
4. The smell of food made me hungry.	

Name _____ Date _____

 **Reader's Guide**

Quest for the Tree Kangaroo

A Kangaroo How-To

Biologists learn about plants and animals by observing
their behavior. They look carefully at causes and effects.
In *Quest for the Tree Kangaroo*, the team of biologists is
observing the causes and effects of behavior in tree kangaroos.

The team is writing a book of instructions to other biologists who
may come to New Guinea to study tree kangaroos in the future.
You will help them write this book based on observations and
experiences with tree kangaroos.

**Read page 179. Under what weather conditions would one most likely
be able to see tree kangaroos? Describe the effect of weather on the
tree kangaroos.**

_____

_____

_____

**Explain the best way to capture tree kangaroos and explain what *not*
to do. Describe the effect of these strategies on the tree kangaroos.**

_____

_____

_____

_____

_____

Name _____ Date _____

Lesson 6
READER'S NOTEBOOK

**Quest for the
Tree Kangaroo**
Independent Reading

Read page 185. Explain how to prepare a tree kangaroo
for an examination. Describe the **effect** of these procedures
on the tree kangaroo.

_____

_____

_____

_____

_____

_____

Explain how to put a radio collar on a tree kangaroo.
Describe what causes them to fall off.

_____

_____

_____

_____

_____

_____

Synonyms and Antonyms

Each item below contains a word that is a synonym or antonym for the underlined word. Circle the synonym or antonym. Then use the synonym or antonym to define the underlined word.

1. The tree kangaroo that the workers rescued was <u>immature.</u>
   Years later, they saw the same tree kangaroo full-grown.

   _____.

2. If we all work together, wild creatures such as the tree kangaroos can
   be safe and no longer <u>threatened.</u> _____

3. The tree kangaroo was almost <u>mutilated</u> by a trap left by careless
   hunters. Luckily the scientists could save its damaged leg.

   _____

4. The tree kangaroo was <u>sluggish</u> and inactive for a while after the
   operation. _____

5. The tree kangaroo's breathing was <u>labored</u> at first but soon became
   easier. _____

6. Because they thought the tree kangaroo was in danger, they
   <u>accelerated</u> their efforts to reach it, speeding through the jungle in
   their jeep. _____

7. The <u>indifference</u> of some people to the animals' suffering
   is discouraging. We should care for all creatures.

   _____

8. I felt <u>fulfilled</u> by my participation in the expedition. It was a very
   satisfying experience. _____

Vowel + /r/ Sounds

Basic   Write the Basic Word that best completes each analogy.

1. *King* is to *robe* as *knight* is to _____ .

2. *Bulb* is to *lamp* as *fire* is to _____ .

3. *Meat* is to *butcher shop* as *milk* is to _____ .

4. *Ride* is to *elevator* as *walk* is to _____ .

5. *Attack* is to *defend* as *condemn* is to _____ .

6. *Exciting* is to *thrill* as *difficult* is to _____ .

7. *Run* is to *dash* as *fly* is to _____ .

8. *Soup* is to *can* as *eggs* are to _____ .

9. *Hate* is to *detest* as *love* is to _____ .

10. *Chef* is to *cook* as *actor* is to _____ .

Challenge 11–14.   Write about what it would be like if you went on a trip to study an unusual animal. Use four of the Challenge Words. Write on a separate sheet of paper.

Spelling Words

1. glory
2. aware
3. carton
4. adore
5. aboard
6. dairy
7. ordeal
8. pardon
9. warn
10. vary
11. barely
12. torch
13. barge
14. soar
15. beware
16. absorb
17. armor
18. stairway
19. perform
20. former

Challenge
discard
forfeit
orchestra
rarity
hoard

64

Name _____ Date _____

Spelling Word Sort

Write each Basic Word beside the correct heading.

/ôr/ spelled *or, ore, oar, ar*	Basic Words:
	Challenge Words:
	Possible Selection Words:
/âr/ spelled *ar, air*	Basic Words:
	Challenge Words:
	Possible Selection Words:
/är/ spelled *ar*	Basic Words:
	Challenge Words:
	Possible Selection Words:

Challenge Add the Challenge Words to your Word Sort.

Connect to Reading Look through *Quest for the Tree Kangaroo.*
Find words that have the vowel + /r/ spelling patterns on this page.
Add them to your Word Sort.

Spelling Words

1. glory
2. aware
3. carton
4. adore
5. aboard
6. dairy
7. ordeal
8. pardon
9. warn
10. vary
11. barely
12. torch
13. barge
14. soar
15. beware
16. absorb
17. armor
18. stairway
19. perform
20. former

Challenge
discard
forfeit
orchestra
rarity
hoard

Name _____ Date _____

Lesson 6
READER'S NOTEBOOK

Quest for the Tree
Kangaroo
Spelling: Vowel + /r/ Sounds

Proofreading for Spelling

**Find the misspelled words and circle them. Write them correctly
on the lines below.**

Scientists worn us not to go near the tree kangaroos. The
kangaroos might fall and get hurt. After all, they do not have any
armer to protect them if they fall. If you do happen to go near
one, bewear! There may also be a baby tree kangaroo abord.
That young one faces an ordele if it falls out of its mother's
pouch. Baby tree kangaroos need their mothers for a long time.
Instead of getting close to them, enjoy tree kangaroos from a safe
distance. You can see the glorie of nature and adoor its wonders
without harming it. Try to be awear of everything around you.
Your heart will sore if you ever do see a tree kangaroo. The tree
kangaroo bearly disturbs the trees as it climbs up. It looks so free!
Remember, a discarded drink carten and other trash can hurt tree
kangaroos. They may mistake it for food. Left undisturbed, the
tree kangaroo prefroms graceful motions up in the trees. It is safe
there.

Spelling Words

1. glory
2. aware
3. carton
4. adore
5. aboard
6. dairy
7. ordeal
8. pardon
9. warn
10. vary
11. barely
12. torch
13. barge
14. soar
15. beware
16. absorb
17. armor
18. stairway
19. perform
20. former

Challenge
discard
forfeit
orchestra
rarity
hoard

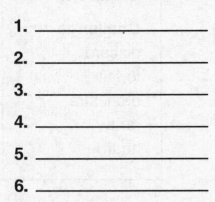
1. _____
2. _____
3. _____
4. _____
5. _____
6. _____

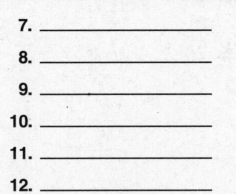
7. _____
8. _____
9. _____
10. _____
11. _____
12. _____

Action Verbs

> An **action verb** shows what the subject does or did.
>
> **action verb**
>
> *The tree kangaroo <u>climbed</u> the tree.*

Thinking Question
What has the subject of the sentence done?

Activity   Underline the action verb in each sentence.

1. I studied about the animals.
2. The scientists searched the forest for tree kangaroos.
3. We finally found a specimen in a tree.
4. The man barked like a dog.
5. The tree kangaroo bit one of the scientists.
6. I worry about the future of these animals.
7. We placed a collar on the tree kangaroo.
8. The team marched through the forest.
9. We followed the old path.
10. The team boarded a plane for home.

Name _____ Date _____

Main Verbs and Helping Verbs

A main verb tells what the subject is thinking or doing. A **helping verb** comes before the main verb and adds detail. Some helping verbs are *may, might, must, been, is, do, should, have, will,* and *can.*

> helping verb and main verb
> *We may go to the rainforest soon.*

Thinking Question
Which verb describes the action and which verb helps it?

Underline the main verb of each sentence once. Then underline the helping verb of each sentence twice.

1. I would love to see a tree kangaroo.
2. We will study the animals of Papua New Guinea in class.
3. We have learned about forest habitats.
4. The biologist will share the findings of the study.
5. The tree kangaroos can return to their home in the trees.
6. The workers have located two tree kangaroos.
7. I would enjoy the presentation very much.
8. I have seen a program about those animals on TV.

Verb Tenses

> **Verb tense** can help convey times, sequences, conditions, or states.
>
> **verb tenses**
> *After the scientists have found a tree kangaroo, they will examine it.*

Thinking Question
Do the verb tenses help convey time, sequence, condition, or state?

For each of the following sentences, identify whether the verb tenses are helping to convey time, sequence, condition, or state.

1. We walk through the forest in search of tree kangaroos.

   _____

2. We flew to Papua New Guinea and will drive to the camp.

   _____

3. The men had to capture the animal before examining it.

   _____

4. We will have completed a full week's worth of work in the forest.

   _____

5. I will be delighted to be done with this project.

   _____

6. We will be flying to a remote part of the island.

   _____

7. I followed the animal I spotted in the trees.

   _____

8. The tree kangaroos will recover if they are given enough time.

   _____

69

Subjects, Predicates, and Complete Sentences

	Subject	Predicate
Sentence	Many marine animals	are endangered.
Fragment	An unusual forest creature	

Activity Underline the subject of each sentence once and the predicate of each sentence twice. If the sentence does not have a subject and predicate, write *fragment*.

1. The scientists work for a vital cause. _____

2. Tree kangaroos are shy and secretive. _____

3. In the trees, the golden-haired animal. _____

4. Tromping through the woods, hoping to spot tree kangaroos.

 _____

5. I have always been interested in these special creatures.

 _____

6. The reporter followed the crew as they searched the forest.

 _____

7. The team of researchers working at the camp. _____

8. Many animals spend most of their lives in the trees. _____

9. Experts on animals do research in many parts of the world.

 _____

10. Many mammals that live in rain forests. _____

Connect to Writing

Choosing exact verbs of the proper tense can help
make writing clear and more interesting.

Vague	Exact
The tree kangaroo sat in the tree.	The tree kangaroo was lounging in the tree.

1–5. Choose the verb or tense that gives more detail about the action.

1. (moved, had moved) The animal _____ to another
   tree.

2. (analyze, will analyze) The scientists _____ the data they
   collect.

3. (seemed, felt) I _____ extremely happy to have made the
   trip.

4. (changed, darkened) Suddenly, the color of the sky _____.

5. (went, zoomed) The plane sped down the runway and
   _____ away.

6–10. Complete each sentence with a word from the box. Choose the verb
that best brings out the meaning of the sentence.

> had taken   was   scrambled   said   reviews
>
> expressed   exclaimed   would be   had studied   gave
>
> examined

6. The tree kangaroo _____ higher into the tree.

7. The scientist _____ samples that
   _____ later.

8. "I am so thrilled to have seen this!" she _____.

9. Oscar _____ the information before taking the test.

10. I _____ gratitude for the help of the workers.

Focus Trait: Organization
Creating a Clear Sequence

Events	Sequence
The tracker put the tree kangaroo in a burlap bag. Holly and Lisa examined the animal. Gabriel attached a radio collar to the kangaroo.	First, the tracker placed the squirming tree kangaroo into a burlap bag. Next, Holly and Lisa conducted an examination of the animal. When they finished, Gabriel attached a radio collar that they would use to track the kangaroo.

Organize the events into a sequence. Add or change words to make the sequence clearer and more interesting.

Events	Sequence
1. Tess was released into the wild.	
2. The hired trackers searched for kangaroos.	
3. The scientists traveled to the forests of Papua New Guinea.	
4. Scientists examined the animal.	
5. They placed a radio collar around Tess's neck.	
6. They searched for three days and captured a female kangaroo.	
7. They named the tree kangaroo Tess.	
8. They determined its weight, temperature, and heart rate.	

Reader's Guide

Old Yeller

Evaluate Word Choice

Authors try to build drama and suspense in a story through their word choice. In *Old Yeller*, vivid sensory language helps build tense, suspenseful moments. We can feel how Travis and Arliss experienced these moments.

Read page 211. Choose three phrases that you think use good sensory language to describe the action, and write them in column 1. For each phrase, explain why it is a good word choice and write the explanation in column 2. Try to think of a different reason for each phrase. The first row has been completed for you.

Author's Word Choice	Characteristics of Good Word Choices
I felt my heart flop clear over.	describes a physical feeling

Write each of the characteristics of good word choices from the table on page 73 in the checklist below. Choose your favorite page of the story. Write three examples of good word choices in column 1 of the checklist. Then, check the characteristics that each example has.

Page number: ____	Characteristic 1	Characteristic 2	Characteristic 3	Characteristic 4
Author's Word Choices	describes a physical feeling			

Give your review of the page. Explain why you think it does or does not show good word choices.

_____

_____

_____

_____

Name _____ Date _____

Lesson 7
READER'S NOTEBOOK

Old Yeller

Vocabulary Strategies:
Adages and Proverbs

Adages and Proverbs

Choose a word from the box to complete each adage or proverb.
Then write the meaning of the sentence below.

succeed	change	receive
misery	honesty	light
earned	safe	join
	end	

1. It is better to give than to _____ .

_____

2. A _____ is as good as a rest. _____

_____

3. A penny saved is a penny _____ .

_____

4. Many hands make _____ work.

_____

5. All good things must come to a(n) _____ . _____

6. If you can't beat them, _____ them. _____

_____

7. _____ loves company.

_____

8. If at first you don't _____ , try, try again. _____

9. _____ is the best policy. _____

10. It is better to be _____ than sorry.

_____

More Vowel + /r/ Sounds

Basic   Write the Basic Word that best completes each group.

1. wiggle, shake, _____

2. pray, meditate, _____

3. tired, exhausted, _____

4. look, gaze, _____

5. spin, whirl, _____

6. mumble, whisper, _____

7. ground, dirt, _____

8. investigate, explore, _____

9. smudge, streak, _____

10. perceptive, attentive, _____

11. dock, wharf, _____

Challenge 12–14.   Write a journal entry about your career goals.
Use at least three Challenge Words. Write on a separate sheet
of paper.

Spelling Words

1. earth
2. peer
3. twirl
4. burnt
5. smear
6. further
7. appear
8. worthwhile
9. nerve
10. pier
11. squirm
12. weary
13. alert
14. murmur
15. thirsty
16. reverse
17. worship
18. career
19. research
20. volunteer

Challenge
yearn
engineer
interpret
dreary
external

Spelling Word Sort

Write each Basic Word beside the correct heading.

/ûr/ spelled *ear*	**Basic Words:** **Challenge Words:** **Possible Selection Words:**
/ûr/ spelled *ir*	**Basic Words:** **Possible Selection Words:**
/ûr/ spelled *ur*	**Basic Words:** **Possible Selection Words:**
/ûr/ spelled *er*	**Basic Words:** **Challenge Words:**
/ûr/ spelled *or*	**Basic Words:**
/îr/ spelled *eer*	**Basic Words:** **Challenge Words:**
/îr/ spelled *ear*	**Basic Words:** **Challenge Words:** **Possible Selection Words:**
/îr/ spelled *ier*	**Basic Words:** **Possible Selection Words:**

Spelling Words

1. earth
2. peer
3. twirl
4. burnt
5. smear
6. further
7. appear
8. worthwhile
9. nerve
10. pier
11. squirm
12. weary
13. alert
14. murmur
15. thirsty
16. reverse
17. worship
18. career
19. research
20. volunteer

Challenge

yearn
engineer
interpret
dreary
external

Challenge Add the Challenge Words to your Word Sort.

Connect to Reading Look through *Old Yeller*. Find words with /ûr/ and /îr/ spelling patterns. Add them to your Word Sort.

Name _____ Date _____

Proofreading for Spelling

Old Yeller
Spelling: More Vowel
+ /r/ Sounds

**Find the misspelled words and circle them. Write them correctly
on the lines below.**

My great-grandpa Virgil grew up in coastal Texas in the 1880s.
As a boy, he had a dog, Grizzle, who was bigger than
the biggest dog you ever saw. They apear to have been good
buddies, according to some old letters my mom found in the attic
during her family resurch. Grizzle once fell down a well, and
Virgil pulled him out. To repay this worthwile favor, Grizzle
went for help later when Virgil was nearly bernt in a fire. Grizzle
had a long, happy carear as a dog-of-all-trades and master
voluntier. He had more nearve than most people. A ferther
valuable trait was his sense of direction. He always led the weery
wanderers home, no matter how far away Virgil and his friends
strayed. Always aleart, Grizzle had no peare on this eairth.

Spelling Words

1. earth
2. peer
3. twirl
4. burnt
5. smear
6. further
7. appear
8. worthwhile
9. nerve
10. pier
11. squirm
12. weary
13. alert
14. murmur
15. thirsty
16. reverse
17. worship
18. career
19. research
20. volunteer

Challenge
yearn
engineer
interpret
dreary
external

1. _____   7. _____

2. _____   8. _____

3. _____   9. _____

4. _____   10. _____

5. _____   11. _____

6. _____   12. _____

Direct Objects

In a sentence, a **direct object** is a person, place, or thing that receives the action of the verb. The direct object can be either a noun or a pronoun (*it, someone, him*).

direct object

The dog loved the <u>boy</u>.

Thinking Question
What word tells who or what receives the action of the verb?

Activity   Underline the direct object in each sentence.

1. Papa is herding cattle.

2. Mama will fix the fence.

3. Last month, a mountain lion attacked our neighbors' cow.

4. Their hired man saw it.

5. That story frightened me.

6. Our parents warned us to stay on the ranch.

7. I will never forget the bear we met in the woods.

8. After that time, we paid attention.

Compound Direct Objects

A **compound direct object** is two or more objects that receive the action of the same verb. The objects can be nouns, pronouns, or both. The object forms of personal pronouns are *me, you, her, him, it, us, you, them.*

Mama called Papa, the hired man, and my brother.
Mama called my brother and me. (Not my brother and I)

Thinking Question
What words tell who or what receives the action of the verb?

1–5. **In each sentence, underline the compound direct object.**

1. I gathered a hammer, nails, and glue.

2. I fixed the fence, the barn, and the front door.

3. We welcomed our neighbors and some traveling musicians.

4. The musicians entertained our neighbors and us.

5. After the music and some dancing, we served food and drink.

6–8. **Underline the incorrect object pronouns. Write the correct ones.**

6. Papa says the darkness never scared Mama or he. _____

7. The moon and stars helped they and us see better. _____

8. Still, you won't find my brother or I out after dark. _____

Indirect Objects

An **indirect object** is a noun or a pronoun that comes
between the verb and the direct object. An indirect
object tells to or for whom or what the action of the verb
is done.

A sentence that has an indirect object must have a
direct object.

   indirect object   direct object
Papa gave his <u>horse</u> a <u>pat</u> on the head.

Thinking Question
*To whom or what or
for whom or what is
the action of the
verb done?*

Activity Underline the indirect object and draw two lines under the
direct object.

1. Our cousins showed us the swimming hole on their ranch.

2. They handed us fishing poles.

3. We brought the ducks and geese small pieces of bread.

4. I showed Papa my catch of the day, a piece of wood!

5. We took the cows and horses their feed.

6. When we returned to our cousins' house, they got us a snack.

7. In the evening, our aunt gave our cousins and us supper.

8. After dinner, we told our aunt, uncle, and cousins the tale of Old

   Yeller and Arliss.

Kinds of Sentences

Four Kinds of Sentences

Declarative sentence	There are bears in the forest.
Interrogative sentence	Did you see the bear?
Imperative sentence	Do not go near the bear.
Exclamatory sentence	Watch out for the bear!

Activity Write each sentence. Add the correct end punctuation. The kind of sentence is shown in parentheses.

1. Bears hunt for blueberries in the woods (declarative)

   _____

2. Did you find any blueberry bushes (interrogative)

   _____

3. Pick some blueberries (imperative)

   _____

4. I love blueberries (exclamatory)

   _____

5. The campers saw a bear near the tents (declarative)

   _____

6. The bear is looking for food (declarative)

   _____

7. Put your food in a bear bag (imperative)

   _____

8. Can unwrapped fresh food attract bears (interrogative)

   _____

Connect to Writing

Direct Objects and the Same Verb	Combined Sentence with Compound Direct Object
The bear ate some berries. The bear ate a fish.	The bear ate some berries and a fish.
Direct Objects and the Same Verb	**Combined Sentence with Compound Direct Object**
I could plant tomatoes. I could plant corn. I could plant lettuce.	I could plant tomatoes, corn, or lettuce.

Activity Combine each set of sentences to form one sentence that includes all the direct objects.

1. Papa rode the big red stallion. Papa rode the bay mare. Papa rode the palomino.

   _____

2. Mama made quilts for our beds. She made cloth for our curtains. She made soap for our baths.

   _____

   _____

3. When we were in the wagon train, we saw hawks circling. We saw mountain lions watching. We saw deer running.

   _____

   _____

4. I want fried chicken for supper. I want corn for supper.

   _____

5. While walking, don't disturb birds' nests. Don't disturb other wildlife.

   _____

Focus Trait: Elaboration
Adding Direct Quotations and
Precise Details

General Detail (Weak)	Precise Detail (Strong)
Old Yeller growled at the bear. He looked fierce.	Old Yeller's lips pulled back from his teeth in a vicious snarl. He snapped and lunged with all his weight at the bear.

A. Read each statement without support on the left. Then add quotations from "Old Yeller" that elaborate on and support the statement.

Without Support (Weak)	With Support (Strong)
1. Travis cared for his brother.	
2. Travis's feelings about Old Yeller changed.	

B. Read each sentence. Then rewrite it to make the detail more precise. Add words that show rather than tell the information.

Pair/Share Work with a partner to brainstorm more exact ways to elaborate on each detail.

General Detail	Precise Detail
3. He heard the sound of the bear.	
4. He got ready to act.	
5. He felt relieved.	

Everglades Forever: Restoring America's Great Wetland

Think Like a Conservationist

Conservationists study how humans' actions affect plants and animals. The author of "Everglades Forever" writes about how the plants and animals of the Everglades depend on water. She wants us to understand how our use of water affects the Everglades. She is thinking like a conservationist.

Think about being one of the students on the field trip in the story. Read page 240. What do you observe that shows how the animals in the slough depend on water?

_____

_____

_____

Read page 241. What do you observe that shows how the animals in the mangrove swamp depend on water?

_____

_____

_____

Name _____ Date _____

Lesson 8
READER'S NOTEBOOK

Everglades Forever:
Restoring America's
Great Wetland
Independent Reading

Read page 244. Ranger Jim says it is important to conserve water.
How do your observations about the slough and the mangrove swamp
support what Ranger Jim says about water?

_____

_____

_____

_____

Think about the details that you found to explain the importance of
water in the slough and mangrove swamp. How might a student like
you on the field trip use those details to persuade people to protect
the water?

_____

_____

_____

_____

Prefixes *en-*, *re-*, *pre-*, *pro-*

The words in the box begin with a prefix. Choose a word to fill in
the blank and complete each sentence. Use the meanings of the prefixes
and base words to help you select the correct word for each sentence.

endangered	proactive	enrage	entangle	review
remove	reaction	precaution	prohibit	preset

"put in"

1. A park ranger can teach us about species that are _____.

2. Treat the alligators with respect so you do not _____ them.

3. Used fishing line can _____ a turtle or bird.

"again"

4. Some types of plants may cause an allergic skin _____.

5. _____ your equipment list before an outdoor journey.

6. It is against the law to _____ wild animals from
   the park.

"before"

7. As a safety _____, make sure you have a first-aid kit with
   you before you go on a nature trip or hike.

8. Give your friends and family a _____ date and time
   when you will return.

"in front of/forward"

9. Park rangers are _____ about taking care of the
   environment before problems occur.

10. Park rules _____ activities that are harmful to the
    environment.

Homophones

Basic Write the Basic Word that best replaces the underlined word or words in each sentence.

Spelling Words

1. steel
2. steal
3. aloud
4. allowed
5. ring
6. wring
7. lesson
8. lessen
9. who's
10. whose
11. manor
12. manner
13. pedal
14. peddle
15. berry
16. bury
17. hanger
18. hangar
19. overdo
20. overdue

Challenge
canvass
canvas
site
sight
cite

1–2. Chris tends to <u>do too much</u> work in the garden.
Some of his planting is <u>late</u> because the weather was too cold.

_____

3–4. Father bought several <u>small fruit</u> seeds for him.
He and Chris are going to <u>plant them underground</u> in the garden.

_____

5–6. Chris digs with a tool made of <u>metal</u>.
He digs a deep hole so birds won't <u>take</u> the seeds.

_____

7–8. The garden project has been a kind of science <u>learning experience</u> for Chris.
Once his garden begins growing, his worry should <u>decrease</u>.

_____

9–10. Chris may <u>sell</u> his plants at a farmer's market.
He can use the money to buy a new <u>foot-lever</u> for his bike.

_____

Challenge 11–14. Suppose your family is going to a boat show. Write a paragraph about what you see and do. Use four of the Challenge Words. Write on a separate sheet of paper.

Spelling Word Sort

Write each Basic Word beside the correct heading.

One-syllable homophones	**Basic Words:** **Challenge Words:** **Possible Selection Words:**
Two-syllable homophones	**Basic Words:** **Challenge Words:** **Possible Selection Words:**
Three-syllable homophones	**Basic Words:**

Challenge Add the Challenge Words to your Word Sort.

Connect to Reading Look through *Everglades Forever: Restoring America's Great Wetland.* Find homophones for the following words: *blew, floes, tales, mourning.* Add them to your Word Sort.

Spelling Words

1. steel
2. steal
3. aloud
4. allowed
5. ring
6. wring
7. lesson
8. lessen
9. who's
10. whose
11. manor
12. manner
13. pedal
14. peddle
15. berry
16. bury
17. hanger
18. hangar
19. overdo
20. overdue

Challenge
canvass
canvas
site
sight
cite

Proofreading for Spelling

Find the incorrect or misspelled words and circle them. Write them correctly on the lines below.

I slide my shirt from its hangar and run outside to meet my uncle. Uncle Harry, whose a diver, is taking me snorkeling. We visit the coral reef offshore from the private landing strip hangarr on the peninsula. A sign reads "No fishing alowed."

The coral reef is an ecosystem that is a home to more kinds of life than any other marine environment. Through my mask, I see a wring of brightly colored coral and many fish. The coral reef, in its maner, protects life and produces food and sand. The reef is endangered because of developers whos pollution has threatened it. After we climb back on the boat, I dry off and wringe out my towel. I wonder alloud about the reef's future. Then Uncle Harry gives me a leson in how to lesen pollution so the coral reef will remain healthy. I feel relieved and am able to burry my fears.

Spelling Words

1. steel
2. steal
3. aloud
4. allowed
5. ring
6. wring
7. lesson
8. lessen
9. who's
10. whose
11. manor
12. manner
13. pedal
14. peddle
15. berry
16. bury
17. hanger
18. hangar
19. overdo
20. overdue

Challenge
canvass
canvas
site
sight
cite

1. _____   7. _____
2. _____   8. _____
3. _____   9. _____
4. _____   10. _____
5. _____   11. _____
6. _____   12. _____

Using *And*, *But*, and *Or*

Conjunctions are words that connect other words or groups of words in a sentence. The words *and*, *but*, and *or* are coordinating conjunctions. *And* joins together. *But* shows contrast. *Or* shows choice.

conjunction

Alligators use their tails and feet to dig holes in the shore.

> **Thinking Question**
> What word's function is to connect other words or groups of words in a sentence?

1–5. Underline the conjunction in each sentence. Tell whether it connects subjects, predicates, direct objects, or sentences.

1. Soon the animals will need to migrate, or they will die. _____
2. The mangrove trees have special roots and bark. _____
3. Lichen spreads on the tree but does not kill it. _____
4. Marlberry bushes and cabbage palms cover the land. _____
5. The heron caught the fish, but the egret stole it. _____

6–10. Write the conjunction that best performs the function shown in parentheses.

6. Crocodiles quietly watch _____ wait for their prey. (joins together)
7. A hawk dove into the river _____ did not catch the fish. (shows contrast)
8. You can conserve water by taking shorter showers _____ by doing full laundry loads. (shows choice)
9. Plants _____ animals rely on each other in the wild. (joins together)
10. Governments _____ businesses must cooperate to achieve conservation goals. (joins together)

Conjunctions in Compound Sentences

When two complete sentences are joined using a comma and a conjunction, they form a compound sentence. If the sentences are related to the same subject or similar idea, use the conjunction *and*. If they present contrasting ideas, use the conjunction *but* or *or*.

I am interested in conservation, **but** I have never studied it before.

I am interested in conservation, **and** I hope to study it in college.

I will study conservation, **or** I will pursue botany.

Thinking Questions
How are the two sentences related? What conjunction can I use to connect them?

Activity Form compound sentences, using a comma and a conjunction. **Write your new sentence on the line.**

1. Dad and I toured the Everglades my sister visited the museum.

   _____

2. The tour lasted three hours I was glad Dad brought snacks.

   _____

3. I liked seeing the wild animals. Dad enjoyed looking at the plants.

   _____

4. I wish we could stay longer our trip will end in two days.

   _____

5. We could go home now. We could stay for the slide show.

   _____

Using Subordinating Conjunctions

Subordinating conjunctions are words that connect one sentence part to another. The subordinating conjunction makes one part of the sentence dependent on the other part. When two sentences are connected using a subordinating conjunction, they form a complex sentence. Some subordinating conjunctions are *if, because, although, after, when,* and *where.*

<u>*Because*</u> *the hawk is desperate for food, it waits patiently to seize its prey.*

Thinking Question
Which part of the sentence is dependent on the other part?

Activity Use a subordinating conjunction to write each pair of sentences as a complex sentence. Add commas where needed.

1. I wrote my report on the Everglades. I researched my topic thoroughly.

    _____

    _____

2. Our class saw the sun set over the still water. We all sighed in amazement.

    _____

    _____

3. We were on our best behavior. Going on the field trip was a privilege for our class.

    _____

    _____

4. We were all tired after our day. We continued to talk enthusiastically about our experiences.

    _____

    _____

93

Lesson 8
READER'S NOTEBOOK

Complete Subjects and Predicates

Everglades Forever
Grammar: Spiral Review

Complete Subject	Complete Predicate
Many of the park's alligators	gather at the edge of this swamp.
(You)	Look at the alligators.

1–10. Underline the complete subject once. Underline the complete predicate twice. If the complete subject is the understood *You*, write it on the line.

1. The state of Florida protects Everglades National Park. _____

2. Many visitors appreciate the park's natural beauty. _____

3. All of us observing the alligators must remain in our seats. _____

4. The hungry alligators will attack their prey. _____

5. Be careful around the alligators! _____

6. The Everglades ecosystem is important to the state of Florida. _____

7. Scientists want to learn about the park's natural resources. _____

8. The alligators are the highlight of their trip to the park. _____

9. Birds, such as the heron, attract observers also. _____

10. Learn how to protect and preserve the Everglades. _____

Connect to Writing

Run-on Sentence
The alligator could have captured the trout it chose to wait for a larger one.
Compound Sentence
The alligator could have captured the trout, but it chose to wait for a larger one.
Complex Sentence
Although the alligator could have captured the trout, it chose to wait for a larger one.

Activity   Rewrite each run-on sentence as a compound sentence and as a complex sentence. Punctuate correctly.

1. The Florida panther is endangered it is on the endangered species list.

_____

_____

_____

2. It is possible to camp in the Everglades you will need a permit.

_____

_____

3. Park rangers are the best guides they know a lot of information about the park.

_____

_____

_____

4. We paddle on the waterways we see unusual fish.

_____

_____

Focus Trait: Evidence
Describing Causes and Effects

Weak Paragraph	Strong Paragraph
Small plants called phytoplankton live in the ocean. They are important. Humans eat large fish. Small fish eat them.	Microscopic plants called phytoplankton live on the ocean's surface. They are important to the survival of most organisms on the planet. They are the basis of the food chain. Small fish eat them; then large fish eat the small fish. Humans, in turn, eat the large fish.

Add details that explain the cause-and-effect relationship between dry weather and the migration of animals within the Everglades. Then organize your evidence logically and use the details to write a paragraph. Remember to include transitions that will connect ideas.

1. During dry weather, water levels in parts of the Everglades fall.

2. _____

3. Large birds and alligators look for the fish and smaller animals to eat.

4. _____

Paragraph: _____

_____

_____

_____

_____

_____

_____

_____

Storm Warriors

Get the Scoop!

When reporters investigate a newspaper story, they interview people who were involved in the events. When they write the story, they use quotes from those people to support their conclusions. Quotes are the actual words of the people involved.

You are a newspaper reporter investigating the rescue of the *E.S. Newman* by the Outer Banks surfmen. You are interviewing Nathan to get some good quotes for your story.

Reporter's Notebook

Read page 268. What can help your readers draw the conclusion that the rescue would be unusual? Write an exact quote from the text.

_____

_____

Now write about the rescue from the point of view of a news reporter. Use the quote from Nathan to support your conclusion.

_____

_____

_____

_____

Reporter's Notebook

Read page 274. What information can help your readers draw the conclusion that the sailor was severely injured? Write an exact quote from the text.

_____

_____

_____

_____

Now write another paragraph for your article describing the rescue of the injured sailor. Write about it from a reporter's point of view. Quote from Nathan within your paragraph.

_____

_____

_____

_____

_____

Greek and Latin Roots *tele*, *photo*, *scrib*, and *rupt*

The listed words have a Greek or Latin root. The Greek root *tele* means *distance*, and *photo* means *light*. The Latin root *scrib* means *write*, and *rupt* means *break*. Choose a word from the list to complete each sentence.

telephone	telescope	interrupt	ruptured
scribble	telegram	describe	photography

1. Before telephones and e-mail were invented, people shared urgent news by sending a _____ .

2. She promised to _____ the rest of her trip in her next letter.

3. It is very rude to _____ someone while he or she is speaking.

4. The sailor used a _____ to scout for land and to identify distant ships.

5. Before the _____ became popular, people had to meet in person to talk.

6. The sail _____ during the storm and had to be sewn.

7. When sea captains kept written records, it was very important to write neatly and not _____ .

8. One of the first things you learn in _____ class is when to use the flash.

99

Name _____ Date _____

Compound Words

Basic Read the letter. Write the Basic Words that best replace the underlined numbers in the sentences.

Dear Kyle Fleetly:

You are the greatest soccer player ever! After watching a televised (1) of highlights from your soccer game against Chicago recently, a (2) went off in my head. I want to be a (3) soccer player like you when I grow up. I read news about you every day to have (4) information. The fans yell and create such an (5) when you play! It must be fun to play with you as your (6)! I'm usually quiet and not (7) about my sports heroes. But I'm amazed and (8) at how well you've played (9) your career. Well, it's time to mail this letter at the (10). Please write back.

Thanks,

Wendel

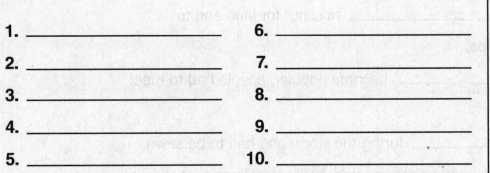

1. _____   6. _____

2. _____   7. _____

3. _____   8. _____

4. _____   9. _____

5. _____   10. _____

Challenge 11–14. What would make an adventurous vacation?
Write a few sentences about things you would like to see or do.
Use four Challenge Words. Write on a separate sheet of paper.

Spelling Words

1. wildlife
2. uproar
3. home run
4. headache
5. top-secret
6. teammate
7. wheelchair
8. light bulb
9. well-known
10. throughout
11. life preserver
12. barefoot
13. part-time
14. warehouse
15. overboard
16. post office
17. outspoken
18. up-to-date
19. awestruck
20. newscast

Challenge

motorcycle
overseas
quick-witted
stomachache
bulletin board

Spelling Word Sort

Write each Basic Word beside the correct heading.

Compound words spelled as one word	**Basic Words:** **Challenge Words:** **Possible Selection Words:**
Compound words spelled with hyphens	**Basic Words:** **Challenge Words:** **Possible Selection Words:**
Compound words spelled as separate words	**Basic Words:** **Challenge Words:** **Possible Selection Words:**

Spelling Words

1. wildlife
2. uproar
3. home run
4. headache
5. top-secret
6. teammate
7. wheelchair
8. light bulb
9. well-known
10. throughout
11. life preserver
12. barefoot
13. part-time
14. warehouse
15. overboard
16. post office
17. outspoken
18. up-to-date
19. awestruck
20. newscast

Challenge
motorcycle
overseas
quick-witted
stomachache
bulletin board

Challenge Add the Challenge Words to your Word Sort.

Connect to Reading Look through *Storm Warriors*. Find words that have the compound word spelling patterns on this page. Add them to your Word Sort.

Name _____ Date _____

Proofreading for Spelling

Storm Warriors
Spelling: Compound Words

Find the incorrect or misspelled words and circle them. Write them correctly on the lines below.

After school, when we're not running bearfoot on the beach, my friend Larry and I are parttime helpers at the U.S. Coast Guard shipwreck museum wherehouse, next to the old post ofice. We were awstruck to see all of the salvaged artifacts for the first time: an early whealchair, a 19th-century shipboard remedy for a head-ache, a lite bulb from a sunken ship, and a life preservor thrown overbored from the *Harriet Lane*. There are many other artifacts: a photo of the winning home-run in a big game against Navy, a top-secrat Civil War document, a collection of wild life drawings by a Coast Guard admiral, and the microphone from the first ship-to-shore newscaste. It is an amazing but not wellknown resource for history buffs.

Spelling Words

1. wildlife
2. uproar
3. home run
4. headache
5. top-secret
6. teammate
7. wheelchair
8. light bulb
9. well-known
10. throughout
11. life preserver
12. barefoot
13. part-time
14. warehouse
15. overboard
16. post office
17. outspoken
18. up-to-date
19. awestruck
20. newscast

Challenge
motorcycle
overseas
quick-witted
stomachache
bulletin board

1. _____   9. _____
2. _____   10. _____
3. _____   11. _____
4. _____   12. _____
5. _____   13. _____
6. _____   14. _____
7. _____   15. _____
8. _____

Subordinating Conjunctions

A **subordinating conjunction** connects two thoughts to make a **complex sentence**. The thought with the subordinating conjunction cannot stand on its own. It needs the rest of the sentence to make sense.

subordinating conjunction

(Because) a storm was coming, we went home early.

Some subordinating conjunctions are *if*, *because*, *when*, *while*, and *although*.

Thinking Questions
Which part of the sentence cannot stand on its own? What word does it begin with?

Activity   Circle the subordinating conjunction in each sentence.

1. Although it was cloudy, we decided to go for a drive.

2. We wanted to go to the beach since the weather was still warm.

3. Because it looked like it might rain, we took our umbrellas.

4. We planned to head home if the rain became too heavy.

5. While we were at the beach, we picked up some seashells.

6. When the first raindrops fell, we walked back to the car.

Activity   Write a sentence explaining what subordinating conjunctions do.

_____

_____

Dependent and Independent Clauses

A **complex sentence** is made up of a
dependent clause and an independent clause.
A **dependent clause** begins with a
subordinating conjunction and needs the
rest of the sentence to make sense. An
independent clause can stand on its own.

dependent clause   independent clause

When it started to rain, we went inside.

Thinking Questions
*Which part of the sentence
can stand on its own?
Which part just gives extra
information?*

Activity Circle the dependent clause and underline the independent clause
in each sentence.

1. We boarded up the windows because a hurricane was coming.

2. After we were finished, we went to the store for supplies.

3. Because the storm could knock down power lines, we bought
   flashlights.

4. We wanted to hurry back before the storm started.

5. When we returned home, the rain began to fall.

6. While the hurricane raged, we stayed safe inside.

Correlative Conjunctions

Correlative conjunctions always work in pairs. They connect two words, phrases, or clauses that are parallel. Correlative conjunctions include *both/and, either/or, neither/nor, not only/but also, whether/or.*

Correlative conjunctions
Not only did they make the station a museum, **but** they **also** created a special exhibit.

Thinking Question
What two words work together to connect parallel parts of the sentence?

Activity   Circle the correlative conjunctions. Then underline the words, phrases, or clauses they connect.

1. Neither the museum nor the historian could find more than one picture of the surfmen.

2. Both the crew and the surfmen felt relieved.

Activity   Use the correlative conjunctions in parentheses to join the two sentences. Write the new sentence.

3. Nathan would become a surfman depending on the outcome of his training. He would become a doctor depending on the outcome of his training. (whether/or)

   _____

   _____

4. Rescues were often long. They were often dangerous. (both/and)

   _____

5. He was a good swimmer. He was a tremendous leader. (not only/but also)

   _____

Kinds of Nouns

A **common noun** is the name of a person, place, or thing. A **proper noun** is the name of a particular person, place, or thing. A proper noun always begins with a capital letter. A **singular noun** names one person, place, or thing. A **plural noun** names more than one person, place, or thing. It is usually formed by adding *s* or *es* to the end of the noun.

singular common nouns: ship, sailor, surfer, watch

plural common nouns: ships, sailors, surfers, watches

singular proper nouns: *E.S. Newman,* Roanoke, Captain Etheridge

plural proper noun: Americans

1–4. **Circle the common noun in each sentence. Underline any proper nouns. Identify them as singular or plural.**

1. The lighthouse is located in North Carolina. _____

2. Herbert Greenley built it to help sailors. _____

3. It helps them see during strong storms. _____

4. Greenley was proud of the building he created. _____

5–10. **Correct six errors in this paragraph. Circle the errors and write the words correctly on the lines below.**

The *lusitania* was the name of a ship. It was built in great Britain over a hundred years ago and made several trips across the atlantic. In 1915, it was hit with torpedos from a submarine. At the time, Britain was in a War with germany. Eighteen minutes after it was struck, the ship sank.

5. _____

6. _____

7. _____

8. _____

9. _____

10. _____

Connect to Writing

Sentence with Related Ideas	Subordinating Conjunction	Correlative Conjunctions
I used the computer in the library. I found more books on the surfmen.	After I used the computer in the library, I found more books on the surfmen.	Not only did I use the computer in the library, but I also found more books on the surfmen.

Activity Combine each pair of sentences. Use the subordinating conjunctions *when*, *because*, *while*, *although*, or *since*. Write the new sentence on the line below.

1. Luis wrote a report on the surfmen. He wanted to learn more about them.

   _____

   _____

2. He had read about the surfmen. There was still a lot he did not know.

   _____

   _____

3. He visited the museum's web site. He learned some interesting facts.

   _____

   _____

Activity Combine each pair of sentences using correlative conjunctions.
Write the new sentence on the line.

4. His cousin was a Coast Guard officer. His cousin knew about the surfmen.

   _____

   _____

5. He could work on his report. He could listen to music.

   _____

   _____

6. The teacher enjoyed the report. She thought it was well done.

   _____

Focus Trait: Evidence
Organizing Main Ideas and Details

Main Idea: Richard Etheridge's early life was unremarkable.
Detail: He was born into slavery in the mid-1800s.
Detail: He learned to read and write.
Detail: He fought in the Civil War.

Read the following details and sort them according to the part of the topic that they develop. Write the details on the lines below each main idea.

Details

- The surfmen could not use their equipment because of the storm.
- He made the crew practice with the equipment.
- There was no dry land close by the ship from which to launch a rescue.
- He supervised the building of a new station.
- The ocean currents were very strong.
- His station was called "one of the tautest on the Carolina Coast."
- His crew became very skilled.

Main Idea: Under Richard Etheridge, the Pea Island Life-Saving Station became one of the best.

1. _____
2. _____
3. _____
4. _____

Main Idea: The rescue of the *E.S. Newman* occurred under seemingly impossible conditions.

1. _____
2. _____
3. _____

Name _____ Date _____

Reader's Guide

Cougars

What's the Take-Away?

The main idea is the most important thing the paragraph says about the topic. All the other information in the paragraph is meant to support that main idea. Writers sometimes call the main idea the take-away. It is the one idea the author wants the reader to take away from the paragraph.

Read the last paragraph on page 296. The main idea, or take-away, of this paragraph is that cougars have adapted to many different habitats. Find three details that support this take-away.

Take-Away	Details
Cougars have adapted to many different habitats.	1. _____ _____ 2. _____ _____ 3. _____ _____

Can you figure out the take-away by using details in
the paragraph? Read the last paragraph on page 303.
Write three details from the paragraph. Think about what
these details are mostly about. Then write the take-away
of the paragraph.

Details	Take-Away
1. _____ _____ _____	_____ _____
2. _____ _____ _____	_____ _____ _____
3. _____ _____ _____	

Name _____ Date _____

Shades of Meaning

Rewrite each sentence, replacing the underlined word with the synonym in parentheses. Then identify the new word as weaker, stronger, or similar in meaning.

watched	shrieked	interesting	unfriendly	hurried
studied	tasty	fascinating	ate	walked
called	delicious	hostile	devoured	

1. The cougar <u>watched</u> its prey. (studied)

_____

2. The bird <u>called</u> a warning. (shrieked)

_____

3. The dessert was <u>tasty</u>. (delicious)

_____

4. We found the cougars' behavior to be <u>interesting</u>. (fascinating)

_____

5. The animals were <u>hostile</u> toward each other. (unfriendly)

_____

6. The cougar <u>ate</u> the steak. (devoured)

_____

7. The children <u>hurried</u> to the cougar exhibit. (walked)

_____

Final Schwa + /r/ Sounds

Basic Write the Basic Words that best complete the analogies.

1. *Hours* is to *clock* as *months* is to _____ .

2. *Governor* is to *state* as _____ is to *city*.

3. *Lincoln* is to *penny* as *Washington* is to _____ .

4. *Cat* is to *cougar* as *minor* is to _____ .

5. *Ear* is to *sound* as *tongue* is to _____ .

6. *Sun* is to *solar* as *moon* is to _____ .

7. *Firefighter* is to *fire truck* as *farmer* is to _____ .

8. *Attic* is to *above* as _____ is to *below*.

9. *Play* is to *scene* as *book* is to _____ .

10. *Harsh* is to *soft* as *sweet* is to _____ .

Challenge 11–14. You are one of the first reporters to arrive at the scene of an earthquake. Write a news story about it. Use four of the Challenge Words. Write on a separate sheet of paper.

Spelling Words

1. cellar
2. flavor
3. cougar
4. chapter
5. mayor
6. anger
7. senator
8. passenger
9. major
10. popular
11. tractor
12. thunder
13. pillar
14. border
15. calendar
16. quarter
17. lunar
18. proper
19. elevator
20. bitter

Challenge
stellar
clamor
tremor
circular
adviser

Spelling Word Sort

Write each Basic Word beside the correct heading.

Words with an *er* pattern for final schwa + *r*	**Basic Words:** **Challenge Words:** **Possible Selection Words:**
Words with an *or* pattern for final schwa + *r*	**Basic Words:** **Challenge Words:**
Words with an *ar* pattern for final schwa + *r*	**Basic Words:** **Challenge Words:** **Possible Selection Words:**

Challenge   Add the Challenge Words to your Word Sort.

Connect to Reading   Look through *Cougars.* Find words that have final schwa + /r/ spelling patterns. Add them to your Word Sort.

Spelling Words

1. cellar
2. flavor
3. cougar
4. chapter
5. mayor
6. anger
7. senator
8. passenger
9. major
10. popular
11. tractor
12. thunder
13. pillar
14. border
15. calendar
16. quarter
17. lunar
18. proper
19. elevator
20. bitter

Challenge
stellar
clamor
tremor
circular
adviser

Name _____ Date _____

Proofreading for Spelling

Find the misspelled words and circle them. Write them correctly on the lines below.

The wolf, bear, and couger are large North American predators. These animals have decreased over the years, even approaching the bordar of extinction. Bears can run 30 miles per hour. Imagine being a passinger in an express elevater and you'll get some sense of that speed. Cougars can run even faster and can leap up to 18 feet high. Wolves and cougars prey on other animals in the wild. Sometimes they might eat a domestic animal when their regular diet sources are scarce. While a rancher feels angre at this, others consider it a small price to pay for a healthy, balanced ecosystem, despite occasional thundar from a senator, congressman, or other piller of the community. Wild predators aren't always populer, but they rarely threaten humans, having a natural, propper fear of people.

1. _____   6. _____

2. _____   7. _____

3. _____   8. _____

4. _____   9. _____

5. _____   10. _____

Spelling Words

1. cellar
2. flavor
3. cougar
4. chapter
5. mayor
6. anger
7. senator
8. passenger
9. major
10. popular
11. tractor
12. thunder
13. pillar
14. border
15. calendar
16. quarter
17. lunar
18. proper
19. elevator
20. bitter

Challenge
stellar
clamor
tremor
circular
adviser

Direct Quotations

A **direct quotation** presents the exact words of another writer or a speaker.

A direct quotation is enclosed in quotation marks. The first word of a direct quotation is capitalized. The end punctuation of a quotation (period, question mark, or exclamation point) appears before the ending quotation mark.

"Look out for cougars as you drive through the park!"

Place a comma between other words in the sentence and the direct quotation.

The ranger said, "Look out for cougars as you drive through the park."

"Look out for cougars as you drive through the park," the ranger said.

Thinking Questions
Does the sentence give a speaker's exact words? How can I separate the exact words from the rest of the sentence?

Activity   Add quotation marks and commas where they are needed.

1. Uncle Robert exclaimed   I would love to visit Big Bend National Park!

2. He said, This is one of the biggest desert areas in America!

3. I asked him   Have you ever seen a mountain lion?

4. Rachel echoed, Did you ever, Uncle Robert?

5. He laughed. Yes, I have, and that was a great day!

Place quotation marks where they are needed in the paragraph below.

Uncle Robert said, When I was walking on Emory Peak, I saw a large animal running in the distance. I knew right away it was a cougar.

Rachel interrupted him, Weren't you scared?

Rachel is my baby sister, and sometimes we think alike.

Uncle Robert told us both to relax. Then he said, In this park, the cougars are not used to humans. They don't want to meet us either.

Quotations from Text

When you include parts of another text in your work, copy the words exactly and include any internal punctuation marks. Then enclose the quote in quotation marks.

The Author's Words

The experience was a once-in-a-lifetime thrill.

Quoted Sentences

Use a comma and capitalize the first letter of the quotation.

The ecologist wrote, "**The** experience was a once-in-a-lifetime thrill."

Use *that* or *as* to introduce the quotation.

The ecologist wrote that "the experience was a once-in-a-lifetime thrill."

Thinking Questions
What part of the text do I want to quote? How can I include it smoothly in my writing?

Complete each sentence with a quoted phrase or sentence taken from the direct quotation that follows it.

1. The cougar might be called an antisocial animal, _____

("The cougar is a solitary diner, preferring to eat alone.")

2. The author describes the cougar's leaping ability saying, _____

_____

("Its legs are like compressed springs that propel it great distances.")

3. Small animals even far away are not safe from the cougar, which is

_____ ("The cougar is favored with acute eyesight.")

4. Unlike a cat, the purr of a cougar is _____ ("Its purr is deceptive.")

5. Although they're hard to spot, _____

("Cougars populate much of North America.")

Interjections and Dialogue

Interjections show strong feelings, such as urgency, disbelief, annoyance, pain, shock, or surprise. They usually appear at the beginning of sentences and include such words as *Hey, Ouch, Wow,* and *No way.* They are followed by exclamation points or commas.

Thinking Questions
Which words tell who is speaking? Do they split the quotation, or come before or after it?

Interjection

Great! My book on cougars is in at the library. (shows excitement, happiness)

Split quotations are direct quotes divided into two parts. Begin and end both parts of the quotation with quotation marks. Capitalize and punctuate the first part the same way as a regular quotation. Place a comma, a space, and quotation marks before the first word of the second part.

Split Quotation

"The cougar moves soundlessly and speedily," said Ms. Smith, "giving it a great hunting advantage."

Add the missing punctuation to each sentence. Then identify the interjection and the emotion it expresses.

1. Ouch! Your cat just scratched me, cried Julia, and I was only petting her!

   _____

2. What! I can't even see a mark, replied Belle, even with my magnifying glass.

   _____

3. Huh! I am just glad she isn't a cougar, moaned Julia, because then I would really be hurt!

   _____

4. Oh, Julia, said Belle, do you really think you would be petting a cougar?

   _____

5. All right! muttered Julia, I was just saying!

   _____

Verb Tenses

Time: conveys past, present, or future
The cougar <u>went</u> to its lair.(*action verb*)

Sequence: conveys order of events
<u>Read</u> the book, and then we <u>will</u> <u>discuss</u> courgars.(*action verb; helping verb*)

Condition: conveys that one action or state of being depends on a condition being met

If the trackers <u>catch</u> a cougar, they <u>will</u> <u>tag</u> it. (*action verb; helping verb*)

State: conveys a subject's state of being
The cougar <u>felt</u> frightened without its mother. (*linking verb*)

On the line following each sentence, tell if the verb or verbs express time, sequence, condition, or state.

1. The cubs greedily **drank** the milk. _____

2. After they **play**, they **will eat** again. _____

3. If they **go** to the watering hole, they **may fall** in. _____

4. The mother cougar **watches** their moves carefully. _____

5. She **feels** anxious about their safety. _____

Write one paragraph about cougars that shows verb tenses used to convey time, sequence, condition, and state.

_____

_____

_____

_____

_____

Connect to Writing

Incorrect	Correct
Oh, when can we see the snakes asked Jeremy?	"Oh, when can we see the snakes?" asked Jeremy.

Activity   Write each statement as a direct quotation. Add quotation marks, capital letters, punctuation, and spaces. Also add an interjection to at least one sentence. You can change words to improve your writing.

1. Ms. Lin told us that the tallest animal on Earth is the giraffe. She said its long neck helps it reach leaves high in the trees.

   _____

   _____

2. One journalist reported that scientists had discovered a new rainforest in Borneo. The animals there had never seen humans.

   _____

   _____

3. The hyena stalks herds of wild animals. According to the tour guide, hyenas attack the sick or weak animals that stray behind the herd.

   _____

   _____

4. This book, according to Jamal, is full of facts about wild animals. He says he will read the whole thing.

   _____

   _____

Focus Trait: Conventions
Using Summaries and Paraphrases

Original	Rewritten
"Cougars face few threats from other animals because they have no natural predators."	Cougars are at the top of the food chain because no other animals prey on them.

Paraphrase or summarize each quotation in your own words. Check your spelling, grammar, and punctuation.

1. "By preying upon various animals, cougars perform the function of keeping the populations of other species in check."

   _____

   _____

2. "Cougars are competent but reluctant swimmers."

   _____

   _____

3. "Cougars conceal large prey they have caught, and feed on it for days."

   _____

   _____

4. "Cougars vocalize in many ways."

   _____

   _____

5. "The cougar population is distributed across North America."

   _____

   _____

Name _____ Date _____

Unit 2
READER'S NOTEBOOK

Hound Dog True
Segment 1
Independent Reading

Reader's Guide

Hound Dog True

Make a Comic Strip

Mattie Breen is adjusting to life in a new place. Retell what has happened to Mattie so far by creating a comic strip. Include details from the text on pages 1–22.

What Happens to Mattie

Name _____ Date _____

Sometimes an author interrupts a story to tell about something that happened to a character before the story began. Use details from the text on pages 3–22 to describe things that happened to Mattie in the past and how they made her feel.

Event from Mattie's Past	What Happened and How Mattie Probably Felt
being new to Mrs. D'Angelo's class	
her name written on the whiteboard	
seeing Star in the coatroom	

Lessons should be helpful, but sometimes they are hurtful. What hurtful lessons do you think Mattie learned from events in her past?

_____
_____
_____
_____

Review the Decision

Mama decided to move with Mattie to her brother's home, so they are now living with Uncle Potluck. What does each of these people think about this decision? As you evaluate the decision from each person's point of view, include details from the text on page 7–11.

Mama

Was this a good decision? _____ 👍   _____ 👎   _____ 👉

Tell your side of the story:

_____

_____

_____

_____

_____

_____

_____

_____

What evidence from the text supports your answer?

_____

_____

_____

_____

_____

Name _____ Date _____

Unit 2
READER'S NOTEBOOK

Hound Dog True
Segment 1
Independent Reading

Mattie

Was this a good decision? _____ 👍   _____ 👎   _____ 👉

Tell your side of the story:

_____

_____

_____

_____

What evidence from the text supports your answer?

_____

Uncle Potluck

Was this a good decision? _____ 👍   _____ 👎   _____ 👉

Tell your side of the story:

_____

_____

_____

_____

What evidence from the text supports your answer?

_____

Name _____ Date _____

Unit 2
READER'S NOTEBOOK

Hound Dog True
Segment 1
Independent Reading

Write Letters from Uncle Potluck and Mattie

Sometimes people don't say exactly what is on their minds.
Consider what Uncle Potluck and Mattie might really be thinking
when they talk about whether Mattie and Quincy should hang out.
Use information from the text on pages 17–22 to write two letters:
one from Uncle Potluck to Mattie and one from Mattie to Uncle Potluck.

Dear Mattie,

_____

_____

_____

_____

_____

_____

_____

_____

_____

_____

Love,
Uncle Potluck

Name _____ Date _____

Unit 2
READER'S NOTEBOOK

Hound Dog True
Segment 1
Independent Reading

Dear Uncle Potluck,

_____

_____

_____

_____

_____

_____

_____

_____

Love,
Mattie

In the story, Mattie also thinks she might not want to hang out with Quincy because Quincy seems a lot older than her. Do you think this is a good reason? Explain why or why not.

_____

_____

_____

Name _____ Date _____

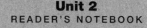

Unit 2
READER'S NOTEBOOK

Hound Dog True
Segment 2
Independent Reading

Reader's Guide

Hound Dog True

Imagining Mattie's World

As Mattie learns about her new surroundings, she finds some distinct, different places. Review pages 23–43 and identify four important places in Mattie's new world. Sketch what each place might look like to Mattie. Give each place a label.

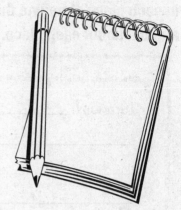

Mattie's World

Name _____ Date _____

Unit 2
READER'S NOTEBOOK

Hound Dog True
Segment 2
Independent Reading

Think about the places in Mattie's new world. How does she feel about each location? Does she feel comfortable or uncomfortable in each place? Imagine that you are Mattie writing a journal entry and tell about each place.

Location 1: _____

_____

_____

_____

Location 2: _____

_____

_____

_____

_____

Location 3: _____

_____

_____

_____

Location 4: _____

_____

_____

_____

Name _____ Date _____

Unit 2
READER'S NOTEBOOK

Hound Dog True
Segment 2
Independent Reading

Make a List

In Mattie's notebook, she takes notes about custodial wisdom and lists tasks that a custodial apprentice might need to do. Use the descriptions on pages 32–37 to create a list about things to know about the school.

Each morning, follow these steps:

1. _____

2. _____

3. _____

Cafeteria Information

Number of tables: _____

Total number of seats available: _____

Lunch Menu	Number of Buckets Needed for Compost

Name _____ Date _____

Unit 2
READER'S NOTEBOOK

Hound Dog True
Segment 2
Independent Reading

Make a Drawing with Labels

At the flat rock, Mattie imagines what a Royal Garbage Wedding
would be like. Read the descriptions of the event on pages 42–43.
Use the descriptions to create a drawing of the wedding. Use quotes
from the text to label the drawing.

Examine Motives and Approaches

Everyone has motives, or reasons for doing something or wanting something to happen. Use details from the text on pages 27–50 to answer the questions below.

Why do the teachers and Principal Bonnet come to visit Uncle Potluck?

_____

_____

_____

_____

Why does Uncle Potluck say he will have to be careful now that Mattie is keeping notes about what he does?

_____

_____

_____

Why does Mama tell Mattie and Uncle Potluck about how she tried to act smart and tough when she had her first real office job?

_____

_____

_____

_____

Name _____ Date _____

Unit 2
READER'S NOTEBOOK

Hound Dog True
Segment 2
Independent Reading

Think about how each character behaves around others.
Write a statement that each character might use to describe
how he or she speaks and behaves around other people.

Principal Bonnet

Uncle Potluck

Mama

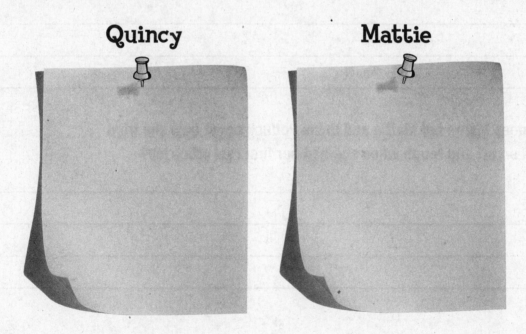

Quincy

Mattie

Name _____ Date _____

Unit 2
READER'S NOTEBOOK

Hound Dog True
Segment 3
Independent Reading

Reader's Guide

Hound Dog True

Write an Advice Column

Imagine that Uncle Potluck writes an advice column for teachers and students at the school in which he offers ideas about ways to solve problems. Think about what Uncle Potluck says and does on pages 63–68 to help him give advice to others.

Dear Uncle Potluck,

I'm new here at school. I thought it would be hard to make friends, but kids have been really friendly. One girl asked me to eat lunch with her my first day, and every day, someone else has invited me to eat lunch with him or her. I really liked that first girl, but I've been too busy to have lunch with her again. What should I do?

New Girl

Dear New Girl,

_____

_____

_____

_____

_____

Your friend,

Uncle Potluck

Name _____ Date _____

Unit 2
READER'S NOTEBOOK

Hound Dog True
Segment 3
Independent Reading

Use the text on pages 63–68 to help Uncle Potluck give advice.

Dear Uncle Potluck,

I'm a teacher here at school. Recently, one of my students was sick with a cold. After she got better, I let her turn a couple of assignments in late because I felt sorry for her. Now she's always late with her homework. Should I let it go, or should I talk to her?

Teacher X

Dear Teacher X,

_____

_____

_____

_____

_____

_____

Your friend,

Uncle Potluck

Name _____ Date _____

Unit 2
READER'S NOTEBOOK

Hound Dog True
Segment 3
Independent Reading

Write an Invitation

Suppose that Mattie had to make an invitation to ask Quincy to come to the sleepover. Use the text from pages 51–60 to help you create an invitation for the sleepover.

You're invited to a sleepover.

Where: _____

_____

When: _____

_____

What we'll have to eat and what we can do:

_____

_____

_____

Do you think Mattie would want to give Quincy this invitation? Why or why not?

_____

_____

How do you think Quincy would respond if she got this invitation? Why?

_____

_____

Unit 2
READER'S NOTEBOOK

Hound Dog True
Segment 3
Independent Reading

Draw Meaningful Items

Some items, such as the button, her notebook, and the silver pipe bracelet are meaningful to Mattie. Use details from pages 52–68 to draw a picture of each item. Write what you think each item means to Mattie.

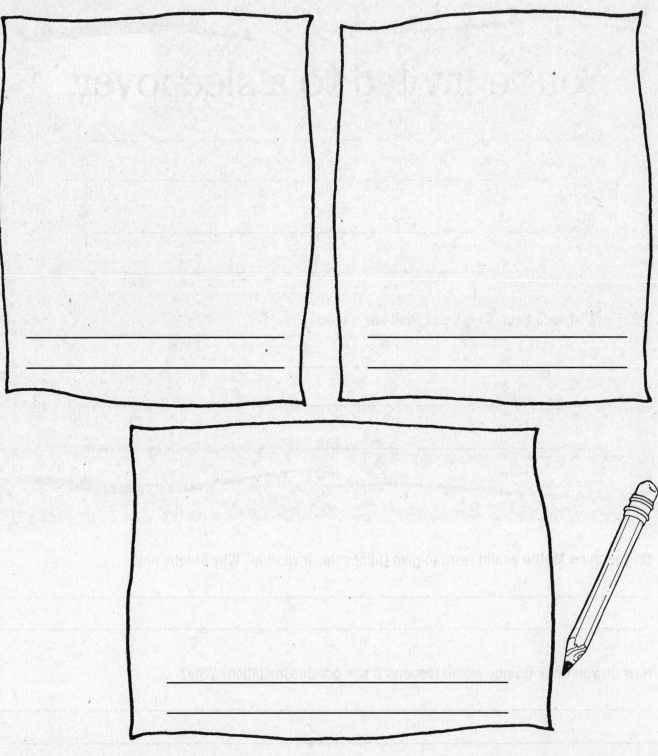

Name _____ Date _____

Unit 2
READER'S NOTEBOOK

Hound Dog True
Segment 3
Independent Reading

Be a Detective

By the end of page 72, some big questions have come up.
Think about mysteries you might want to solve about Mattie
and Quincy. First, review pages 51–72. Use each clue to write a
question about a mystery that has yet to be solved.

? the open notebook **? ? ?**

_____

_____

_____

_____

? Quincy leaving with Aunt Crystal **? ? ?**

_____

_____

_____

_____

? Mattie and Quincy in the future **? ? ?**

_____

_____

_____

_____

Name _____ Date _____

Unit 2
READER'S NOTEBOOK

Hound Dog True
Segment 3
Independent Reading

A detective has to examine clues and evidence to solve a mystery. Now, examine clues in the text on pages 51–72. Write to tell whether you can answer the questions you wrote on page 137, based on evidence in the text.

Your question: _____
_____
_____
_____

Your question: _____
_____
_____
_____

Your question: _____
_____
_____
_____

Name _____ Date _____

Unit 2
READER'S NOTEBOOK

Hound Dog True
Segment 4
Independent Reading

Reader's Guide

Hound Dog True

Write E-Mails

Uncle Potluck has an accident and has to go to Boone County Hospital. Mattie believes that it is all her fault. What do you think they would say if they could write an e-mail to each other?

Use the text on pages 84–94 to help Mattie write an e-mail to Uncle Potluck.

New Message

To: **Uncle Potluck**

From: **Mattie**

Subject: **It's My Fault**

_____
_____
_____
_____
_____
_____
_____
_____
_____

Name _____ Date _____

Unit 2
READER'S NOTEBOOK

Hound Dog True
Segment 4
Independent Reading

Use the text on pages 84–94 to help Uncle Potluck
write an e-mail to Mattie.

New Message
To: **Mattie**
From: **Uncle Potluck**
Subject: **It's Not Your Fault**

_____

_____

_____

_____

_____

_____

_____

_____

_____

_____

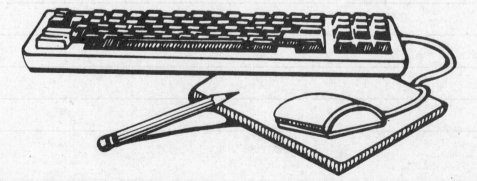

Name _____ Date _____

Unit 2
READER'S NOTEBOOK

Hound Dog True
Segment 4
Independent Reading

Write Diary Entries

Principal Bonnet had an unusual day when Uncle Potluck had his accident. Use the text from pages 88–94 to help you write a diary entry about the day from Principal Bonnet's point of view.

Dear Diary,

_____

_____

_____

_____

_____

_____

_____

_____

_____

_____

_____

_____

_____

_____

_____

Name _____ Date _____

Unit 2
READER'S NOTEBOOK

Hound Dog True
Segment 4
Independent Reading

Now write another diary entry from Mattie's point of view, using details from pages 90–94.

Dear Diary,

_____

_____

_____

_____

_____

_____

_____

_____

_____

_____

_____

_____

Name _____ Date _____

Unit 2
READER'S NOTEBOOK

Hound Dog True
Segment 4
Independent Reading

Complete a Chain of Events Organizer

Mattie tries to show she can be useful, but her idea doesn't work as planned. Review what Mattie does on pages 84–86. Complete the graphic organizer below to show how she ends up locked in Principal Bonnet's office.

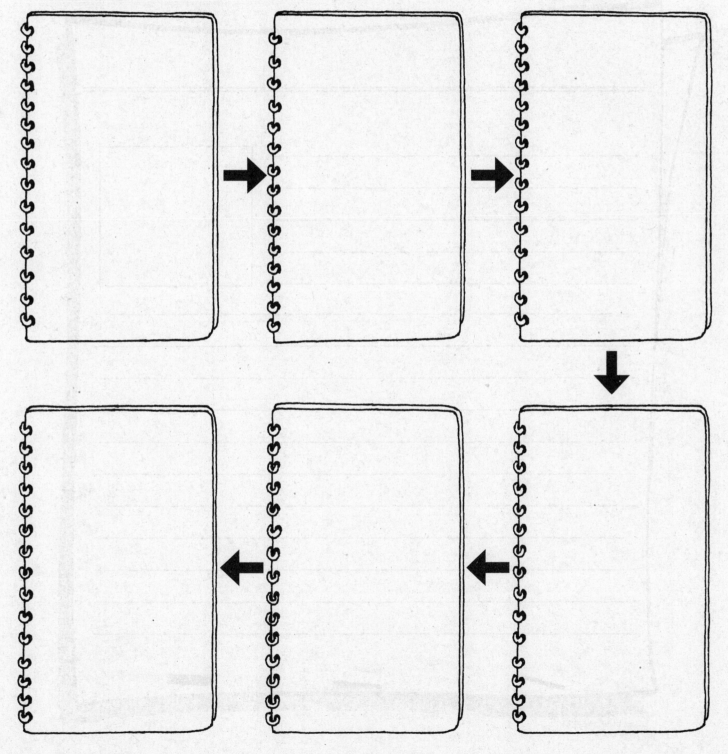

Name _____ Date _____

Unit 2
READER'S NOTEBOOK

Hound Dog True
Segment 4
Independent Reading

Write a Newspaper Article

Write a newspaper article to describe what happened to Uncle Potluck.
Include a quote from Principal Bonnet. Be sure your headline captures
the readers' attention. Draw an illustration to go with the article.

Name _____ Date _____

Unit 2
READER'S NOTEBOOK

Hound Dog True
Segment 5
Independent Reading

Reader's Guide

Hound Dog True

Make an Advertisement for a Laundryville Adventure

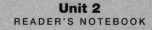
Laundryville

Mattie and Quincy imagine and act out adventures for Moe in Laundryville. Use the text on pages 101–105 to jot notes about how the girls describe their ideas.

Use details from the text to describe Laundryville.

_____

_____

_____

Use details from the text to describe the heroes.

_____

_____

_____

Use details from the text to describe the villain.

_____

_____

_____

Use details from the text to describe why Moe wants to defeat the Lint Monster.

_____

_____

_____

Name _____ Date _____

Unit 2
READER'S NOTEBOOK

Hound Dog True
Segment 5
Independent Reading

Use the notes you created and the rest of the text from pages 101–105 to create an advertisement for an adventure in Laundryville. The advertisement should be descriptive and make readers want to join in an adventure there. Include text and illustrations.

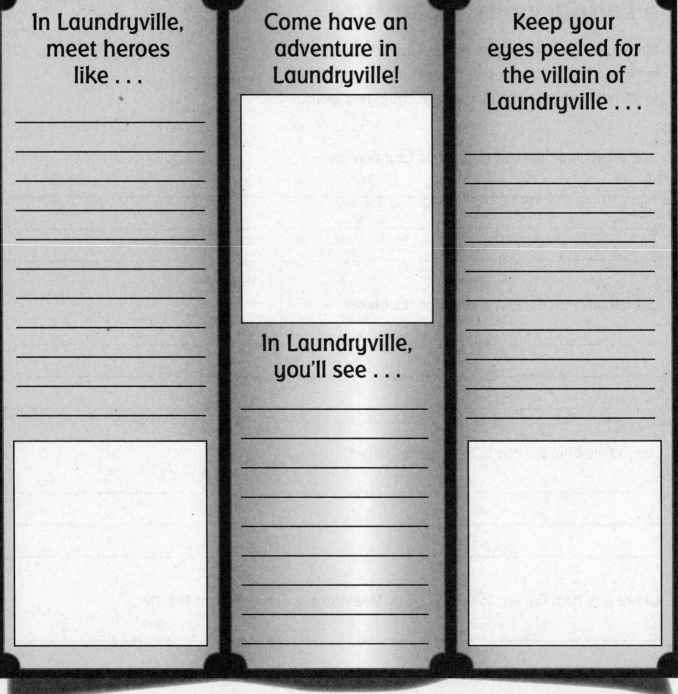

In Laundryville, meet heroes like . . .

_____
_____
_____
_____
_____
_____
_____
_____

Come have an adventure in Laundryville!

In Laundryville, you'll see . . .

_____
_____
_____
_____
_____
_____
_____

Keep your eyes peeled for the villain of Laundryville . . .

_____
_____
_____
_____
_____
_____
_____
_____

Name _____ Date _____

Unit 2
READER'S NOTEBOOK

Hound Dog True
Segment 5
Independent Reading

Retell the Story from Quincy's Point of View

Quincy and Mattie spent the afternoon together. Use the text from pages 97–105 to tell about what they did. Tell the story from Quincy's point of view.

Name _____ Date _____

Unit 2
READER'S NOTEBOOK

Hound Dog True
Segment 5
Independent Reading

Read pages 106–108. As Quincy, tell what you and Mattie did.

_____

_____

_____

_____

As Quincy, tell what you think of Mattie.

_____

_____

_____

_____

_____

As Quincy, tell what you think about trusting the moon.

_____

_____

_____

_____

_____

Name _____ Date _____

Unit 2
READER'S NOTEBOOK

Hound Dog True
Segment 5
Independent Reading

Cause-and-Effect Graphic Organizer

Mama has been thinking over her past. She thinks about what things were like for her when she was young. She thinks about her actions and how they have affected her daughter, Mattie. Use details from pages 112–116 to help you complete the cause and effect organizer.

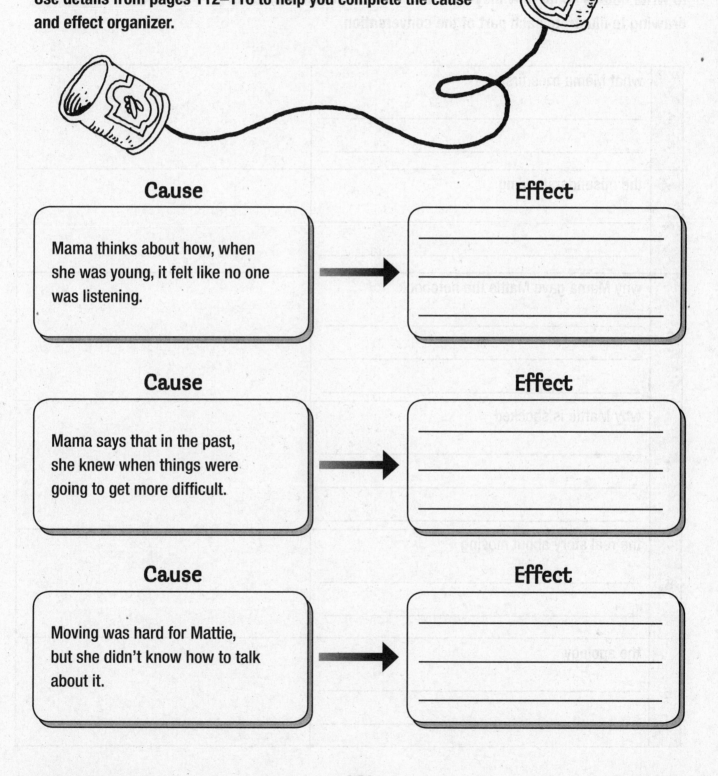

Cause

Mama thinks about how, when she was young, it felt like no one was listening.

Effect

_____
_____
_____

Cause

Mama says that in the past, she knew when things were going to get more difficult.

Effect

_____
_____
_____

Cause

Moving was hard for Mattie, but she didn't know how to talk about it.

Effect

_____
_____
_____

Name _____ Date _____

Unit 2
READER'S NOTEBOOK

Hound Dog True
Segment 5
Independent Reading

How Do Things Get Sorted Out?

It can be difficult for two people to talk about a problem, and there can be misunderstandings. Read the clues about what happens during Mama's conversation with Mattie. Then use the text on pages 112–118 to write details about how they work things out together. Include a drawing to illustrate each part of the conversation.

1.	what Mama tries first _____ _____	
2.	the misunderstanding _____ _____	
3.	why Mama gave Mattie the notebook _____ _____	
4.	why Mattie is shocked _____ _____	
5.	the real story about moving _____ _____	
6.	the apology _____ _____	

Name _____ Date _____

Unit 2
READER'S NOTEBOOK

Hound Dog True
Segment 6
Independent Reading

Hound Dog True

Weigh the Decision

When Quincy gets up and leaves the dinner table, Mattie has an opportunity to do something. Use the text on pages 135–138 to help you understand her choices. List the factors that Mattie might use to decide what to do.

do nothing
_____
_____
_____
_____
_____
_____
_____

go to Quincy
_____
_____
_____
_____
_____
_____

Why do you think Mattie decides to go to Quincy?

_____

_____

_____

Stella's Story

On pages 125–127, Uncle Potluck tells the rest of the story about
Stella the dog. Think about why Stella might have behaved the way
she did. Then write the ending of Stella's story as she might tell it.

The Story that Stella Might Tell

_____

_____

_____

_____

_____

_____

_____

_____

_____

_____

_____

_____

_____

_____

Name _____ Date _____

Unit 2
READER'S NOTEBOOK

Hound Dog True
Segment 6
Independent Reading

Write Thank-You Notes

Mattie and Quincy have helped each other, and their friendship
seems stable and strong. Use the text from pages 134–144
to write a thank-you note from Quincy to Mattie.

Dear Mattie,

_____

_____

_____

_____

_____

_____

_____

_____

_____

_____

_____

_____

_____

Friends Forever,
Quincy

Name _____ Date _____

Unit 2
READER'S NOTEBOOK

Hound Dog True
Segment 6
Independent Reading

Use the text from pages 134–144 to write a thank-you note from Mattie to Quincy.

Dear Quincy,

_____
_____
_____
_____
_____
_____
_____
_____
_____
_____
_____
_____
_____
_____

Friends Forever,
Mattie

Name _____ Date _____

Corncob Futures

Potluck says you can tell a person's future from their corncob. Think about the story characters. What might their corncobs tell about what will happen to them in the future? Write about the future of each character. Use an example from the text to support your prediction.

Potluck

_____

_____

_____

_____

_____

Mama

_____

_____

_____

_____

_____

Name _____ Date _____

Unit 2
READER'S NOTEBOOK

Hound Dog True
Segment 6
Independent Reading

Principal Bonnet

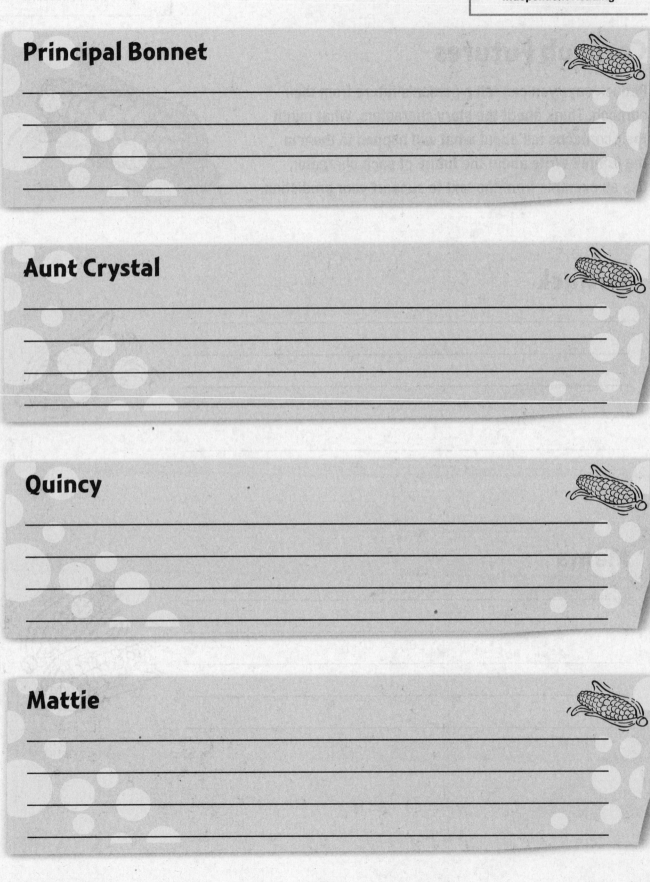

_____

_____

_____

_____

Aunt Crystal

_____

_____

_____

_____

Quincy

_____

_____

_____

_____

Mattie

_____

_____

_____

_____

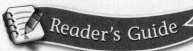
Reader's Guide

Dangerous Crossing

Illustrate Historical Fiction

An illustrator creates images that help readers understand
the meaning and events of a story. Greg Harlin, the illustrator
of *Dangerous Crossing,* has created beautiful paintings that
help capture the events of the story. The illustrations have
an emotional effect on the readers.

Look at the illustrations on pages 334 and 335. How does the
color and light in these images affect you?

_____

_____

_____

_____

Now look at the illustrations on pages 336 and 338. How do these
illustrations show a cause-effect relationship in the story?

_____

_____

_____

_____

Read page 337. What is a cause-effect relationship described on the page?

_____

_____

_____

You are working with the illustrator, Greg Harlin. Create an illustration that would help the reader visualize the cause-effect relationship you just described.

Name _____ Date _____

Lesson 11
READER'S NOTEBOOK

Dangerous Crossing
Vocabulary Strategies:
Using Reference Sources

Using Reference Sources

> ¹ **sur-vey** /sər vā′/ v. [ME, from *surveien*, to look over + to see]
> 1. To question a group of people to gather their opinions
> 2. To look closely at someone or something to make a decision
> 3. To measure a plot of land
> ² **sur-vey** /sûr′ vā/ n.
> 4. A specific set of questions used to gather information

1–4. Read the dictionary entry for *survey*. Write the number of the definition that best fits the meaning of the underlined word.

1. The captain <u>surveyed</u> the valley looking for a place to camp. _____

2. The revolutionary conducted a <u>survey</u> of all townspeople to see how they felt about the British laws. _____

3. The engineer will <u>survey</u> the land before the new bank is built. _____

4. Jane will <u>survey</u> the girls, and Dan will <u>survey</u> the boys about their interest in student government. _____

bracing *adj.* Causing or giving energy and liveliness **Synonyms** energizing, refreshing, invigorating, renewing	**embark** *v.* To set out on an adventure **Synonyms** begin, launch, approach, commence, enter, initiate

5–6. Replace the underlined word with a synonym from the sample thesaurus entries above.

5. The <u>bracing</u> wind felt good on the soldier's hot face. _____

6. Before <u>embarking</u> on the journey across the Delaware River, General Washington worried about the enemy soldiers following his troops.

_____

> **shattered** *adj.* Broken into pieces by force; smashed

Write a sentence using the glossary word above. Use the word in the same way as given.

7. _____

VCCV Pattern

Basic   Write the Basic Word that best completes each sentence.

Spelling Words

1. My family is beginning a _____ to the country.

2. First, we drive through a winding _____ under the bay.

3. I tap my mother on her _____ and ask how much farther we have to go.

4. She shrugs and says _____ 40 miles.

5. I _____ we stop for a snack, and Mom says we'll be at the picnic grounds shortly.

6. We buy three pounds of peaches from a farmer for one dollar. What a _____ !

7. Soon we pass forests full of beautiful, sturdy _____ .

8. Few trees grow around our house, but they are _____ in the country.

9. When we finally _____ at the picnic grounds, I feel a little sad.

10. I _____ that getting somewhere is half the fun!

Challenge 11–14.   Write a paragraph about something you learned while on a trip or an outing. Use four of the Challenge Words. Write on a separate sheet of paper.

Spelling Words
1. bargain
2. journey
3. pattern
4. arrive
5. object
6. suppose
7. shoulder
8. permit
9. sorrow
10. tunnel
11. subject
12. custom
13. suggest
14. perhaps
15. lawyer
16. timber
17. common
18. publish
19. burden
20. scissors

Challenge
narrate
mentor
attempt
collide
ignore

Spelling Word Sort

Write each Basic Word beside the correct heading.

VC/CV: divide between double consonants	**Basic Words:** **Challenge Words:** **Possible Selection Words:**
VC/CV: divide between different consonants	**Basic Words:** **Challenge Words:** **Possible Selection Words:**

Challenge   Add the Challenge Words to your Word Sort.

Connect to Reading   Look through *Dangerous Crossing.* Find words that have the VCCV syllable patterns on this page. Add them to your Word Sort.

Spelling Words

1. bargain
2. journey
3. pattern
4. arrive
5. object
6. suppose
7. shoulder
8. permit
9. sorrow
10. tunnel
11. subject
12. custom
13. suggest
14. perhaps
15. lawyer
16. timber
17. common
18. publish
19. burden
20. scissors

Challenge
narrate
mentor
attempt
collide
ignore

Proofreading for Spelling

Find the misspelled words and circle them. Write them correctly on the lines below.

I, Ben Franklin, was born in Boston and attended the Latin School. As is the custem, I was apprenticed to my older half-brother, James, a printer in Philadelphia. Since age 12, I have helped publisch the colonies' first independent newspaper, *The New-England Courant.* Using a patern, I cut paper to size with big scisors and set lead type. Our last job was an announcement for a new lawer. I was bold enough to sugest that I write a column. To my sorow, James didn't permitt it, so I write under a pseudonym, Mrs. Silence Dogood. Her letters to the editor are the talk of the town. Will James purhaps obgect when he learns the truth? I supose he might. Someday I will speak openly on any subjeck that pleases me. But until I arive at that day, I will continue to speak through my secret pen name, Silence.

Spelling Words

1. bargain
2. journey
3. pattern
4. arrive
5. object
6. suppose
7. shoulder
8. permit
9. sorrow
10. tunnel
11. subject
12. custom
13. suggest
14. perhaps
15. lawyer
16. timber
17. common
18. publish
19. burden
20. scissors

Challenge
narrate
mentor
attempt
collide
ignore

1. _____   8. _____

2. _____   9. _____

3. _____   10. _____

4. _____   11. _____

5. _____   12. _____

6. _____   13. _____

7. _____

Subject Pronouns

A **pronoun** is a word that takes the place of a noun. A **subject pronoun** performs the action of the verb in a sentence.

subject pronoun

singular	plural
I	we
you	you
he, she, it	they

Thinking Questions
Who or what is the subject of the sentence? What word can you replace the subject with?

Jane read her history text.   She read her history text.
Ed and Mark studied for the test.   They studied for the test.

1–5. Underline the subject and circle the verb in each sentence. Replace the noun(s) with a subject pronoun.

1. Ken, Lee, and Martha want to write a play about the Revolutionary War.

    _____

2. Ken begins researching the topic. _____

3. The play takes many weeks to plan. _____

4. Harry builds the sets for the play. _____

5. The story focuses on the ride of Paul Revere. _____

6–10. Underline the correct subject pronoun(s) in each sentence.

6. (They, Them) are changing the rehearsal schedule.

7. (We, You) would like to hear your opinion.

8. (You, I) were just voted director of the play.

9. Mark and (me, I) will make the costumes.

10. However, (he, him) and (I, me) will ask others to help.

Object Pronouns

A **pronoun** is a word that takes the place of a noun. An **object pronoun** takes the place of a noun used after an action verb or after a word such as *to, for, with, in,* or *out.*

singular object pronouns: me, you, him, her, it
plural object pronouns: us, you, them

History is easy for Liam. History is easy for him.
Lars went with Mike and Aiden. Lars went with them.

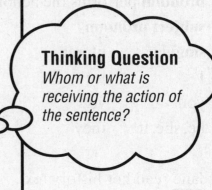

Thinking Question
Whom or what is receiving the action of the sentence?

Activity Read each sentence pair. Put an (X) on the blank by the sentence with the correct object pronoun.

1. _____ Ken wanted me to play Paul Revere.

   _____ Ken wanted I to play Paul Revere.

2. _____ He offered parts in the play to he and she.

   _____ He offered parts in the play to him and her.

3. _____ Martha emailed copies of the script to we.

   _____ Martha emailed copies of the script to us.

4. _____ It was a good way for them to study history.

   _____ It was a good way for they to study history.

5. _____ Sarah didn't like the way the costume fit she.

   _____ Sarah didn't like the way the costume fit her.

6. _____ The director called they on the phone.

   _____ The director called them on the phone.

7. _____ My parents applauded loudly for I.

   _____ My parents applauded loudly for me.

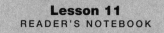
Pronoun and Antecedent Agreement

A **pronoun** is a word that takes the place of a noun. An **antecedent** is the word the pronoun replaces or refers to. A pronoun and its antecedent must agree in number and gender.

pronoun	sentence	antecedent
I	I am (Emily.)	Emily
you	You are (Jana.)	Jana
he	He is (Jarrod.)	Jarrod
she	My (dog) barks when she plays.	dog
they	My (dogs) rest after they exercise.	dogs

Thinking Questions
Whom or what is the pronoun representing? Is the noun singular or plural? Male or female?

Activity   Underline the pronoun and circle the antecedent in each sentence.

1. Joshua said he would dim the lights from backstage.
2. Mary turned on the flashlight, but it did not work.
3. Lucy hoped she had extra batteries in her pocket.
4. Andy's friends helped him practice his lines for the play.
5. The class shouted, "We are going to be great tonight!"
6. "Bart and Gary, you will help people in the audience find their seats," said the principal.

Correlative Conjunctions

> **Correlative conjunctions** are used in pairs. They connect two parallel parts of a sentence, such as two nouns, two adjectives, or two clauses.
>
> **Neither** General Washington **nor** his soldiers knew how the battle would turn out.
> **Whether** they would win **or** they would lose, they knew they had to fight.

either/or	whether/or
neither/nor	not only/but also
both/and	

Activity Fill in the blanks. Choose a pair of correlative conjunctions from the word box to complete each sentence.

1. The rough water of the river _____ rolled the boat from side to side _____ pitched it back and forth.

2. The men worried that the boats would _____ capsize _____ break apart before they reached the other side.

3. They wondered _____ to keep going _____ to turn back.

4. General Washington endured the same suffering as his soldiers, but he _____ complained _____ gave up hope.

5. Washington was concerned about _____ his men's physical safety _____ their mental well-being.

Connect to Writing

> Pronouns are useful words. Good writers use pronouns to avoid repeating the same nouns in every sentence.
>
> Dana always calls me when Dana wants to do history homework.
> Dana always calls me when she wants to do history homework.

Activity   Rewrite each sentence. Replace the repeated noun(s) with the correct pronoun(s).

1. Kara will be unhappy if Kara is late to class.

   _____

2. Will and Matt took notes when Will and Matt read about John Adams.

   _____

3. Both students were nervous before both students presented to the class.

   _____

4. Matt does research every night after Matt eats dinner.

   _____

5. "Let me read your paper when your paper is done," said Mother.

   _____

6. Matt mailed Will's notes to Will on Thursday.

   _____

7. Will felt proud after Will presented to the class.

   _____

8. Matt and Will won awards and put the awards on a shelf.

   _____

Focus Trait: Elaboration
Use Convincing Words

Clear Position	Unclear Position
People should be willing to adopt shelter animals of all ages, not only puppies and kittens.	People usually adopt just puppies and kittens from animal shelters.

A.   Read the given topic and write a sentence that clearly states and elaborates on your position on the issue. Use words that are clear and convincing.

1. Using bicycles for transportation

_____

_____

2. Picking teams for gym class

_____

_____

Position: The library should buy the books students want to read.	
Persuading Classmates	**Persuading a Newspaper Editor**
Wouldn't you use the library more if it had better books?	If the library had books by popular authors, students would use the library more often.

B.   Read the given position below. Write a supporting sentence to connect with and persuade each target audience.

Pair/Share   Work with a partner to brainstorm arguments that each audience might have with your position.

Position: Students should be able to use the school gym on weekends.

3. Persuading the school principal:

_____

_____

4. Persuading a caregiver:

_____

_____

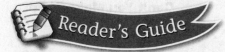
Reader's Guide

Can't You Make Them Behave, King George?

Editorial

Write an Editorial

Usually, newspaper stories tell about facts, not opinions. But sometimes newspapers feature a few stories that express opinions. These stories are called editorials. When expressing an opinion, an editorial writer often uses words that show judgments, feelings, or beliefs. Sometimes, to persuade others, they use adjectives that sound extreme.

Read page 363. What words are used to express an opinion?

_____

_____

_____

_____

_____

Read page 366. What facts show that the Americans would not easily be defeated?

_____

_____

_____

_____

_____

Name _____ Date _____

You are a member of the British government. You are writing a three-paragraph editorial in a British newspaper to persuade the government to make peace with the Americans. Use facts to support your opinion but also use a persuasive tone.

Figurative Language

Read the set of sentences in each item. Circle context clues that help you understand the underlined expression. Then rewrite the underlined expression in your own words.

1. The king's face was like a thundercloud when he heard the news. He frowned at the messenger and slammed the door.

   _____.

2. The colonists were a thorn in the side of the king. Every time he thought of their rebellion, he became irritated.

   _____

3. He swallowed his pride. Then he said he was sorry for losing the colonies. _____

4. The battle took them a step further down the road to independence. They were excited about their victory.

   _____

5. The soldier felt like a limp dishrag after the long march. He could barely stand upright.

   _____

6. The darkness blanketed the sleeping soldiers lying on the field. Only the white hospital tent could be seen.

   _____

7. The king was caught off guard by the defeat of his army. It took him a long time to understand what happened.

   _____

8. The king's advisors clucked at him like hens. Finally, the king plugged his ears and walked away.

   _____

VCV Pattern

Basic   Write the Basic Word that best completes each analogy.

1. *Fire department* is to *fire* as _____ *department* is to *crime*.

2. *Job* is to *task* as *prize* is to _____ .

3. *Noise* is to *quiet* as *calm* is to _____ .

4. *Quick* is to *slow* as *good* is to _____ .

5. *Old* is to *young* as *ancient* is to _____ .

6. *Nile* is to *river* as *United States* is to _____ .

7. *Thick* is to *thin* as *drab* is to _____ .

8. *Separate* is to *split* as *choose* is to _____ .

9. *Program* is to *television* as *food* is to _____ .

10. *Memo* is to *note* as *object* is to _____ .

11. *Special* is to *ordinary* as *approximate* is to _____ .

12. *Oak* is to *tree* as _____ is to *family*.

Challenge 13–15.   Make a poster that encourages students at your school to participate in a Clean-Up Day for the environment. Use three of the Challenge Words. Write on a separate sheet of paper.

Spelling Words

1. human
2. exact
3. award
4. behave
5. credit
6. basic
7. vivid
8. evil
9. modern
10. nation
11. robot
12. panic
13. select
14. cousin
15. item
16. police
17. prefer
18. menu
19. novel
20. deserve

Challenge
autumn
nuisance
logic
column
laser

Spelling Word Sort

Write each Basic Word beside the correct heading. Show where
the word is divided into syllables.

V/CV: Divide before the consonant	**Basic Words:**	
	Challenge Words:	
	Possible Selection Words:	
VC/V: Divide after the consonant	**Basic Words:**	
	Challenge Words:	
	Possible Selection Words:	

Challenge   Add the Challenge Words to your Word Sort.

Connect to Reading   Look through *Can't You Make Them Behave,
King George?* Find words that have the VCV syllable patterns on
this page. Add them to your Word Sort.

Spelling Words

1. human
2. exact
3. award
4. behave
5. credit
6. basic
7. vivid
8. evil
9. modern
10. nation
11. robot
12. panic
13. select
14. cousin
15. item
16. police
17. prefer
18. menu
19. novel
20. deserve

Challenge
autumn
nuisance
logic
column
laser

Proofreading for Spelling

**Find the misspelled words and circle them. Write them correctly
on the lines below.**

Thomas Paine wasn't happy in England, his homeland. He
tried to beheave in a way that would please his superiors, but he
wasn't a robott. He had his own ideas—but they kept getting
him in trouble. Then Paine met Ben Franklin, who told him to
go to America. Franklin thought Paine would perfer the New
World to England. Once in America, Paine discovered he could
write well—not a novell, but vived prose. He wrote a pamphlet
called *Common Sense* to encourage people to rise up against
evill King George. To his creddit, Paine felt he did not diserve
an aword for his work. He just wanted to live in a nashion with
a moderne government that tried to meet the basick needs of
all humman beings. He wrote other pamphlets, too, always
encouraging people to be involved in government. He was glad
he came to America.

Spelling Words

1. human
2. exact
3. award
4. behave
5. credit
6. basic
7. vivid
8. evil
9. modern
10. nation
11. robot
12. panic
13. select
14. cousin
15. item
16. police
17. prefer
18. menu
19. novel
20. deserve

Challenge
autumn
nuisance
logic
column
laser

1. _____   8. _____

2. _____   9. _____

3. _____   10. _____

4. _____   11. _____

5. _____   12. _____

6. _____   13. _____

7. _____

Name _____ Date _____

Present and Past Tense

Can't You Make Them Behave, King George?
Grammar: Verb Tenses

The **tense** of a verb shows the time of an action or event. Verbs in **present tense** show that an event is happening now or regularly. Verbs in **past tense** show that an event has already happened. To form the past tense of most verbs, you can add *-d* or *-ed*.

present tense
Today, most Americans <u>live</u> in or near cities.

past tense
Most of the American colonists <u>lived</u> on farms.

Thinking Questions
When is the action occurring? Is it happening now, or is it over?

Activity Write the verbs in each sentence and tell whether they are in present or past tense.

1. Pedro shared how the New England colonists lived.

   _____

2. During the summer break, he travels to Virginia and visits a living history museum.

   _____

3. He bought a bottle that a glassblower created from melted sand.

   _____

4. Pedro's little sister traveled with him, and she still remembers the trip.

   _____

5. They both decided that the furniture in the houses seemed tiny.

   _____

Future Tense

Verbs in **future tense** show that an event is going to happen. To form the future tense, use a helping verb such as **will**.

present tense
She <u>learns</u> about American history.
future tense
She <u>will learn</u> about American history.

To shorten a future tense verb, you can use a contraction. <u>She will learn</u> contracts to <u>she'll learn</u>.

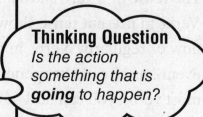

Thinking Question
*Is the action something that is **going** to happen?*

Activity Write the future tense of the verb in parentheses. Write both the full future tense and the contraction.

1. She (takes) a field trip with her class.

   _____

2. They (visit) the site of a famous battle.

   _____

3. She (sees) the bridge that she read about in school.

   _____

4. They (talk) to the park ranger about the battle.

   _____

5. The teacher calculates how much it (costs) to buy copies of a historic map for their classroom.

   _____

Consistent Tenses

Verb tenses help readers understand when different events in a story happen. To clearly show when events take place, choose the best tense for the situation. Change the tense only when you want to show a change in time.

Yesterday, we **started** to research our history project. Today, we **make** a poster for the presentations. We **will complete** the project next week.

Thinking Questions
Does the paragraph make sense? Is the order of events clear?

Activity Read the sentences and think about the relationship between events. Underline the verb that is in the wrong tense. Then write the correct verb.

1. Last weekend, Max finds an old diary in the attic and showed it to his mother. _____

2. The diary was dusty and they will wonder how old it was. _____

3. Max's mother reads the date on the first entry. She was so surprised, she almost dropped the diary on the floor. _____

4. Max couldn't believe that the diary will belong to someone who lived in 1774. _____

5. "This diary was older than the U.S.!" he says, and his mother laughs. _____

Complex Sentences

A **complex sentence** contains two groups of words: an **independent clause** that can stand on its own, and a **dependent clause** that adds meaning but cannot stand on its own. The dependent clause begins with a **subordinating conjunction**, such as *when, because, if,* or *although.* These conjunctions show the relationship between the two clauses.

Independent clause: Dave is working on his report.

Dependent clause: Because it is due next week.

Subordinating conjunction: Because

Compound Sentence (Note that it can either begin or end with the dependent clause.):

Dave is working on his report because it is due next week.

Because it is due next week, Dave is working on his report.

1–4.   Circle the subordinating conjunction in each sentence.

1. Dave found a book about women patriots while he was researching the Boston Tea Party.

2. Although women rarely took part in political protests at that time, a group of women got together in 1774 in Edenton, NC.

3. The women decided to boycott tea and other British goods because they thought the taxes were unfair.

4. When people in Britain heard about the Edenton protest, they did not take the women seriously.

5–8.   Underline the independent clause and circle the dependent clause in each sentence.

5. Dave will return the book to the library after he completes his project.

6. He wants to read about some of the other patriots because their stories are very interesting.

7. If no other students need the book, Dave will ask the librarian if he can check it out for another week.

8. Although math is his favorite subject, Dave is very interested in this chapter of history.

Name _____ Date _____

Lesson 12
READER'S NOTEBOOK

Can't You Make Them
Behave, King George?
Grammar: Connect to Writing

Connect to Writing

Using Present Tense
In this movie, a boy <u>carries</u> messages between army camps during the Revolutionary War.
Using Past Tense
I <u>thought</u> the best part was when the boy got lost at night.
Using Future Tense
People probably <u>will like</u> the overhead shots of the battlefield.

Activity   Choose the best tense for the verbs in parentheses. Rewrite the sentences to make the meaning clear.

1. The movie (begin) when the boy's older brother (join) the militia.

    _____

2. The firing cannons (be) so loud, I missed what the brother (tell) his captain.

    _____

    _____

3. The story gets exciting when the boy (borrow) a horse after he (hurt) his ankle.

    _____

    _____

4. When I (leave) the theater, I (want) to learn how to ride a horse.

    _____

5. I (like) the movie so much that I (tell) my friends to see it.

    _____

Focus Trait: Organization
Presenting Reasons and Evidence

Good writers can persuade readers by giving the pros and cons of different solutions to a problem. Reasons and evidence must be organized clearly and logically.

Clearly Organized Reasons:

The American colonists felt that their opinions did not matter to the British government. They thought they needed more power within the government. They decided that the American colonies should ask for representation in British government. That way the colonists could better accept the government's decisions about taxes and other matters that affected them.

Read the problem below. Explain why you think it is a problem. Then write one pro and one con for each given solution.

Problem: Students have no variety in what they are able to buy for lunch.

Reason: _____

Solution: Students vote for a student representative who will help the cafeteria workers decide what to serve for lunch.

Pro: **Con:**

_____   _____

_____   _____

Solution: The cafeteria could offer several different types of lunches.

Pro: **Con:**

_____   _____

_____   _____

Now write a reasonable solution to the problem.

_____

_____

Name _____ Date _____

Lesson 13
READER'S NOTEBOOK

They Called Her
Molly Pitcher
Independent Reading

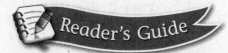

They Called Her Molly Pitcher

She's in the Army Now!

Before deciding to make Molly Hays a sergeant, George
Washington investigated her actions by talking to his soldiers.

**Read page 396. General Washington asked Corporal Banks if he saw
Molly doing anything he would consider brave or special. Write details
that would support the conclusion that Molly was a hero.**

Sir, you are not going to believe this, but I saw Molly

_____

_____

_____

**Read page 399. Ensign Wiggins was an artillery officer who saw Molly
that day. General Washington asked Ensign Wiggins if he saw Molly doing
anything outstanding. Write details that would support the conclusion that
Molly was a hero.**

Sir, I looked across the battlefield and could not believe my eyes.

I observed that woman

_____

_____

_____

Name _____ Date _____

Lesson 13
READER'S NOTEBOOK

**They Called Her
Molly Pitcher**
Independent Reading

Read page 401. Sergeant Wells was an infantry officer who saw Molly
from his position on the battlefield. General Washington asked Sergeant
Wells if he saw Molly doing anything important that day. What would
Sergeant Wells tell him? Write details that would support the conclusion
that Molly was a hero.

> Sir, you might think the heat has gone to my head, but
> I saw something incredible. Over by one of the cannons,
> I saw _____
> _____
> _____
> _____
> _____

George Washington is writing his report to the Continental Congress about the
Battle of Monmouth. He is explaining his decision to award Molly Hays the rank
of sergeant. Write his conclusion and the reasons supporting his conclusion.

> I have concluded that Molly Hays deserves the rank of
> sergeant in our army. The reasons for my conclusion are as
> follows: _____
> _____
> _____
> _____
> _____

Lesson 13
READER'S NOTEBOOK

**They Called Her
Molly Pitcher**
Vocabulary Strategies:
Reference Materials

Reference Materials

Consult a thesaurus to help you choose a word from the list to complete each series of synonyms, or words that have similar meanings. Following each series is another word. Is it a synonym or antonym of the other words? Circle it if it is an antonym. Underline it if it is a synonym.

> magnificent   wounded   substitute   courageous
> facilitate   precedent   legend   feminine

1. grand, _____ , splendid   wonderful

2. female, _____ , ladylike   masculine

3. _____ , myth, story   tale

4. bold, brave, _____   cowardly

5. harmed, hurt, _____   injured

6. example, _____ , standard   instance

7. replacement, alternate, _____   regular

8. aid, _____ , help   obstruct

VCCCV Pattern

Basic   Write the Basic Word that best completes each group.

1. storekeeper, seller, _____

2. battle, fight, _____

3. friend, teammate, _____

4. buy, pay for, _____

5. grumble, nag, _____

6. trouble, misbehavior, _____

7. giggles, chuckles, _____

8. easily, plainly, _____

9. difficult, complicated, _____

10. thief, crook, _____

11. shiver, shake, _____

Challenge 12–14.   Write a letter to a friend about a cause or effort that you might support. Use three of the Challenge Words. Write on a separate sheet of paper.

Spelling Words

1. conflict
2. orphan
3. instant
4. complex
5. simply
6. burglar
7. laundry
8. laughter
9. employ
10. anchor
11. merchant
12. improve
13. arctic
14. mischief
15. childhood
16. purchase
17. dolphin
18. partner
19. complain
20. tremble

Challenge
anthem
illustrate
function
conscience
apostrophe

Spelling Word Sort

Write each Basic Word beside the correct heading. Show where
the word is divided into syllables.

	Spelling Words

VC/CCV pattern: **divide between** **first consonant** **pair**	**Basic Words:** **Challenge Words:** **Possible Selection Words:**
VCC/CV pattern: **divide between** **second consonant** **pair**	**Basic Words:** **Challenge Words:** **Possible Selection Words:**

Challenge Add the Challenge Words to your Word Sort.

Connect to Reading Look through *They Called Her Molly Pitcher.*
Find words that have the VCCCV syllable patterns on this page. Add
them to your Word Sort.

Spelling Words

1. conflict
2. orphan
3. instant
4. complex
5. simply
6. burglar
7. laundry
8. laughter
9. employ
10. anchor
11. merchant
12. improve
13. arctic
14. mischief
15. childhood
16. purchase
17. dolphin
18. partner
19. complain
20. tremble

Challenge
anthem
illustrate
function
conscience
apostrophe

Name _____ Date _____

Proofreading for Spelling

**Find the misspelled words and circle them. Write them correctly
on the lines below.**

Spelling Words

Born in 1760, Deborah Sampson was about five years old
when her father disappeared, making her practically an orfan
and ending a chilhood of fun and laufghter. By the time she
was ten, she was a servant, doing lawndry and working in the
fields. During the winters, which had an arktic feel to them, she
was able to go to school and improove herself. School was her
ancher and way out of a hard life. At 16, she became a teacher.

When the conflickt between the Americans and the British
began, Deborah wanted to join the fight. Though there were
no woman soldiers, Deborah was ready to imploy any effort
to reach her goal. She put on a disguise and enlisted in the
Continental Army as Robert Shurtlieff. She took to the army
like a dolphan to water. She fought alongside the other soldiers
and did not complaine when things got rough. No one suspected
she was a woman until the instent she got wounded.

1. conflict
2. orphan
3. instant
4. complex
5. simply
6. burglar
7. laundry
8. laughter
9. employ
10. anchor
11. merchant
12. improve
13. arctic
14. mischief
15. childhood
16. purchase
17. dolphin
18. partner
19. complain
20. tremble

Challenge
anthem
illustrate
function
conscience
apostrophe

1. _____   7. _____
2. _____   8. _____
3. _____   9. _____
4. _____   10. _____
5. _____   11. _____
6. _____   12. _____

Regular Verbs

Most verbs are **regular verbs**. They form their past
tense by adding *–ed* or *–d*. A regular verb also adds
–ed when it is used with the helping verbs *has*, *have*,
or *had*.

  walk, walked, have walked   live, lived, has lived

If a verb ends in a vowel followed by a consonant,
double the consonant and add *–ed*. If a verb ends
in a consonant followed by *y*, change the *y* to *i* and
add *–ed*.

stop, stopped, has stopped   **cry**, cried, had cried

Thinking Questions
*Does adding –ed or –d
form the past tense?
Does the verb have a
helping verb?*

Activity Write the past tense of each verb listed. Then write a
sentence using the verb in the past tense.

1. travel _____

_____

2. beg _____

_____

3. use _____

_____

4. carry _____

_____

5. injure _____

_____

Irregular Verbs

Some verbs are **irregular**. These verbs don't add *–ed* or *–d* to form the past tense. Some very common verbs are irregular.

Thinking Question
Is the past tense formed by adding –ed or –d, or some other way?

be: was/were   have: had
go: went   do: did
eat: ate   buy: bought
become: became   leave: left

Activity Write the verbs and tell whether they are regular or irregular.

1. Annie went to the library every weekend because she liked it there. _____

2. She spent her time reading stories about people who fought in the Revolution. _____

3. Sometimes hours passed before Annie stopped to check the time. _____

4. The librarian always smiled when Annie suddenly rushed out.

_____

5. Annie's family ate at six o'clock and Annie always got home just before that. _____

Name _____ Date _____

Lesson 13
READER'S NOTEBOOK

They Called Her
Molly Pitcher
Grammar: Regular and
Irregular Verbs

Forms of Irregular Verbs

For many irregular verbs, the form that is used with a helping verb is the same as the past tense. For others, it is different from the past tense.

verb	past tense	with a helping verb
be	was (were)	has been
go	went	have gone
do	did	has done
know	knew	has known
ride	rode	have ridden

Thinking Question
What form of the verb belongs in a sentence that begins with Yesterday?

Activity   Read the sentence and think about what form the irregular verbs should take. Underline the verb that is in the wrong form. Then write the correct verb form. Item 5 has more than one verb in the wrong form.

1. Samuel had went to take food to the soldiers. _____

2. His father had knew that he wanted to do it. _____

3. Still, he been surprised that he had left the house so early.

   _____

4. He had came downstairs to find him already gone.

   _____

5. However, Samuel had forgot the food money he had gave him.

   _____

Name _____   Date _____

Lesson 13
READER'S NOTEBOOK

They Called Her
Molly Pitcher
Grammar: Spiral Review

Interjections

An **interjection** is a word that is used to express surprise, excitement, or other emotions. Interjections are usually followed by an exclamation point. If an interjection expresses a mild emotion, a comma can be used to set it apart from the sentence.

Exclamation Points
Hey! The British are coming!
Wow! He is sure riding that horse quickly!
We won that battle. **Hooray!**

Commas
Yes, I'm going to support the soldiers.
Oh, that was such a surprise.

1–4.   Add an interjection to the sentence, using an exclamation point.

1. Many of the soldiers got sick.

_____

2. This would be a set back for the division.

_____

3. The soldiers soon felt better.

_____

4. That was a close call!

_____

5–6.   Add an interjection using a comma.

5. My brother is due home tomorrow.

_____

6. I guess I can wait one more day.

_____

Name _____ Date _____

Lesson 13
READER'S NOTEBOOK

They Called Her
Molly Pitcher
Grammar: Connect to Writing

Connect to Writing

Action verbs describe what a person or thing does.
The more exact or vivid an action verb is, the better it
describes the action.

Instead of **said**, use **exclaimed**, **cried**, or **replied**.
Instead of **make**, use **wrote**, **built**, or **invented**.
Instead of **went**, use **raced**, **trudged**, or **strolled**.

cooked, sewed, strolled, ate, exclaimed

**Activity   Replace each underlined verb with an exact verb from
the box. Rewrite each sentence to use the exact verb and make
the author's meaning clear.**

1. The soldier <u>went</u> all the way back to camp. He wasn't in
   a hurry.

   _____

2. She <u>made</u> him a new coat. She used her needle and
   thread.

   _____

3. "I love the coat!" her husband <u>said</u>. He was excited.

   _____

4. Later, they <u>had</u> the dinner she <u>made</u>.

   _____

Focus Trait: Purpose
Presenting Ideas to an Audience

Good writers think about their audience and their purpose for writing.
An argument made to one audience may not be right for another. You should
also think about your letter's greeting or salutation and closure.

To Parents	To the General
Dear Mom, My sisters and I want to start sewing clothes for the soldiers. We heard that our brother Jeremiah doesn't have any warm clothes at Valley Forge! It wouldn't be good for him to get sick while he's there. So, after our lessons and chores are done, can we borrow your sewing basket and some fabric? Thanks, Lisbeth	Dear Sir, I am writing to ask permission to send some warm clothing to you and your troops at Valley Forge. My brother Jeremiah is there with you now. My sisters and I have been sewing some coats and pants and gloves for a month now. We would like you to have them so you can all stay healthy. Thank you for considering my request. Sincerely yours, Lisbeth Howe

The letter below is written to a fabric company. Read the letter and
underline the salutation, ideas, and closure that you think are right
for the audience.

(Hi/To Whom It May Concern),
My sisters and I recently got permission from our mother to start sewing. We want to
make warm clothing for our soldiers at Valley Forge. (Would it be possible for you to
donate/Could your company please give) some fabric to us? (That would be awesome/
I would really appreciate the donation). It would allow (people/soldiers) to get the
clothing they need.
(Thanks/Sincerely yours),
Lisbeth Howe

Name _____ Date _____

Lesson 14
READER'S NOTEBOOK

"James Forten" from
Now Is Your Time!
Independent Reading

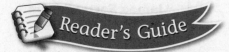
Reader's Guide

"James Forten" from *Now Is Your Time!*

The Log of the *Royal Louis*

When researching historical events, historians often look at official records from that time for details about how and when events occurred. The official record on a ship is called a log. The captain of the ship writes in the log exactly what happened on each day. Help Captain Decatur write in the log of the *Royal Louis*.

Read page 425 and the first paragraph from page 426. What would Captain Decatur record in his log on that date?

August 5, 1781

_____

_____

_____

_____

Read the rest of page 426. What would Captain Decatur record in his log on that date?

August 23, 1781

_____

_____

_____

_____

Name _____ Date _____

Lesson 14
READER'S NOTEBOOK

"James Forten" from
Now Is Your Time!
Independent Reading

Read page 427. What would Captain Decatur record in his log
on that date?

October 16, 1781

_____

_____

_____

_____

_____

_____

Read the details that you wrote in the ship's log. How do these details
support a main idea of the story of James Forten?

Main Idea: _____

_____

_____

_____

_____

Name _____ Date _____

Lesson 14
READER'S NOTEBOOK

James Forten
Vocabulary Strategies:
Greek and Latin Roots

Greek and Latin Roots:
graph, *meter*, *port*, and *ject*

The words in the box have Greek and Latin roots. Some are formed using the Greek roots *graph* (meaning *to write*) and *meter* (meaning *to measure*). Others use the Latin roots *port* (meaning *to carry*) and *ject* (meaning *to throw*). Use each word's parts to determine its meaning. Then complete each sentence by filling in the blank with a word from the box.

thermometer	autographs	project	portable
injection	graphics	imported	kilometer

1. The ship stayed in the deep water a _____ from shore.

2. The colonists _____ goods they could not make themselves from Europe.

3. Large and heavy items such as stoves and tractors are less _____ than others.

4. The doctor gave the patient an _____ to help her heal.

5. In colonial times, you could not use a _____ to see if a person had a fever.

6. The signed copy of the Constitution has the _____ of some of our first presidents.

7. I will _____ the slides onto the screen so everyone can see them.

8. Some of the slides have _____ that show what a colonial port may have looked like.

VV Pattern

Basic   Write the Basic Word that best fits each clue.

1. intentionally unkind _____

2. sound _____

3. variety of foods to eat _____

4. a place to watch a play or movie _____

5. happening every year _____

6. a building that displays historic or artistic objects

   _____

7. a disturbance caused by a large crowd _____

8. destroy something _____

9. informal, comfortable _____

10. relating to sight _____

Challenge 11–14.   Read the headline. On a separate sheet of paper, write about it using four Challenge Words.

SCIENTISTS DISCOVER
AMAZING CURE

Spelling Words
1. actual
2. cruel
3. influence
4. diet
5. museum
6. casual
7. ruin
8. pioneer
9. trial
10. visual
11. realize
12. create
13. riot
14. genuine
15. area
16. annual
17. audio
18. dial
19. theater
20. patriot
Challenge
diagnose
media
appreciate
society
prior

Name _____ Date _____

Spelling Word Sort

Write each Basic Word beside the correct heading.

V/V with two syllables: Divide between vowel pairs	**Basic Words:** **Challenge Words:**
V/V with three syllables: Divide between vowel pairs	**Basic Words:** **Challenge Words:**
V/V with more than three syllables: Divide between vowel pairs	**Challenge Words:**

Challenge   Add the Challenge Words to your Word Sort.

Spelling Words

1. actual
2. cruel
3. influence
4. diet
5. museum
6. casual
7. ruin
8. pioneer
9. trial
10. visual
11. realize
12. create
13. riot
14. genuine
15. area
16. annual
17. audio
18. dial
19. theater
20. patriot

Challenge
diagnose
media
appreciate
society
prior

Proofreading for Spelling

Find the misspelled words and circle them. Write them correctly on the lines below.

Growing up enslaved in Framingham, Massachusetts, Crispus Attucks never dreamed that he would be famous. Today, he is remembered in an anual reenactment of the Boston Massacre of 1770. Working in the harbor areya, Attucks was part of a cazual group that gathered in protest of British tyranny. He served as a pionear in the exercise of free speech. When Attucks saw the British aim their guns, he couldn't diel 911. He stood his ground, becoming the first of five genuwine martyrs to fall during the riat and chaos that followed. There was a triall to examine the actuel facts of these crual deaths. John Adams defended the British soldiers, and they were found not guilty of murder. Nevertheless, Paul Revere's engraving of the massacre had a major influance on the independence movement. Americans today relize that Crispus Attucks was a patreot who gave his life to help creat our independent nation.

Spelling Words

1. actual
2. cruel
3. influence
4. diet
5. museum
6. casual
7. ruin
8. pioneer
9. trial
10. visual
11. realize
12. create
13. riot
14. genuine
15. area
16. annual
17. audio
18. dial
19. theater
20. patriot

Challenge
diagnose
media
appreciate
society
prior

1. _____ 8. _____

2. _____ 9. _____

3. _____ 10. _____

4. _____ 11. _____

5. _____ 12. _____

6. _____ 13. _____

7. _____ 14. _____

Commas and Semicolons in a Series

Commas and semicolons are used to separate three or more items within a series or list. A semicolon is used when the items in the series already contain a comma.

Thinking Question
Do the items in the series or list contain commas?

Items separated by commas: He was shocked by the dirt, the smell, and the noise on the ship.

Items separated by semicolons: The documentary aired on Channel 11, PBS; Channel 35, WGN; and Channel 70, HMN.

Insert commas or semicolons to correctly punctuate each sentence.

1. When James signed up to be a sailor, he had no idea of the discomfort danger and hard work involved.

2. He carried gunpowder ran errands and helped the wounded.

3. The four officers on the ship were from Malvern, Pennsylvania Trenton, New Jersey Lebanon, Pennsylvania and Baltimore, Maryland.

4. The captain the first mate and the cabin boys remained on deck during the battle.

5. The wind rain thunder and lightning made the battle worse.

6. Finally, the sea calmed down the skies cleared and the battle ended.

7. James felt relieved grateful and exhausted.

8. To find out more about this battle, we looked for these three books at the library: *War Heroes, Then and Now Sailors, Soldiers, Heroes How They Fought, How They Won.*

Introductory Elements

Introductory elements are words, phrases, or clauses that appear at the beginning of a sentence. They add information, but they are not part of the main sentence. To show they are introductory elements, they are set off by commas.

introductory word
Truly, I believe it is important to know about James Forten and other patriots.

Thinking Question
Is there a word or group of words that introduces the sentence but is not part of the main sentence?

Underline each introductory word or phrase. Then correctly punctuate the sentence.

1. Like James Forten many successful African Americans worked to abolish slavery.

2. For example Frederick Douglass, who lived in the 1800s, became a famous abolitionist.

3. In the 1700s it was difficult for African Americans to become successful.

4. For many African Americans going to school was not an option.

5. In fact enslaved people could be punished for learning to read and write.

6. Well that is because education opens people's eyes to what is right and wrong.

7. As a result they may recognize injustice and work for change.

8. "Yes you are right. That makes me appreciate my education more."

Direct Address and Tag Questions

Commas are used to set off names that indicate direct address, or someone being spoken to. If the name appears in the middle of the sentence, commas should be placed both before and after it.

Commas are also used to set off short questions that appear at the end of sentences.

direct address   **tag question**
Class, take out your history books, would you please?

> **Thinking Questions**
> *Is there a name in the sentence that shows someone is being addressed? Is there a short question joined on to the end of a sentence?*

Rewrite each sentence with the correct punctuation.

1. "Please pass me the index cards Roberto."

   _____

2. "I want to get started on my research don't you?"

   _____

3. "Tara said the paper is due tomorrow Bill."

   _____

4. "I need to find one more web site Andrea before I can begin to write."

   _____

5. "You should have all your research done by now shouldn't you?"

   _____

6. "I have Henry and I have found out a lot about Molly Pitcher and James Forten."

   _____

Present and Past Tense Verbs

> **Present tense verbs** tell what is happening now.
>
> **Past tense verbs** tell what has already happened.
>
> **Consistent verb tense** clearly shows readers the order of events.

Inconsistent	Consistent
He hurried up the steps and loads the cannon.	He hurries up the steps and loads the cannon.
Last week, they fought a fierce battle, and they win.	Last week, they fought a fierce battle, and they won.

Circle the four verbs in each paragraph that are inconsistent in their tense. Write them in the correct tense on the line following the paragraph.

1. James Forten was a hero because he carries out his responsibilities even in the heat of battle. He acted on the values that his parents instill in him. They want him to go to school and to work hard. He did. His hard work leads him to achieve success as a businessman.

   _____

2. History never went out of date. When we study history, we gained wisdom. We learned from others' mistakes. We are presented with examples of men and women who used their abilities to change the world for the better. Knowing about these historical figures helped us to be better people too.

   _____

Connect to Writing

Good writers insert commas and semicolons to clarify the meaning of their sentences.

Use commas or semicolons to separate items in a series.

John Adams, Molly Pitcher, and James Forten all contributed to the war effort.

Use commas to set off introductory words or phrases, direct address, and tag questions.

Henrietta, whom do you admire most?

In my opinion, all three were very brave, wouldn't you say?

Rewrite the paragraph, inserting commas and semicolons where necessary.

We have read about some exceptional Americans in Lesson 11, Unit 3 Lesson 13, Unit 3 and Lesson 14, Unit 3. For example James Forten fought in the war built up a business and worked to abolish slavery. At the time he lived African Americans had few rights or opportunities. In my mind this makes him even more extraordinary wouldn't you agree?

_____

_____

_____

_____

_____

Focus Trait: Organization
Presenting Evidence Clearly

James Forten
Writing: Opinion Writing

Argument: It took courage for African Americans to fight in the Revolutionary War on the side of the Patriots.	
Weak Evidence	**Strong Evidence**
War is scary. They could die. If they were on a ship, it might sink.	If they were captured by the British, they might be sold as slaves in the West Indies. Also if they were captured by the British, they could be executed for being traitors. They risked being injured or killed or dying from the diseases that spread through the camps.

A. Choose a side of the argument below. List three pieces of strong evidence that you can use to support your argument.

Argument: Biographies of historical figures (should/should not) be

        included in every reading textbook.

1. _____

2. _____

3. _____

B. Use your evidence to write a well-organized persuasive paragraph.
Organize the ideas in a way that is easy to understand.
Pair/Share Work with a partner to brainstorm smooth transitions.

_____

_____

_____

_____

Name _____ Date _____

Lesson 15
READER'S NOTEBOOK

We Were There, Too!
Joseph Plumb Martin
and Sybil Ludington
Independent Reading

Reader's Guide

We Were There, Too! Joseph Plumb Martin and Sybil Ludington

Make an Illustrated Glossary

A glossary is a feature at the back of a nonfiction book that gives the meanings of words found in the text. Usually, authors include words that are important to understanding the main ideas of the text.

Read the second paragraph on page 451. The word *scrawling* means writing quickly or carelessly. What does this word tell you about how the boys were signing up for the army?

_____

_____

_____

Read the first paragraph on page 452. An indenture is an agreement to work for someone for a fixed period of time. Why do you think Joseph used the word *indenture* to describe his enlistment?

_____

_____

_____

Name _____ Date _____

Lesson 15
READER'S NOTEBOOK

We Were There, Too!
Joseph Plumb Martin
and Sybil Ludington
Independent Reading

The author of "We Were There, Too!" has asked you to make an illustrated glossary for the book. Choose six words from the stories of Joseph Plumb Martin and Sybil Ludington. Each must be a word that helps you understand the characters and what they experienced. Remember that glossary entries are listed in alphabetical order. After you write the words, draw an illustration that shows what each word means.

Illustrated Glossary

Word	Meaning	Illustration

Name _____ Date _____

Prefixes *in-*, *im-*, *il-*, and *ir-*

The words in the box begin with a prefix that means *not* or *in*.
Choose a word from the list to fill in the blank and correctly complete
each sentence.

inefficient	indirect	informal	imbalance	impersonal
impure	illogical	illegible	irregular	irresponsible

1. If Sybil had ridden back and forth, it would have been

_____ because it would have taken up extra time.

2. The border shown on the map was jagged and _____.

3. Chemicals dumped in the stream made the watering hole

_____.

4. The yearly neighborhood picnic was a fun, _____ event.

5. Too much air in one of the bicycle's tires can create a pressure

_____.

6. The order of events was _____ and made no sense.

7. To forget an appointment twice is considered _____.

8. Compared to a handwritten note, a typed one can seem a bit

_____.

9. We were forced to take an _____ route because the

bridge was closed for repairs.

10. Blurred ink and poor penmanship made the address

_____.

Final Schwa + /l/ Sounds

Basic Complete the puzzle by writing the Basic Word for each clue.

Spelling Words

1. formal
2. whistle
3. label
4. puzzle
5. legal
6. angle
7. normal
8. needle
9. angel
10. pupil
11. struggle
12. level
13. local
14. bicycle
15. channel
16. global
17. stumble
18. quarrel
19. article
20. fossil

Challenge

identical
vehicle
mineral
colonel
artificial

Across

1. remains of a plant or animal from an earlier age
4. to trip and nearly fall
6. relating to a specific nearby area
8. related to the law
10. a figure made by two lines that extend from the same point or line
12. a thin, metal tool that is used for sewing

Down

2. a great effort
3. to make a sound by forcing air out between the teeth or lips
5. a vehicle with two wheels, a seat, and pedals
7. a connecting body of water
9. concerning the whole world
11. a tag on an object that tells what it contains

Challenge 13–15. Write a brief journal entry describing what it would be like to visit another planet. Use at least three of the Challenge Words. Write on a separate sheet of paper.

Spelling Word Sort

Write each Basic Word beside the correct heading.

Final /əl/ spelled *el*	Basic Words:
	Challenge Words:
	Possible Selection Words:
Final /əl/ spelled *al*	Basic Words:
	Challenge Words:
	Possible Selection Words:
Final /əl/ spelled *le*	Basic Words:
	Challenge Words:
	Possible Selection Words:
Other spellings for final /əl/	Basic Words:

Spelling Words

1. formal
2. whistle
3. label
4. puzzle
5. legal
6. angle
7. normal
8. needle
9. angel
10. pupil
11. struggle
12. level
13. local
14. bicycle
15. channel
16. global
17. stumble
18. quarrel
19. article
20. fossil

Challenge

identical
vehicle
mineral
colonel
artificial

Challenge   Add the Challenge Words to your Word Sort.

Connect to Reading   Look through *We Were There, Too!* Find words with the final /əl/ spelling patterns on this page. Add them to your Word Sort.

Proofreading for Spelling

Find the misspelled words and circle them. Write them correctly on the lines below.

Elizabeth Zane was a heroine of the last battle of the American Revolution. Betty was considered normle—a colonial girl with little formel education, but a pupill of the world nonetheless. In 1782, when she was 17, her family was under siege by Native American allies of the British in Fort Henry (now Wheeling, West Virginia). The powder supply was exhausted, and the nearest supply was 100 yards away. How to retrieve the powder was a puzzel. There was a quarel among the men about who should go. Betty suggested her own angul. She pointed to a handy artikle of clothing she wore—her apron. It was perfect for holding the black powder. All watched nervously as she took a slight stumbel on her way back to the fort with her apron filled to the top with gunpowder. She was hailed as an anjel. Her story is a lokal legend of the struggel for our nation's independence.

Spelling Words

1. formal
2. whistle
3. label
4. puzzle
5. legal
6. angle
7. normal
8. needle
9. angel
10. pupil
11. struggle
12. level
13. local
14. bicycle
15. channel
16. global
17. stumble
18. quarrel
19. article
20. fossil

Challenge
identical
vehicle
mineral
colonel
artificial

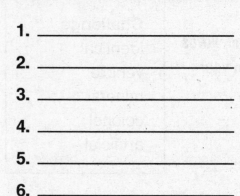

1. _____
2. _____
3. _____
4. _____
5. _____
6. _____

7. _____
8. _____
9. _____
10. _____
11. _____

Transitions

Transitions are connecting words or phrases used to show relationships between ideas. Transitions may appear anywhere in a sentence. They may link ideas within a sentence or between sentences. Common transitions include *however, moreover, similarly, in addition to, on the other hand, also*.

Thinking Question
Which word or group of words links ideas?

transition

We learned the national anthem. **Then** we learned about flag etiquette.

Circle each transition and write it on the line.

1. We carefully carried the flag out. Next we fastened it to the pole, first unfolding it. We raised the flag just as we were taught. We saluted and finally returned to our classroom. Afterwards we said the Pledge of Allegiance and later discussed the subject of patriotism.

   _____

2. As a result of our discussion, I understand more about why we honor the flag. I also know that the flag should never touch the ground. Similarly it should not be placed carelessly over something, for example, a car hood.

   _____

Transitions and Relationships

Transitions signal different types of relationships between details and ideas.

time order	first, next, later, soon, after eventually, then	He **first** told his grandparents. **Later** he packed.
comparison/ contrast	unlike, like, similarly, in contrast to, moreover, although	They had many soldiers. **Moreover,** they had better weapons.
cause and effect	therefore, as a result, consequently, unless, if	If wounded, he would not reenlist.

Thinking Questions
What is the transition? How does it relate the ideas?

Write the transition that shows the relationship indicated in parentheses.

1. _____ James Forten, Joseph Martin is a hero. (comparison)

2. He was a patriot. _____ he served his country. (cause and effect)

3. _____ horrified by his first sight of battle, he continued to fight. (contrast)

4. _____ chaos was everywhere. (time order)

5. The Americans rallied and _____ pushed the British back. (cause and effect)

6. _____ experiencing several battles, Joseph Martin _____ grew less nervous. (time order)

7. _____ life on his peaceful farm, the war seemed like a nightmare. (contrast)

8. He had time to reflect on his experiences _____ (time order)

Transitions in Writing

> **Opinion writing:** Use transitions that link reasons and supporting details to the opinion: *consequently, because, as a result, due to, furthermore, specifically, first of all.*
>
> **Informative writing:** Use transitions that link examples and facts to main ideas: *for example, also, in fact, in addition to, in contrast, similarly, especially, besides.*
>
> **Narrative writing:** Use transitions that show the sequence of events: *first, at the beginning, next, then, later, finally.*
>
> **example**
>
> **Informative text:** Sybil Ludington was different from many 18th century women. **Although** she took care of the house and children for her father, she could also ride a horse well. **In addition,** she was independent. **For example,** she didn't ask anyone to go with her on her ride.

Thinking Questions
What is the purpose of my writing? Which transitions will show the organization of my ideas?

Insert transitions to connect the ideas in each paragraph.

1. I am going to write a report on Sybil Ludington. _____ I will reread the selection. _____ I will check the Internet and other books for more information. _____ I will take notes on what I find. _____ I will write up my report. _____ it is done, I will hand it in.

2. Sybil Ludington is a great role model for students. _____ she was smart. _____ she thought of taking a stick to knock on doors. _____ she didn't have to waste time getting off her horse. She showed courage _____ in the way she fearlessly rode through the rainy night.

Irregular Verbs

> **Irregular verbs** do not add *-ed* to form their past or past participle forms. It is a good idea to memorize the forms of each irregular verb.

Fill in the missing form for each verb.

Present	Past	Past Participle
ring	rang	(have)
break		(have) broken
swim		(have) swum
take		(have) taken
throw	threw	(have)
speak	spoke	(have)
write		(have)

Circle the four errors in verb form in this paragraph.

He keeped a journal. He had telled his nephew about it. The nephew read the journal. Then he wrote about his uncle's war experience. Many people boughten the book. They were surprised to learn what the war was like. They thinked the book was very interesting. _____

Connect to Writing

Good writers use transitions to help readers understand how ideas are connected and to create smoother flowing sentences.

The study of history is valuable. It gives us a chance to learn from others' mistakes.	The study of history is valuable. **For instance,** it gives us a chance to learn from others' mistakes.

Insert transitions to link the ideas and sentences in the paragraph.

The new recruits marched many miles _____ they set up their camp. _____ they cooked their dinner over the campfire, they cleaned their rifles. _____ some of the recruits wrote letters home, others patched their boots. _____ they went to sleep. _____ the camp was quiet and still. _____ they woke up, they ate breakfast and prepared for battle.

Focus Trait: Evidence
Reducing and Combining Sentences

Separate Sentences	Combined Sentences
Eight companies made up a regiment. A regiment was also called a battalion.	A regiment, or a battalion, was made up of eight companies.

Rewrite each pair of sentences to make one combined sentence that cites evidence more effectively.

1. Continentals often fought in battle. They fought together with militiamen.

   _____

   _____

2. A group of boys he knew saw him coming. When the boys saw him, they began to taunt him.

   _____

   _____

3. His grandparents were unhappy, but they outfitted him with clothing. They gave him a musket and powder, too.

   _____

   _____

4. Hundreds of British warships were arriving at nearby Staten Island. On Staten Island, the warships were unloading redcoated soldiers.

   _____

   _____

Reader's Guide

Lunch Money

Make an Advertisement

The purpose of an advertisement is to persuade a reader or viewer to buy a product. Advertisements often have a few facts about the product, but the ad usually shows only positive facts. Advertisements also use powerful visual elements to make a product look exciting or attractive.

Greg's comic book business had a great start, but sales are dropping. He wants you to help him create an advertisement for his comic books.

Read page 484. What information about Chunky Comics would you include in an advertisement about them? Remember, it must be information that will make buyers more interested in them.

_____

_____

_____

_____

Read pages 490–491. What information about the *stories* in Chunky Comics would you include in an advertisement about them? What information about these stories would make buyers excited to read them?

_____

_____

_____

_____

_____

Now review the information you wrote about Chunky Comics and their stories. Choose three of your best pieces of information and rewrite them, using a persuasive tone. Use positive adjectives to persuade your readers.

_____

_____

_____

_____

Use the three sentences you wrote about Chunky Comics to create an advertisement. Remember to write the sentences to generate interest in the comics. Use exciting visuals to capture your readers' attention.

Name _____ Date _____

Lesson 16
READER'S NOTEBOOK

Lunch Money
Vocabulary Strategies:
Word Origins

Word Origins

The sentences below describe English words that come from other languages. Choose the word from the box that each sentence describes.

> villain   absurd   cafeteria   fiasco   finale
>
> solo   banana   guitar   patio   encyclopedia

1. This word, meaning *an evil or wicked person*, is taken from the Latin word *villānus*: _____.

2. In Spanish, this word means *an inner court that is open to the sky*: _____.

3. In Italian, this word is a noun that means *last* or *final*: _____.

4. This word for *tropical plant* is taken from Spanish: _____.

5. This word is taken from Latin and Greek words that describe *a course of learning*: _____.

6. This word means *flask* in Italian, but it means *a complete failure* in English: _____.

7. This musical word originally came from the Greek word *kithára*: _____.

8. The Latin origin of this word means *not to be heard of*: _____.

9. This word for *alone* is taken from both Italian and Latin: _____.

10. This is a Spanish-American word for *coffee shop*: _____.

Words with *-ed* or *-ing*

Basic   Read the paragraph. Write the Basic Word that best replaces the underlined numbers in the sentences.

My sister and I arrived at the movie theater and found the line where people were (1) for tickets. When my sister asked me what I wanted to see, I (2) because I didn't know. She bought two tickets to *A Pirate Story*. When we saw that two tickets (3) more than $20.00, we were (4) at how expensive they were. We still had a little money left, so my sister (5) over to the food counter to buy snacks. While she (6) popcorn for us, I began (7) to a conversation taking place among a group of teenagers. They were (8) and laughing about a movie they had just seen—*A Pirate Story*. They gave away the surprise ending!

"The movie is (9) soon," my sister called to me.

"I don't know if I want to see it anymore," I said. "I know how it ends!"

I watched the movie anyway, but I learned that tuning in to other people's conversations can be (10)!

1. _____   6. _____

2. _____   7. _____

3. _____   8. _____

4. _____   9. _____

5. _____   10. _____

Challenge 11–14.   Write a letter to a television station stating reasons why it should not cancel a program that you enjoy. Use four of the Challenge Words. Write on a separate sheet of paper.

Spelling Words

1. scrubbed
2. listening
3. stunned
4. knitting
5. carpeting
6. wandered
7. gathering
8. beginning
9. skimmed
10. chatting
11. shrugged
12. bothering
13. whipped
14. quizzed
15. suffering
16. scanned
17. ordered
18. totaled
19. answered
20. upsetting

Challenge
compelling
deposited
occurred
threatening
canceled

Name _____ Date _____

Spelling Word Sort

Write each Basic Word beside the correct heading.

Adding -ed: Final consonant doubled	**Basic Words:** **Challenge Words:** **Possible Selection Words:**
Adding -ing: Final consonant doubled	**Basic Words:** **Challenge Words:**
Adding -ed: Final consonant not doubled	**Basic Words:** **Challenge Words:** **Possible Selection Words:**
Adding -ing: Final consonant not doubled	**Basic Words:** **Challenge Words:** **Possible Selection Words:**

Spelling Words

1. scrubbed
2. listening
3. stunned
4. knitting
5. carpeting
6. wandered
7. gathering
8. beginning
9. skimmed
10. chatting
11. shrugged
12. bothering
13. whipped
14. quizzed
15. suffering
16. scanned
17. ordered
18. totaled
19. answered
20. upsetting

Challenge
compelling
deposited
occurred
threatening
canceled

Challenge   Add the Challenge Words to your Word Sort.

Connect to Reading   Look through *Lunch Money*. Find words that have -ed or -ing. Add them to your Word Sort.

Name _____ Date _____

Proofreading for Spelling

Find the misspelled words and circle them. Write them correctly on the lines below.

Dear Aunt Lenore,

I'm reviewing whether or not my behavior needs to improve. Maybe you can help me decide. Here are some good things I did last week: answred 11 out of 12 questions correctly when we were quized in math; skimed bugs from the backyard pool; totalled earnings of $25 from mowing lawns; kept the yarn ball away from the cat while Grandma was nitting; and put carpetting in the doghouse so Fang won't keep sufforing from splinters. I think that's pretty good!

There are also some things that weren't so good. I had to be asked by the teacher to stop chating during class; took pleasure in bothoring my little brother; skrubbed the paint off the porch steps; and stood by while Fang wipped Grandma's flowers with his wagging tail. I haven't been *too* upseting, have I?

Love,

Sammy

Spelling Words

1. scrubbed
2. listening
3. stunned
4. knitting
5. carpeting
6. wandered
7. gathering
8. beginning
9. skimmed
10. chatting
11. shrugged
12. bothering
13. whipped
14. quizzed
15. suffering
16. scanned
17. ordered
18. totaled
19. answered
20. upsetting

Challenge
compelling
deposited
occurred
threatening
canceled

1. _____   7. _____

2. _____   8. _____

3. _____   9. _____

4. _____   10. _____

5. _____   11. _____

6. _____   12. _____

Kinds of Adjectives

An **adjective** is a word that describes a noun or a pronoun. It tells *what kind* or *how many*. Adjectives that tell us *what kind* are called **descriptive adjectives**. Capitalize a descriptive adjective that gives the origin of the person, place, or thing being described.

> **Thinking Questions**
> *Which word gives information about a noun? Does it describe the noun or tell the origin of the noun?*

what kind	Emily enjoys <u>suspense</u> stories.
origin	Kimberly likes to read <u>Japanese</u> comics called *manga*.
how many	The <u>three</u> girls share their books.

Underline the adjective or adjectives in each sentence. For each adjective, write *what kind*, *origin*, or *how many* to show the kind of information given.

1. The hero in this adventure story is named Gregory.

   _____

2. He carries a tiny computer with him.

   _____

3. His jacket has pictures of Chinese warriors!

   _____

4. Gregory flies an invisible American spaceship.

   _____

5. Did you ever write a story about a comic-book hero?

   _____

6. I tried to write one about a brainy girl two years ago.

   _____

7. I could never draw the right images to tell the story.

   _____

8. Someday I'll start again and find a good, exciting idea for a story.

   _____

Adjectives After Linking Verbs

An adjective does not always come before the noun or pronoun it describes. An adjective can also follow a linking verb, such as any form of *be*. *Smell*, *feel*, *taste*, *look*, and *sound* can also be linking verbs.

subject + linking verb + adjective
Linda is (talented) at art.
Oscar feels (tired) of drawing.
The new book looks (wonderful).

Thinking Questions
What is the subject?
What is the adjective?
What word connects the subject to the adjective?

For each sentence, circle the adjective that follows the linking verb. Then underline the noun or pronoun that the adjective describes.

1. Sarah is excited about creating illustrations to help tell the story in her comic book.

2. After leaving his favorite comic in the rain, Leo felt unhappy.

3. Harry felt lucky because he got the last illustrated copy in the store.

4. The macaroni and cheese tasted delicious and gave me the energy to keep drawing.

5. In my first draft, the battle seems boring.

6. I created a villain whose image appears evil.

7. Ben's new bedroom was small, with no room for his stacks of comic books.

8. Maya's new photographs are exciting and scary.

Articles

The words *the*, *a*, and *an* are adjectives called **articles**. *The* is a **definite article** because it points out a specific person, place, or thing. *A* and *an* are **indefinite articles** because they refer to any person, place, or thing. Use *an* before a noun that begins with a vowel sound.

A newspaper launched a new cartoon strip. The paper is a small, hometown paper.
An edition of the newspaper comes out every day.

Thinking Question
Is the noun general or specific?

Write the correct articles to fill in the blanks. Reread all the sentences to be sure they make sense.

1. Before creating _____ new comic book, you have to come up with _____ idea.

2. It is also helpful if you are _____ artist who can bring characters to life.

3. Perhaps you want _____ book to be about _____ awesome hero.

4. _____ hero has _____ series of adventures.

5. Each illustration can show _____ good quality that _____ hero has.

6. Of course, _____ hero wins _____ conflicts.

7. Finally, _____ villains are vanquished.

8. The book comes to _____ end.

Kinds of Pronouns

Lunch Money
Grammar: Spiral Review

Nouns	Subject Pronouns
Brian and Chris go to the bookstore.	They go to the bookstore.
The one who wants a book is Brian.	The one who wants a book is he.

Nouns	Object Pronouns
Brian bought this book.	Brian bought it.
Brian gave these books to Chris and Anthony.	Brian gave these books to them.

1– 6. Circle the correct pronoun in parentheses. Then label the pronoun
subject **or** *object*.

1. Have (you, her) ever read a comic book? _____

2. The person who reads the most comic books is (him, he).

    _____

3. Kathy listens to (him, he) talk about comic books. _____

4. When a new comic is released, Roger is the first to buy
   (it, them). _____

5. Roger buys an extra copy for (I, me). _____

6. (I, Me) thank Roger! _____

7–10. Circle four errors in this paragraph and write the corrections on
the line below. Subject and object pronouns are misused.

   In my favorite comic book, the images help show the
characters' superpowers. One of they can control the weather
with her mind! Another character can walk through walls. Him is
my favorite character. When I create a comic book someday, I will
include a character like he. In my comic book, all the superheroes
will be able to fly to the planets in outer space in seconds. My
sister can draw and paint really well. I guess her and I can work
together, but only if she remembers that I am the boss!

_____

Connect to Writing

When you write, use precise adjectives to add details and create clear images for your readers.

Vague Adjective	Precise Adjectives
Harry saw an **interesting** movie about jewelry hidden in pyramids.	Harry saw an **adventure** movie about **gold** jewelry hidden in **Egyptian** pyramids.

Activity   Use precise adjectives to rewrite each sentence and add details.

1. Harry drew a comic strip based on the movie.

_____

_____

2. His main character was an archaeologist.

_____

_____

3. The archaeologist figured out the code to open the pyramid.

_____

_____

4. He saw piles of treasure inside the tomb.

_____

_____

5. He fought off the thieves who wanted the treasure.

_____

_____

Focus Trait: Development
Using Informal Language

Formal Language	Informal Language
Children had been talking about his comic book.	Kids had been going on like crazy about his comic book.

A. Read each formal sentence. Replace the formal words or phrases with informal words. Write your new sentence in the box.

Formal Language	Informal Language
1. My father is an illustrator of graphic novels.	
2. Kindly return my printed materials in a timely manner.	

B. Read each formal sentence. Rewrite each sentence to develop a voice, using informal language that shows feelings and personality.

Pair/Share Work with a partner to rewrite each sentence with informal words and phrases that show feelings and personality.

Formal Language	Informal Language
3. I am greatly looking forward to attending the art show.	
4. My mother will not allow me to draw until my homework is done.	

Name _____ Date _____

Lesson 17
READER'S NOTEBOOK

LAFFF from
"Best Shorts"
Independent Reading

LAFFF from "Best Shorts"

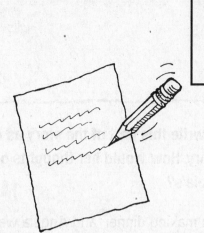

Narrator Swap

When Angela is telling the story, she tells us exactly what she is seeing, feeling, or thinking. But because she is a character in the story, she does not necessarily know what the other characters see, feel, or think.

Read page 513. Rewrite this part of the story as if Peter were telling the story. How would his thoughts or reactions be different from Angela's?

I walked up behind Angela and, speaking in my best mad scientist voice, said, "I am Dr. Lu Manchu, the mad scientist." When Angela turned and looked at me, _____

_____

_____

Read page 515. Rewrite this part of the story as if Peter were telling the story. How would his thoughts or reactions be different from Angela's?

I said, "Okay, Angela. I'll show you!" and stepped inside. I set the machine for June of next year. A few seconds later, I stepped out of the machine and went to the garden, where _____

_____

_____

What additional information about Peter's character, as well as the plot, did you include that was not in the original version?

_____

_____

Name _____ Date _____

Lesson 17
READER'S NOTEBOOK

LAFFF from
"Best Shorts"
Independent Reading

Read page 519. Rewrite this part of the story as if Angela's mother were telling the story. How would her thoughts or reactions be different from Angela's?

I was in the kitchen making dinner, and Angela was upstairs taking a shower. Suddenly I turned and

_____

_____

_____

Now, read page 520. Rewrite this part of the story as if it were told from Angela's mother's point of view.

Then, Angela came down the stairs again, but this time she was in her bathrobe and she was wet! I told her I could not understand what was going on. Angela said,

_____

_____

_____

_____

Think about how the story structure is different when told from her mother's point of view. What information is now missing from the plot?

_____

_____

_____

Name _____ Date _____

Lesson 17
READER'S NOTEBOOK

LAFFF
Vocabulary Strategies:
Reference Materials

Reference Materials

Dictionaries and glossaries contain the meanings of phrases as well as words. Use a print or digital dictionary to define the phrases in the box. Then complete each sentence with the phrase that matches the meaning in parentheses.

come through	come along	sign on	turn away	turn up
come by	sign off on	turn out	make up	turn down

1. They had to _____ many customers. (reject).

2. The supervisor will _____ the project when it is completed. (approve)

3. Angela wanted to _____ the prize at first. (refuse)

4. A good friend will _____ in times of trouble. (help)

5. Did Angela _____ the story of Peter's time machine, or did he really build one? (invent)

6. The workers were able to _____ the equipment that the group needed. (produce)

7. Peter's time machine was starting to _____ after a slow start. (progress)

8. Angela decided to _____ her focus on her school work. (increase)

9. Peter did _____ his idea for the time machine without any help. (get).

10. He will _____ with the company. (join).

More Words with *-ed* or *-ing*

Basic Write the Basic Word that best completes each group.

1. transferred, presented, _____

2. restated, retold, _____

3. linked, joined, _____

4. commented, mentioned, _____

5. exhausting, weakening, _____

6. enacting, presenting, _____

7. anticipated, awaited, _____

8. rehearsing, preparing, _____

9. funny, entertaining, _____

10. murmured, mumbled, _____

11. cold, icy, _____

Challenge 12–14. Write a short review of a school play that raised money for a charity. Use three of the Challenge Words. Write on a separate sheet of paper.

Spelling Words

1. tiring
2. borrowed
3. freezing
4. delivered
5. whispered
6. losing
7. decided
8. amazing
9. performing
10. resulting
11. related
12. attending
13. damaged
14. remarked
15. practicing
16. supported
17. united
18. expected
19. amusing
20. repeated

Challenge
assigned
entertaining
operated
rehearsing
donated

Spelling Word Sort

Write each Basic Word beside the correct heading.

Adding -ed: Final e dropped	**Basic Words:** **Challenge Words:**
Adding -ing: Final e dropped	**Basic Words:** **Challenge Words:** **Possible Selection Words:**
Adding -ed: No spelling change	**Basic Words:** **Challenge Words:**
Adding -ing: No spelling change	**Basic Words:** **Challenge Words:** **Possible Selection Words:**

Challenge   Add the Challenge Words to your Word Sort.

Connect to Reading   Look through *LAFFF*. Find words that have -ed or -ing. Add them to your Word Sort.

Spelling Words

1. tiring
2. borrowed
3. freezing
4. delivered
5. whispered
6. losing
7. decided
8. amazing
9. performing
10. resulting
11. related
12. attending
13. damaged
14. remarked
15. practicing
16. supported
17. united
18. expected
19. amusing
20. repeated

Challenge
assigned
entertaining
operated
rehearsing
donated

Proofreading for Spelling

LAFFF
Spelling: More Words with
-ed or -ing

**Find the misspelled words and circle them. Write them correctly
on the lines below.**

Spelling Words

I remember the day I desided to join the Intergalactic
Space Corps. True, I never expeckted that atending the training
would be easy or amuzing. But I never knew how tiering it
would be prackticing for the demands relatted to space travel.
It helped that my parents reppeated in their letters to me that
they suported my decision. Knowing that I was unitted with
my amayzing new friends also helped. Before long, my fellow
cadets and I were performming quite well. I even heard that an
instructor re-marked that our hard work was ressulting in one of
the best classes she'd seen in years!

1. tiring
2. borrowed
3. freezing
4. delivered
5. whispered
6. losing
7. decided
8. amazing
9. performing
10. resulting
11. related
12. attending
13. damaged
14. remarked
15. practicing
16. supported
17. united
18. expected
19. amusing
20. repeated

Challenge
assigned
entertaining
operated
rehearsing
donated

1. _____
2. _____
3. _____
4. _____
5. _____
6. _____
7. _____

8. _____
9. _____
10. _____
11. _____
12. _____
13. _____
14. _____

LAFFF
Grammar: Adverbs

Adverbs That Tell How, When, and Where

An **adverb** is a word that usually describes a
verb. Adverbs tell *how*, *when*, or *where* an action
happens. Many adverbs end with *–ly*.

	adverbs
how:	They played the music **loudly**.
when:	He came **early**.
where:	He went **inside**.

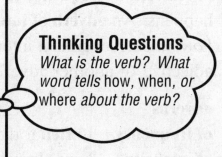

Thinking Questions
*What is the verb? What
word tells* how, when, *or*
where *about the verb?*

Activity   Underline the adverb in each sentence. Write whether the
adverb tells *how*, *when*, or *where*.

1. Nola hoped that she would go far in her career as an engineer. _____

2. She eagerly worked on her designs. _____

3. One day, she finally allowed her friend to look at her

   drawings. _____

4. Her friend jumped ahead in the pages to look at the final design.

   _____

5. She thought Nola thought inventively. _____

6. Nola closed her eyes and soon envisioned herself at an

   awards ceremony. _____

7. She dreamily imagined her parents saying how proud

   they were of her. _____

8. Nola picked up her pen and practiced hard for her future

   goal. _____

Adverbs of Frequency and Intensity

An **adverb of frequency** tells *how often* something happens. An **adverb of intensity** gives information about *how much*. Adverbs of intensity can describe a verb, an adjective, or another adverb.

Thinking Questions
Which word is the verb?
Which word tells how often or how much?

adverbs	
of frequency	I **often** forget to bring my lunch to school.
of intensity	I am **almost** finished with my invention.
	That idea is **too** strange!

Activity Underline the adverb in each sentence. Write whether the adverb tells *how often* or *how much*.

1. Katie could barely believe she had won the science prize. _____

2. She had never achieved such an honor before. _____

3. She thought about how sometimes hard work paid off. _____

4. She had just about given up on her invention at one point. _____

5. She was completely out of new ideas. _____

6. Adam was very encouraging, though. _____

7. He wanted her to win the prize almost as much as she wanted to win it.

   _____

8. Katie will always remember what a good friend he was to her.

   _____

Using Adverbs in Different Parts of Sentences

LAFFF
Grammar: Adverbs

An **adverb** usually gives us more information about the verb in the sentence. When it is used with a verb, it can come in front of the verb or after it.

He **sometimes** works **late** in the laboratory.
Jenny **often** works **alone**.
Do you think Howard will do **well** in the competition?
Since he works **hard**, he **usually** does **brilliantly**.

Thinking Question
Does the adverb describe the action in the sentence?

Activity   Read the sentence and the adverb in parentheses. Decide where the adverb belongs in the sentence. Then rewrite the sentence with the adverb.

1. Roger went to sleep one night. (early)

_____

2. He was dreaming of time machines and space capsules when he awoke. (suddenly)

_____

3. He saw a red line streaking across the yellow moon. (quickly)

_____

4. Roger blinked and then leapt out of bed. (bravely)

_____

5. He had no idea what he had just seen. (really)

_____

6. He leaned out his window and looked for the thing to return. (everywhere)

_____

Simple Verb Tenses

Present Tense	Past Tense	Future Tense
The alien visits Earth. The author writes about aliens.	The alien visited Earth. The author wrote about aliens.	The alien will visit Earth. The author will write about aliens.

1–6. Write which tense of the verb in parentheses correctly completes the sentence. Then write the correct tense of the verb.

1. The author (use) Pluto as the setting of his next book.

_____

2. For his last book, the author (choose) Venus for the setting.

_____

3. My brother (read) a chapter of his favorite science book every day. _____

4. He now (enjoy) reading stories about space travel. _____

5. Last year, he (like) books about dinosaurs. _____

6. I wonder what type of books he (like) next. _____

7–10. This paragraph contains four errors in verb tense. Underline each error. On the line below, correct the errors and tell which verb tense is correct.

    The famous science fiction author signed copies of her book later today at 4:00 p.m. I can't wait! Yesterday my mom tells me about the book signing. I finish reading the book last night. In the book, all the characters live on Earth, but Earth is very different. The characters' things are very small. Their cars and computers are tiny. The characters can enlarge and shrink themselves to fit into their cars or use their computers. When I meet the author, I ask her if she really thinks we will be able to change our own size in the future. Sometimes the work of science fiction authors inspires inventors to create new technologies.

_____

Connect to Writing

Less Precise Adverb	More Precise Adverb
The spaceship crew cheered <u>loudly</u> when they saw Earth.	The spaceship crew cheered <u>ecstatically</u> when they saw Earth.

Activity Look at the underlined adverb in each sentence. Write a more precise adverb on the line.

1. The scientist stood on the street and <u>slowly</u> looked

   around. _____

2. He then walked <u>quietly</u> toward the corner.

   _____

3. At the entrance to a building, he <u>quickly</u> stopped and looked

   around. _____

4. As he went up the front steps, the scientist <u>smoothly</u> brushed off

   the front of his coat. _____

5. When he finally pushed a buzzer, he did it <u>firmly</u>. _____

6. After waiting a while, he <u>softly</u> placed the palm of his hand on

   the glass door. _____

7. <u>Strangely</u> enough, his hand passed right through the glass!

   _____

8. A woman who had observed the use of this amazing invention retreated <u>quickly</u>

   back into her apartment. _____

Focus Trait: Elaboration

Using Concrete Words and Sensory Details

Basic Description	Description with Concrete Words and Sensory Details
Tara had blonde hair.	Tara's <u>long, straight</u> hair was the color of <u>sunlit wheat</u>.

A. Think about the characters Angela and Peter from LAFFF. Read each sentence. Make it more vivid by adding descriptive words and details.

Basic Description	Description with Exact Words
1. Angela felt odd when she looked into the room.	Angela felt _____ when she _____
2. Peter waited to hear about what Angela did.	Peter _____ to hear about _____

B. Rewrite each description, adding details to make it more precise and interesting.

Pair/Share   Work with a partner to brainstorm concrete words and sensory details to elaborate on each sentence.

Basic Description	Description with Exact Words
3. Angela saw something in the kitchen.	
4. Peter laughed at the funny thing.	
5. Angela ran away.	

Name _____ Date _____

Lesson 18
READER'S NOTEBOOK

The Dog Newspaper
from "Five Pages a Day"
Independent Reading

Reader's Guide

The Dog Newspaper from "Five Pages a Day"

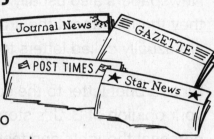

Write Newspaper Headings

Newspaper writers often use headings to break articles into parts. The heading for each section is usually a brief statement of the main idea of that section, or what the section is mostly about. The headings often appeal to readers or create interest in the story. They are not complete sentences, but phrases with the most important information.

Read page 545. If you were helping the author write the newspaper story about B. J., what heading would you write for this section? Remember that the heading should tell what that section is mostly about.

_____

_____

Read page 546. What would be an exciting heading for this section?

_____

_____

A headline provides readers with an interesting and eye-catching summary of the main idea of the entire article instead of just one section. Headlines may be a little longer than headings, but they are still not complete sentences. Again, simply use the most important words. What would make an interesting headline for the story about B. J. on pages 545–546?

_____

_____

Name _____ Date _____

Lesson 18
READER'S NOTEBOOK

The Dog Newspaper
from "Five Pages a Day"
Independent Reading

Write a Letter to the Editor

Newspapers also usually contain letters from readers telling what
they thought about the articles in previous issues. These letters
are usually called letters to the editor.

Write a brief letter to the editor of *The Dog Newspaper,* giving
your opinion of B. J.'s story from pages 545 and 546. Tell your
personal thoughts and feelings about the article. Explain which
part of the story you think was most engaging and why.

Dear *Dog Newspaper,*

I read your article about how B. J. came to the United States in the
first issue of *The Dog Newspaper*, and _____

_____

_____

_____

_____

_____

_____

_____

_____

_____

_____

_____

_____

Homophones and Homographs

1–10. Circle the homophone that correctly completes each sentence.

1. He quickly untied the (not, knot) in the dog's leash.

2. The boy was invited to the party and told to bring his dog, (to, too, two).

3. That edition of the newspaper (won, one) national awards.

4. I (red, read) the headline but not the article.

5. That dog was quite a (site, sight) after he ran through the wet paint.

6. We asked for (to, too, two) dog bones.

7. (There, Their) puppy chewed up the rug.

8. Please put the water dish (there, their).

9. They chose a (site, sight) for the dog clinic.

10. My writing career lasted (won, one) week.

11–14. Read the definitions of each pair of homographs. Then write an original sentence that shows the meaning of each.

> **well** *adv.* skillfully **well** *n.* deep hole dug into the earth to obtain water **light** *v.* to set on fire **light** *adj.* having little weight

11. _____

12. _____

13. _____

14. _____

Changing Final *y* to *i*

Basic Write the Basic Word that best completes each analogy.

1. *Losses* are to *defeats* as *wins* are to _____.

2. *Happy* is to *joyous* as *scared* is to _____.

3. *Close* is to *far* as _____ is to *later*.

4. *Teammates* are to *rivals* as *allies* are to _____.

5. *Talents* are to *strengths* as *skills* are to _____.

6. *Cloudier* is to *darker* as _____ is to *brighter*.

7. *Cleaner* is to _____ as *tidier* is to *messier*.

8. *Sharpest* is to *dullest* as *ugliest* is to _____.

9. *Jets* are to *airplanes* as _____ are to *boats*.

10. *Goals* are to *ambitions* as *plans* are to _____.

Challenge 11–14. Suggest some ways neighbors can get along with one another better. Use four of the Challenge Words. Write on a separate sheet of paper.

Spelling Words

1. duties
2. earlier
3. loveliest
4. denied
5. ferries
6. sunnier
7. terrified
8. abilities
9. dirtier
10. scariest
11. trophies
12. cozier
13. enemies
14. iciest
15. greediest
16. drowsier
17. victories
18. horrified
19. memories
20. strategies

Challenge
unified
dictionaries
boundaries
satisfied
tragedies

Spelling Word Sort

Write each Basic Word beside the correct heading.

Words ending in *-es*	**Basic Words:**
	Challenge Words:
	Possible Selection Words:
Words ending in *-ed*	**Basic Words:**
	Challenge Words:
	Possible Selection Words:
Words ending in *-er*	**Basic Words:**
Words ending in *-est*	**Basic Words:**

Spelling Words

1. duties
2. earlier
3. loveliest
4. denied
5. ferries
6. sunnier
7. terrified
8. abilities
9. dirtier
10. scariest
11. trophies
12. cozier
13. enemies
14. iciest
15. greediest
16. drowsier
17. victories
18. horrified
19. memories
20. strategies

Challenge
unified
dictionaries
boundaries
satisfied
tragedies

Challenge Add the Challenge Words to your Word Sort.

Connect to Reading Look through *The Dog Newspaper*. Find words that have the spelling patterns on this page. Add them to your Word Sort.

Name _____ Date _____

Proofreading for Spelling

The Dog Newspaper
Spelling: Changing Final *y* to *i*

Find the misspelled words and circle them. Write them correctly on the lines below.

Today my cartoons are printed in newspapers from coast to coast. Twenty years ago, when I was in fifth grade, they ran in just one—my school paper, the *Spy*. As I sit by my fireplace, memorys of the awards ceremony that year make me feel even cozyer than the fire does. Before I get drowzier, I will relate that earlyer event. I had abilitys in drawing. My dutyies for the paper were to write and illustrate a cartoon about the icyest bigfoot creature I could create—the greedyest monster ever drawn. I wanted it to make readers feel horiffied and terified. My wish was not denyed. I received the award for scaryest cartoon that year. It was the first of several trophys that I have earned and the most satisfying of my victries. Its reflection casts the lovliest glow into my studio.

1. _____ 9. _____

2. _____ 10. _____

3. _____ 11. _____

4. _____ 12. _____

5. _____ 13. _____

6. _____ 14. _____

7. _____ 15. _____

8. _____

Spelling Words

1. duties
2. earlier
3. loveliest
4. denied
5. ferries
6. sunnier
7. terrified
8. abilities
9. dirtier
10. scariest
11. trophies
12. cozier
13. enemies
14. iciest
15. greediest
16. drowsier
17. victories
18. horrified
19. memories
20. strategies

Challenge

unified
dictionaries
boundaries
satisfied
tragedies

Prepositions

A **preposition** is a word that shows the connection between other words in the sentence. Some prepositions are used to show time, location, and direction. Other prepositions, such as *with* and *about*, provide details.

prepositions

time	We played <u>until</u> bedtime.
location	The dog sleeps <u>on</u> his own bed.
direction	She walked <u>into</u> the corner store.
detail	The dog <u>with</u> the pink collar is mine.

Thinking Question
What words tell about time, direction, or location, or add detail?

Activity Underline the preposition in each sentence. Tell if it describes time, location, direction, or detail.

1. My friends and I built a doghouse in the backyard. _____

2. On the doghouse, we painted a white bone. _____

3. We worked throughout the afternoon. _____

4. We stopped once and drank lemonade with ice. _____

5. My dog Oscar had always slept with me. _____

6. I can see the doghouse from my window. _____

7. Its entrance faces toward the house. _____

8. The elm tree will provide shade during the summer. _____

Prepositional Phrases

A **prepositional phrase** adds information to a
sentence. It can tell *where, when,* or *how,* or it can
add detail. It begins with a preposition and ends
with a noun or pronoun. The noun or pronoun is the
object of the preposition.

Thinking Questions
*What is the prepositional
phrase in the sentence?
What information does it
add?*

prepositional phrase

Holly is the feature editor for our local newspaper.
Where
She became editor in 2011. **When**
She writes her stories on the computer. **How**
She often writes stories about dogs and cats. **Detail**

**Underline the prepositional phrase. Then write the object of the
preposition on the line and *where, when, how,* or *detail* to tell what
information the phrase adds.**

1. Holly interviewed several people about their pets. _____

2. She walked throughout the neighborhood. _____

3. During her interviews, she discovered some interesting facts.

   _____

4. She also took photos with her camera. _____

5. One dog can jump ten feet off the ground. _____

6. To her amazement, she even saw one dog smile. _____

7. One cat with very white teeth helps advertise pet toothbrushes. _____

8. By Tuesday afternoon, Holly had written her article. _____

Prepositional Phrases to Combine Sentences

A prepositional phrase can be used to combine two sentences.

Short sentences:	My dog loves his treats. He has one in the morning and at night.
Combined sentence:	My dog loves his treats in the morning and at night.

Thinking Questions
What is the prepositional phrase in the short sentences? How can it be used to combine the sentences?

Activity Rewrite the two short sentences by combining them into one sentence using a prepositional phrase.

1. Our dog Fritz loves to look out the window. The window is in our living room.

   _____

2. Fritz barks at the mail carrier. The mail carrier is by the front door.

   _____

3. Fritz and I play with the ball. We play in the yard.

   _____

4. I take Fritz for a walk. We walk along the river.

   _____

5. Fritz chased a squirrel at the park. The squirrel ran up a tree.

   _____

6. Fritz jumped into the water to fetch a stick. He jumped over a bench!

   _____

Transitions

Transitions	Relationship
before, now, next, later, finally, then, eventually, soon, first, when	time order
as, likewise, also, similarly, unlike, on the other hand, but	comparison-contrast
because, as a result, consequently, due to, although	cause and effect

Fill in each blank with a transition that logically connects the ideas in the paragraph. Choose from those listed in the chart.

_____ the soldiers _____ found B.J., he was just a ball of fur.

_____ B.J. grew into a fine young dog. _____ other dogs

his age, he was well behaved from the beginning. _____,

the soldiers took him everywhere. _____ the war came to an

end. _____, B.J. needed a new home. Several soldiers

wanted to take him with them, _____ the choice was narrowed

down to one. B.J. bravely boarded the plane with his master

_____ he had never been on one before. _____ his journey

was over. He was in his forever home at last!

Name _____ Date _____

Connect to Writing

You can use prepositional phrases to combine sentences.

Two Sentences	Longer, Smoother Sentence
The green notebook is on the table. The black pen is on top of the notebook.	The black pen is on top of the green notebook on the table.
The car keys are in the purse. The purse is on the desk.	The car keys are in the purse on the desk.

Activity Use prepositional phrases to combine the two sentences. Write the new sentence on the lines below.

1. The dog sat under the oak tree. The oak tree stands beside our house.

   _____

   _____

2. We gave the dogs a bath. We put them in our bathtub.

   _____

   _____

3. Nick bought a newspaper from the stand. He bought it for his mother.

   _____

   _____

4. During the summer, they exercise the dogs after dinner. They run with the dogs on the beach.

   _____

   _____

5. The photograph of Fido is on the shelf. The shelf is above the bed.

   _____

   _____

Focus Trait: Development

The Dog Newspaper
Writing: Narrative Writing

Adding Concrete Words and Sensory Details

Vague	Strong
I gave Spot lots of attention.	I brushed Spot's coat, gave him a red collar, and played catch with him.

A.   Read each vague or weak sentence. Then add concrete words and sensory details that develop the narrative and express feelings.

Vague	Strong
1. Spot was in the newspaper.	_____ when I saw that Spot was _____ _____.
2. Neighbors enjoyed the story, and I liked receiving their compliments on how great Spot looked in the photo.	Neighbors _____ the story, and I _____ compliments on how _____ _____ _____.

B.   Read each weak sentence. Then rewrite it, adding words and details that give the writing a strong voice or personality.

Pair/Share   Work with a partner to brainstorm new words and details.

Weak	Strong
3. Dogs are good pets.	
4. I like to talk about my pet.	
5. I enjoyed taking my puppy to the beach.	

Reader's Guide

Darnell Rock Reporting

Write a Persuasive E-Mail

A person's words tell us a lot about his or her character. We can learn about Darnell's character, as well as his purpose, by the things he says and the way he says them.

Read Darnell's article on page 570. Give two details he tells his readers in order to persuade them about building the garden.

_____

_____

_____

_____

Read Darnell's speech on pages 576–577. Give two details of other arguments that he makes to persuade listeners about the garden.

_____

_____

_____

_____

_____

A local business owner, Paul Rossini, has offered to donate two city lots to build the garden if Darnell can convince him it is a good idea. Help Darnell write an e-mail to Mr. Rossini. Use Darnell's most persuasive arguments to convince Mr. Rossini to donate the lots.

New Message

To: Paul Rossini; P_Rossini@RossinisPizza.com

From: Darnell Rock; D.Rock@PS157.edu

Subject: Community Garden Proposal

Dear Mr. Rossini,

I received your e-mail from a reporter at the *Oakdale Journal.* He told me you may be willing to donate two of your lots to our garden project. I believe that a community garden …

_____

_____

_____

_____

_____

_____

_____

Thank you for your support.

Sincerely,

Darnell Rock

Name _____ Date _____

Lesson 19
READER'S NOTEBOOK

Darnell Rock Reporting
Vocabulary Strategies:
Greek and Latin Suffixes
-ism, -ist, -able, -ible

Greek and Latin Suffixes *-ism*, *-ist*, *-able*, *-ible*

Suffixes give clues about what a word means. The suffixes *-able* and *-ible* mean "able to" or "can do." The suffix *-ism* means "belief in something." The suffix *-ist* means "one who is or does."

reliable	visible	violinist	flexible	heroism
reasonable	convertible	novelist	realist	realism
artist	columnist	acceptable	reversible	

Choose a word from the list to complete the sentences below.

1. The _____ wrote an editorial for the newspaper.

2. A wire that can bend is _____.

3. She was a _____ who did not believe in fairy tales.

4. A friend who is always there is _____.

5. A _____ car can be driven with the top down.

6. Stories about _____ describe actions that help others.

7. He was an _____ who enjoyed painting.

8. A fair argument is _____.

9. Something that is _____ can be seen with the eyes.

10. The _____ played her instrument beautifully.

11. The _____ wrote a book that became very popular.

12. A _____ jacket can be worn inside out.

13. Sometimes, it can be _____ to take a loss.

14. _____ is the belief that paintings should show the world the way it actually looks.

Suffixes: *-ful*, *-ly*, *-ness*, *-less*, *-ment*

Basic Complete the puzzle by writing the Basic Word for each clue.

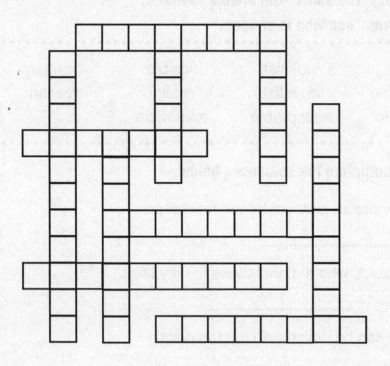

Spelling Words

1. lately
2. settlement
3. watchful
4. countless
5. steadily
6. closeness
7. calmly
8. government
9. agreement
10. cloudiness
11. delightful
12. noisily
13. tardiness
14. forgetful
15. forgiveness
16. harmless
17. enjoyment
18. appointment
19. effortless
20. plentiful

Challenge
suspenseful
merciless
seriousness
contentment
suspiciously

Across

1. alert
5. loudly
8. a decision made together
9. very pleasing
10. without injury

Down

2. without worry, anger, or excitement
3. recently
4. an arrangement to meet with someone
6. in an unchanging way
7. too many to keep track of

Challenge 11–14. Write a suspenseful story that you could tell around a campfire. Use four of the Challenge Words. Write on a separate sheet of paper.

Spelling Word Sort

Write each Basic Word beside the correct heading.

-ful	**Basic Words:**
	Challenge Words:
-ly	**Basic Words:**
	Challenge Words:
	Possible Selection Words:
-ness	**Basic Words:**
	Challenge Words:
-less	**Basic Words:**
	Challenge Words:
	Possible Selection Words:
-ment	**Basic Words:**
	Challenge Words:

Spelling Words

1. lately
2. settlement
3. watchful
4. countless
5. steadily
6. closeness
7. calmly
8. government
9. agreement
10. cloudiness
11. delightful
12. noisily
13. tardiness
14. forgetful
15. forgiveness
16. harmless
17. enjoyment
18. appointment
19. effortless
20. plentiful

Challenge
suspenseful
merciless
seriousness
contentment
suspiciously

Challenge   Add the Challenge Words to your Word Sort.

Challenge   Look through *Darnell Rock Reporting*. Find words that have the suffixes *-ful*, *-ly*, *-ness*, *-less*, or *-ment*. Add them to your Word Sort.

Name _____ Date _____

Proofreading for Spelling

Find the misspelled words and circle them. Write them correctly on the lines below.

Katie's neighborhood had the feeling of closenes that might exist in a small setlement. It seemed almost to have its own goverment, with a homeowners' association group and a neighborhood crime watch. Katie decided to join the neighborhood community and start a babysitting club. She found it to be a nearly efortless job to sign up babysitters who wanted to be in the club. Everybody understood that there would be no forgivness for tardyness on the job—and that nobody could be forgettful. One rainy morning, Katie made flyers to advertise the babysitting club. As soon as she had finished, the rain stopped, and the sun erased all traces of cloudines. She then took enjoiment in distributing the flyers to the plentifull supply of prospective neighborhood clients!

Spelling Words

1. lately
2. settlement
3. watchful
4. countless
5. steadily
6. closeness
7. calmly
8. government
9. agreement
10. cloudiness
11. delightful
12. noisily
13. tardiness
14. forgetful
15. forgiveness
16. harmless
17. enjoyment
18. appointment
19. effortless
20. plentiful

Challenge
suspenseful
merciless
seriousness
contentment
suspiciously

1. _____   6. _____

2. _____   7. _____

3. _____   8. _____

4. _____   9. _____

5. _____   10. _____

Indefinite Pronouns

An **indefinite pronoun** takes the place of a noun. It can stand for a person, place, or thing. The noun that it stands for is unclear or not identified.

Thinking Question
What pronoun refers to a person or thing that is not identified?

indefinite pronoun
Someone wrote a letter to the city council.

Activity Circle the correct pronoun for each sentence.

1. (All, Every) of us wanted to go swimming this summer.

2. However, (someone, something) decided to close the city pool.

3. We asked if (nobody, anyone) on the city council could reopen the pool.

4. The council members said there was (everything, nothing) they could do.

5. We decided to search for (someone, somewhere) else to go swimming.

6. (Everyone, Everything) looked for another place.

7. But we couldn't find (everywhere, anywhere) to go.

8. So we decided to do (something, nothing) else instead.

Name _____ Date _____

Possessive Pronouns

A **possessive pronoun** shows ownership.
Possessive pronouns like *mine*, *yours*, *its*, and
ours can stand alone and take the place of
a noun. Other possessive pronouns such as
my, *your*, *its*, and *our* come before a noun.

possessive pronouns
The speech was <u>his</u> and not <u>hers</u>.
<u>My</u> friends came to the meeting.

Thinking Question
*What is the pronoun
in the sentence that
shows ownership?*

Activity   Underline the possessive pronouns.

1. The donation that helped start the shelter was mine.

2. Shepherd's pie is our favorite dinner at the shelter and spaghetti
   is theirs.

3. Those plates and cups are ours.

4. This seat is yours if you want to join us.

5. Jose made the chicken, and the salad was his, too.

6. Alice brought her sister with her tonight.

7. I know this bag is mine because its zipper is broken.

8. Sometimes people forget their hats or scarves when they leave.

Name _____ Date _____

Interrogative Pronouns

An **interrogative pronoun** replaces a person, place, or thing in a question. Some interrogative pronouns are *who*, *what*, and *which*.

interrogative pronouns

Who wanted to start a community garden?

Thinking Question
What pronoun begins the question in this sentence?

Activity Write an interrogative pronoun to complete each question.

1. _____ planted the flowers in the garden?
2. _____ does she grow there?
3. _____ helped her take all the weeds out?
4. _____ is the best time of year to plant seeds?
5. _____ is the tallest plant you've ever grown?
6. _____ of these flowers does she like most?
7. _____ does she plan to grow next?
8. _____ would like to help me start a vegetable garden?

Commas and Semicolons

Compare how commas and semicolons are used.

Commas in a series	The town needs people to plant trees, rake leaves, and pick up trash.
Commas setting off introductory word or words	Well, nobody told him he couldn't write a letter to the editor.
Commas setting off *yes, no,* or direct address	Yes, I believe we should all help keep our town clean.
Semicolons to separate items in a series	The following people were scheduled to speak: three builders, who spoke about building code violations; Ms. Sanchez, the librarian, who spoke about library funding; Mr. Fisher, a gardener, who spoke about improving the community garden.

1-7. Read each sentence. Add commas or semicolons where they are needed.

1. Lana James and Maria were on time for the meeting.

2. The girl urged the city council to do the following: to support the students, who need a good education support the teachers, who need a new parking lot and support the community.

3. Yes we should all look out for the elderly in our community.

4. Oh I think Mona would make an excellent city councillor.

5. Mr. Boroshok Mr. Williams and half of the city had turned out for the meeting.

6. Well not everyone is cut out for public speaking.

7. No Nasser will not give up his job at the animal shelter.

Connect to Writing

Repeating Nouns	Replacing Nouns with Pronouns
The book you are reading is my book.	The book you are reading is mine.
They drove his car to the city council meeting and returned in her car.	They drove his car to the city council meeting and returned in hers.

Activity Rewrite each sentence. Use possessive pronouns to avoid repeating nouns.

1. The article about homeless people was my article.

_____

2. Is this newspaper your newspaper?

_____

3. The city council members listened to her speech and then to his speech.

_____

4. The teacher graded my story but didn't grade your story.

_____

5. Today it's my turn to help Mrs. Lawson, and tomorrow it's your turn to help.

_____

Focus Trait: Purpose
Adding Thoughts and Feelings

The writer's purpose for a narrative can be made clear by including thoughts and feelings.

Weak Writing	Strong Writing
I stepped up to the podium and prepared to give my speech.	I nervously stepped up to the podium, fearing that no one wanted to hear my speech.

Read each weak sentence. Rewrite the first weak sentence by adding details that show feeling. Rewrite the second weak sentence by adding details that develop a thought.

Weak Writing	Strong Writing
1. I looked at the crowd before speaking.	
2. Before my speech started, many people in the audience were talking.	

Pair/Share Work with a partner to revise the weak writing to make it more interesting. Add thoughts or feelings. Write your new sentences on the right.

Weak Writing	Strong Writing
3. As I began speaking, I started to feel better.	
4. The council members agreed with the ideas in my speech.	

**Reader's Guide**

The Black Stallion

Create a Movie Storyboard

A plot chart can help you visualize the major events in the structure of a story. By creating a plot chart for *The Black Stallion*, you can see the structure of the story. Reread pages 608–613 and write a sentence describing each part of the plot.

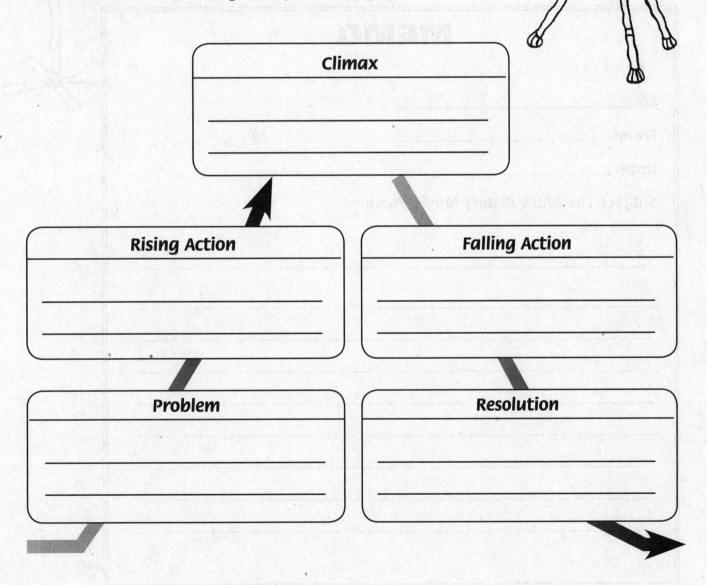

Climax

_____

_____

Rising Action

_____

_____

Falling Action

_____

_____

Problem

_____

_____

Resolution

_____

_____

A movie company is making a movie based on the story of the *The Black Stallion*. You are responsible for designing the movie poster, but you have to get the idea approved first. Write a memo to the movie executives describing your idea for the movie poster. Focus on the climax of the story because that would generate the most audience excitement. Include a few sentences that would make the audience even more interested in the movie.

MEMO

To: _____

From: _____

Date: _____

Subject: The *Black Beauty* Movie Poster

_____

_____

_____

_____

_____

_____

_____

_____

Name _____ Date _____

Figurative Language

Read each sentence and the figurative language
in parentheses. Then rewrite the sentence using
the figurative language. Your new sentence should have the same
meaning as the original one.

Example: The horse's coat was shiny. (gleamed like silver)
New sentence: The horse's coat gleamed like silver.

---

1. A lot of sweat poured off the boy. (like rain)

   _____

2. His face was pale and clammy. (a fish's underbelly)

   _____

3. Suddenly, a loud voice called his number. (boomed out)

   _____

4. Shakily, he made his way to Chestnut, his horse. (on rubber legs)

   _____

5. He got into the saddle stiffly. (like a robot)

   _____

6. His fears disappeared. (melted away)

   _____

7. With confidence, he urged Chestnut into the ring. (cool as a cucumber)

   _____

8. He felt he could win. (the sky was the limit)

   _____

Name _____ • Date _____

Lesson 20
READER'S NOTEBOOK

The Black Stallion
Spelling: Words from Other
Languages

Words from Other Languages

Basic Write the Basic Word that best completes each sentence.

1. A very rich _____ owns the Triple Z ranch.
2. All of the ranch hands work in thick, denim _____.
3. In cooler weather they also wear a warm cloak, or _____.
4. A _____ helps keep sweat off their faces and necks.
5. They use a _____ to rope wild horses and stray cattle.
6. The _____, a flour tortilla with fillings, is a specialty of the ranch's cook.
7. He also prepares a spicy sauce called _____.
8. He chops one ripe, juicy _____ after another.
9. The cook serves lunch on the paved _____.
10. Then the workers take an afternoon nap, or _____.
11. They take turns sleeping in the _____ swinging on the porch.

Challenge 12–14. Write a short travel article for your school paper about things to see and do on a vacation. Use three of the Challenge Words. Write on a separate sheet of paper.

Spelling Words

1. salsa
2. mattress
3. tycoon
4. burrito
5. bandana
6. tomato
7. poncho
8. dungarees
9. lasso
10. patio
11. siesta
12. cargo
13. vanilla
14. tsunami
15. iguana
16. plaza
17. caravan
18. hammock
19. pajamas
20. gallant

Challenge
mosquito
cathedral
alligator
tambourine
sombrero

Spelling Word Sort

Write each Basic Word beside the correct heading.

Two syllables	Basic Words:
Three syllables	Basic Words:
	Challenge Words:
Other syllable counts	Challenge Words:

Challenge   Add the Challenge Words to your Word Sort.

Spelling Words

1. salsa
2. mattress
3. tycoon
4. burrito
5. bandana
6. tomato
7. poncho
8. dungarees
9. lasso
10. patio
11. siesta
12. cargo
13. vanilla
14. tsunami
15. iguana
16. plaza
17. caravan
18. hammock
19. pajamas
20. gallant

Challenge
mosquito
cathedral
alligator
tambourine
sombrero

Name _____ Date _____

Proofreading for Spelling

**Find the misspelled words and circle them. Write them correctly
on the lines below.**

Dear Anna,

   We are having fun in Mexico, despite a stunami of chores
before we left Laredo. I think the cargoe includes everything
but a matress! Our carivan of three left early while it was still
dark. I was still in my pajammas! While we drove along, I read
The Black Stallion. That horse is so gallent. He reminds me
of Old Yeller. For lunch today, I ate a buritto with saulsa and
vannilla flan in a little plazza. Yesterday, during my midday
seista in a woven-rope hammack, I watched a fat, lazy igauna
on the hotel pattio. I named him the Green like how Alec named
the stallion the Black. Today I am shopping for a ponchoe to
protect you in wild weather.

Juan

Spelling Words
1. salsa
2. mattress
3. tycoon
4. burrito
5. bandana
6. tomato
7. poncho
8. dungarees
9. lasso
10. patio
11. siesta
12. cargo
13. vanilla
14. tsunami
15. iguana
16. plaza
17. caravan
18. hammock
19. pajamas
20. gallant

Challenge
mosquito
cathedral
alligator
tambourine
sombrero

1. _____   9. _____

2. _____   10. _____

3. _____   11. _____

4. _____   12. _____

5. _____   13. _____

6. _____   14. _____

7. _____   15. _____

8. _____

The Mechanics of Writing Titles

A **title** is the name of a creative work. Writers indicate titles in certain ways. For longer works, such as books, movies, plays, or the names of newspapers or magazines, writers underline titles when they are writing them by hand. When these titles are printed, they appear in italics.

Book Title

The Girl Who Rode Like the Wind

> **Thinking Question**
> *When writing by hand, how would you show that* The Girl Who Rode Like the Wind *is a book title?*

1–8. **Identify the titles in the following examples, and write them in the space provided.**

1. Our local *Daily Recorder* had a story of a boy who raised horses. _____

2. Allen Verman wrote a book about his childhood pet entitled My Very Best Friend.

   _____

3. The movie about five castaways was called *Trapped on an Island.*

   _____

4. I learned a lot about animals from the movie Friends, Servants, and Saviors.

   _____

5. The film *My Pretty Pony* told the story of a young woman and her horse.

   _____

6. I read a fascinating book called *My Life on a Desert Island.*

   _____

7. My cousin appeared in a play called The Boy Who Loved to Ride.

   _____

8. Barn and Stable is my favorite magazine. _____

The Mechanics of Writing Titles

A **title** is the name given to a creative work. Writers indicate titles in certain ways. The titles of shorter works, such as stories, articles, TV programs, or songs, appear in quotation marks.

TV Program Title
"Animals on the Farm"

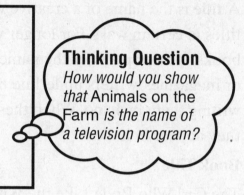

Thinking Question
How would you show that Animals on the Farm *is the name of a television program?*

1–5. **Identify the titles in the following examples, and write them properly in the space provided.**

1. The article in the magazine was called Great Trail Adventures.

   _____

2. Arnold wrote a song called Black Like Coal about his horse.

   _____

3. The castaway passed the time by writing a poem called On This Island.

   _____

4. His favorite program, Animal Adventures, ran on Saturday nights.

   _____

5. The Animal That Saved Me was published in a collection of animal stories.

   _____

6–8. **Decide if the following titles should be underlined or placed in quotation marks.**

6. The class read a fascinating book called What Animals Know

   _____

7. Aisha recited the poem The Boy Who Loved to Ride.

   _____

8. The article came from the magazine Adventure Stories.

   _____

Name _____ Date _____

The Mechanics of Writing Titles

A **title** is the name given to a creative work. Writers follow special rules for capitalizing letters at the beginning of words in titles. The first and last words of a title always begin with a capital letter. Most other words begin with capital letters, too. However, articles, coordinating conjunctions, and short prepositions never begin with capital letters unless they are the first or last word of the title.

The Boy Who Ran for Gold and Glory

Thinking Question
How would you use capital letters in the title, the boy who ran for gold and glory?

1–5. Write the following titles using the proper capitalization.

1. living on a desert island _____

2. the girl who loved to ride in the hills _____

3. racing against the wind and rain _____

4. in the land of the tallest trees _____

5. raising champion horses _____

6–8. Identify the titles in the sentences below, and write them using the proper capitalization and punctuation.

6. After I read the book partners in adventure, I wanted to get a horse.

   _____

7. The poem when the thunder cracks gave me the chills.

   _____

8. I read a short story about horses in the book tales of the wild west.

   _____

Prepositions and Prepositional Phrases

A **preposition** is a word that shows relationships between other words in a sentence. Common prepositions include *above, after, at, during, for, through, in, on, of, to, with.*

1–5. Choose a preposition to complete each of the following sentences.

1. I would like to live ___ a farm.
2. He looked up and saw the birds _____ him.
3. The girl rode her horse ___ the driveway.
4. The castaway built a hut _____ encountering wild dogs.
5. The trainer worked ____ the horse.

A prepositional phrase begins with a preposition and ends with a noun or pronoun.

6–10. Identify the prepositional phrases in the following sentences.

6. I wanted to ride the horse around the track.

_____

7. Eliza dreamed of the animals she would take care of during the summer.

_____

8. Walter knew his cat's life would change after the accident.

_____

9. The horse jumped over the barrier.

_____

10. In the fall, he and his dog were happy.

_____

Connect to Writing

> The titles of books, articles, and other works often appear in writing. The special rules for writing titles help readers know when an essay or research paper is referring to some other work.
>
> *The Black Stallion* is an exciting and inspiring novel.

Activity   If the sentence is incorrect, rewrite it correctly. If it is correct, write correct on the line.

1. The book *The Boy and His Horse* is a powerful tale of adventure. _____

2. When Tina sings <u>Go to sleep, Baby,</u> it calms the horse.

   _____

3. The article "Tips for Training Horses" explains horse

   behavior. _____

4. Elvin Ramirez starred in the play Stranded at Sea.

   _____

5. The movie "The Long Trail over the Mountains" features

   an amazing horse race.

   _____

6. An article in the *Daily Examiner*, our local paper, told this

   story. _____

7. In *galloping in the galaxy*, the poet expresses the freedom

   he feels on his horse.

   _____

   _____

Focus Trait: Conventions
Strengthening Voice

Weak Voice	Strong Voice with concrete words, sensory details, and dialogue
I was frightened but also drawn to the horse.	The great size of the shining, snorting beast thrilled—and frightened—me. "It may be the last thing I ever do," I thought as I drew near the animal. "But it will be the greatest thing I ever do."

Read the following weak sentences. Rewrite them to develop a stronger voice. Include concrete words, sensory details, and dialogue. Pay attention to quotation marks and other punctuation.

1. The horse did not want me to ride him. He threw me off.

_____

_____

_____

2. It was fun to ride the horse. He ran very fast.

_____

_____

_____

3. The horse seemed happy that I was in charge. It was calm.

_____

_____

_____

Name _____ Date _____

Unit 4
READER'S NOTEBOOK

About Time: A First Look
at Time and Clocks
Segment 1
Independent Reading

About Time: A First Look at Time and Clocks

Write Chapter Titles

The author of "About Time" has asked you to
write chapter titles for the book. When coming up
with a chapter title, begin by collecting a list of
key words from the chapter. Key words are those that
are the most important words and ideas in the chapter.

Imagine that one chapter of the book is pages 3–4. What words
seem to be very important? The first word is given for you.

time, _____

How did you decide what words were key words?

_____

_____

_____

_____

Based on these key words, what might be a good chapter title for
the material on pages 3–4?

_____

_____

Name _____ Date _____

Unit 4
READER'S NOTEBOOK

About Time: A First Look at Time and Clocks
Segment 1
Independent Reading

Suppose that pages 5–7 will be the next chapter of the book. What are some key words from this chapter?

_____

_____

_____

Write a title for this chapter. The title should give the reader a good idea about what the chapter is mostly about.

_____

_____

_____

How did the key words help you write the title?

_____

_____

_____

_____

Name _____ Date _____

Unit 4
READER'S NOTEBOOK

About Time: A First Look
at Time and Clocks
Segment 1
Independent Reading

Explaining Time

Read pages 4–6 and look carefully at the diagrams.
Complete the chart by telling how these ancient people
tracked time. The first one is done for you.

Time Unit
A Day *set by where the sun is located in the sky*
A Week
A Season
A Month
A Year

Name _____ Date _____

Unit 4
READER'S NOTEBOOK

About Time: A First Look
at Time and Clocks
Segment 1
Independent Reading

Now use the information you gathered on page 279 to write encyclopedia entries about how units of time were defined. Choose a unit of time and write it on the line. Then write a brief factual description of how the unit of time was originally defined.

Word: _____

_____

_____

_____

Word: _____

_____

_____

_____

Name _____ Date _____

Unit 4
READER'S NOTEBOOK

About Time: A First Look
at Time and Clocks
Segment 1
Independent Reading

Calendar Math

What were the problems ancient peoples discovered by using natural time cycles to measure years? Complete the chart with the correct number of days.

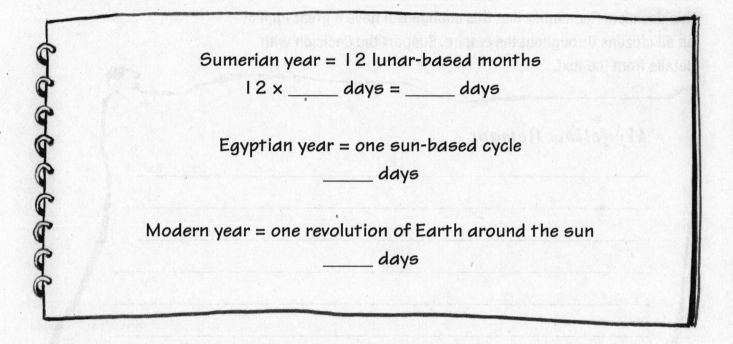

Sumerian year = 12 lunar-based months

12 x _____ days = _____ days

Egyptian year = one sun-based cycle

_____ days

Modern year = one revolution of Earth around the sun

_____ days

Explain the problem of using natural divisions of time for calendars.

_____

_____

_____

How did the Julian calendar attempt to solve the problem of a sun–based calendar?

_____

_____

_____

Name _____ Date _____

Unit 4
READER'S NOTEBOOK

About Time: A First Look
at Time and Clocks
Segment 1
Independent Reading

Caesar's Solution

It is the year 46 B.C. On the advice of his chief astronomer, Emperor Julius Caesar has decided to change the calendar to a new system that includes a leap year every four years. Write the speech that the Emperor will give to the Roman Senate explaining this decision. Remember that this change will have a great impact on all citizens throughout the empire. Support the decision with details from the text.

My fellow Romans,

_____

_____

_____

_____

_____

_____

_____

_____

_____

_____

_____

_____

_____

_____

_____

_____

Name _____ Date _____

Unit 4
READER'S NOTEBOOK

About Time: A First Look
at Time and Clocks
Segment 2
Independent Reading

 **Reader's Guide**

About Time: A First Look at Time and Clocks

Write Chapter Titles

Imagine that the next chapter of the book is pages 8–9.
Find three keywords in the text and show what characteristics
they meet. The first one has been done for you.

Keyword	Used Often in the Chapter	Describes an Important Idea in the Chapter	Necessary to Understanding the Chapter
Egypt	✓		✓

Using these key words, write a title for this chapter. Remember that the title
should give the reader a good idea about what the chapter is mostly about.

_____

_____

Suppose that the next chapter will be pages 10–11. What are some key
words from this chapter?

_____

Think about the key words you found. Using these key words,
write a title for this chapter.

_____

Name _____ Date _____

Unit 4
READER'S NOTEBOOK

About Time: A First Look
at Time and Clocks
Segment 2
Independent Reading

Make a Museum Audio Tour

**Answer the questions below. Then you will write a script for
an audio tour.**

Read page 9. What do the hemicycle systems of the Egyptians,
Greeks, and Romans have in common?

_____

_____

Read page 10. What problems do you think might make using
a clepsydra difficult?

_____

_____

_____

Read page 11. What features make the angel clock more
accurate than the clepsydra?

_____

_____

Read page 13. Compare the oil lamp clock and candle clock.
What did a monk need to do once the oil or candle was used up?

_____

_____

How is this problem similar to the hourglass clock?
What is the main problem with all of these types of clocks?

_____

_____

_____

284

Name _____ Date _____

Unit 4
READER'S NOTEBOOK

About Time: A First Look at Time and Clocks
Segment 2
Independent Reading

Many museums provide audio tours for their visitors. Visitors listen to information about exhibits around the museum on headsets. The audio tour helps the visitor understand the exhibits. Choose one of the clocks from ancient times. Write the script for the audio tour for this type of clock. Describe how it works as well as any problems it has in keeping accurate time.

_____

_____

_____

_____

_____

_____

_____

_____

Name _____ Date _____

Unit 4
READER'S NOTEBOOK

About Time: A First Look
at Time and Clocks
Segment 2
Independent Reading

Write Test Questions

Making test questions can sometimes be a fun
and challenging way to study a text. Each part
of a test question serves an important purpose.
Every multiple-choice question contains a question,
a correct answer, and incorrect answer choices.
The question below is based on the information
on page 8.

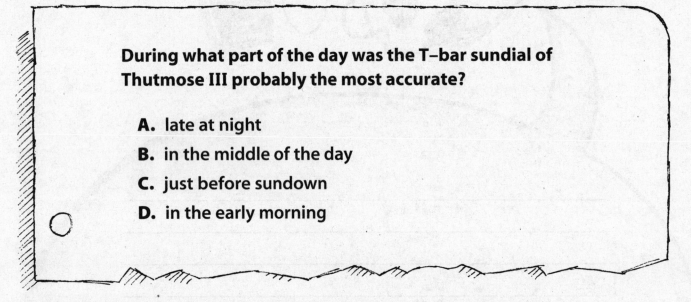

**During what part of the day was the T–bar sundial of
Thutmose III probably the most accurate?**

   A. late at night

   B. in the middle of the day

   C. just before sundown

   D. in the early morning

**A good test question should not have an obvious answer. Notice that the
correct answer, "in the middle of the day," is not stated in the text. What
information in the text helps you infer that this is the correct answer?**

_____

_____

_____

Name _____ Date _____

In a challenging test question, the incorrect answer choices should sound reasonable. The reader will know they are wrong if they read the text carefully.

Read pages 9–10. Then read the question below. The correct answer, B, is given. A sample incorrect answer, A, is given. Write two more incorrect answers for this question.

Why was the clepsydra, or water clock, used by the Greeks and Romans?

A. There was plenty of water.

B. They needed to tell time when the sun was not available.

C. _____

D. _____

What makes your choices both reasonable and wrong?

_____

_____

_____

Name _____ Date _____

Unit 4
READER'S NOTEBOOK

About Time: A First Look
at Time and Clocks
Segment 2
Independent Reading

In test questions, some of the answer choices may appear to be correct, but are not the **best** answer. The question will use words to tell the reader to choose the best answer, such as:

What is the main purpose …   *Which is most important …*   *What is most likely …*

Read page 12 and the answer choices below. Write the question for these choices so students choose the best answer choice.

_____

_____

A. to impress the emperor's subjects ← **correct answer**

B. to precisely measure time

C. to provide water for the people

D. to provide a simple way to tell time

Now write a question that asks the reader to make an inference about hourglasses and write the correct answer. Finally, write the incorrect choices.

Question

_____

_____

A. _____ ← **correct answer**

B. _____

C. _____

D. _____

Name _____ Date _____

Unit 4
READER'S NOTEBOOK

About Time: A First Look
at Time and Clocks
Segment 3
Independent Reading

About Time: A First Look at Time and Clocks

Write Chapter Titles

The next chapter of the book is pages 14–18. Use the checklist below to find keywords for this chapter. Rate the words on a scale from 1–5 for each characteristic. The first one has been done for you.

Keyword	Used Often in the Chapter	Describes an Important Idea in the Chapter	Necessary to Understanding the Chapter
monastery	2	4	3

Think about the key words you found. Using these key words, write a title for this chapter. The title should give the reader a good idea about what the chapter is mostly about.

_____

Suppose that the next chapter will be pages 19–21. What are some key words from this chapter?

_____

Think about the key words you found. Using these key words, write a title for this chapter.

_____

Name _____ Date _____

Unit 4
READER'S NOTEBOOK

About Time: A First Look
at Time and Clocks
Segment 3
Independent Reading

Write a Troubleshooting Guide

A clock maker built an escapement clock for an important German prince in the 1500s. Although this clock was very accurate for its time, it sometimes had problems. The clockmaker wants to include a troubleshooting guide with the clock. This guide will help the prince fix the clock if it stops working. A troubleshooting guide usually explains causes and effects. When the user has a problem, the guide explains the cause.

Read page 15. Look at the diagram of the clock and read the captions.

What causes the drive wheel to move?

Cause:

_____

_____

_____

Effect:
The drive wheel moves.

What makes the clock give a ticktock sound?

Cause:

_____

_____

_____

Effect:
The clock makes a ticktock sound.

When the bell sounds for each hour, what makes the bell stop ringing?

Cause:

_____

_____

_____

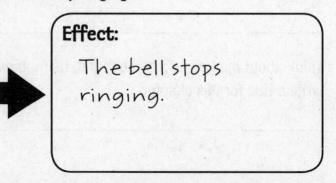

Effect:
The bell stops ringing.

A troubleshooting guide will list common problems with a device. The user looks at the list to find the problem he or she is having, and then looks at the cause of the problem. Use the diagram on page 15 and your notes on the previous page to complete the troubleshooting guide.

Problem	Cause
The drive wheel has stopped turning.	
The drive wheel is turning, but it has stopped making a ticktock sound.	
The bell will not stop ringing.	

291

Name _____ Date _____

Unit 4
READER'S NOTEBOOK

**About Time: A First Look
at Time and Clocks**
Segment 3
Independent Reading

Write a Proposal

In medieval times, a typical German town was ruled by
a council elected by the citizens of the town. Imagine
that it is the year 1345, and you wish to propose that
a mechanical bell tower be built in the center of town.

**Read pages 16–17. Write a letter to the town council,
explaining why you think a bell tower would be a good idea.
Use information from the text to support your letter.**

Dear Fellow Citizens,

I wish to propose that our town build a tower in
the center of town with a mechanical bell clock.

_____

_____

_____

_____

_____

_____

_____

_____

_____

_____

_____

_____

Write a Collector's Guide to Antique Clocks

Collector's guides help collectors identify valuable clocks. A collector is especially interested in features that make each clock unique. You have been asked to help write a guide for identifying important European clocks. The publisher wants you to research particular features that appeared in clocks at different times in history.

Read pages 18–21. For each year on the timeline, write an important development in clocks.

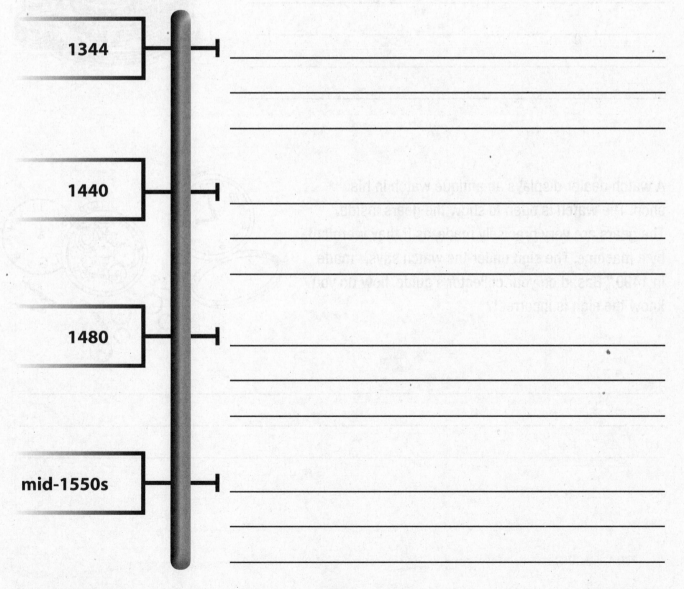

1344 _____

_____

_____

1440 _____

_____

_____

1480 _____

_____

_____

mid-1550s _____

_____

_____

Name _____   Date _____

Unit 4
READER'S NOTEBOOK

**About Time: A First Look
at Time and Clocks**
Segment 3
Independent Reading

At an antique store, an old French clock is displayed for sale. The sign on the clock says it was made in 1342. According to your collector's guide, how do you know the sign is incorrect?

c. 1342

_____

_____

_____

_____

_____

A watch dealer displays an antique watch in his shop. The watch is open to show the gears inside. The gears are very precisely made, as if they were cut by a machine. The sign under the watch says, "made in 1490." Based on your collector's guide, how do you know the sign is incorrect?

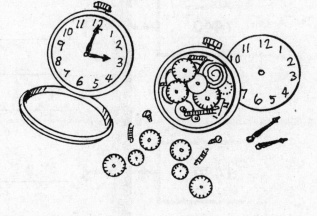

_____

_____

_____

Name _____ Date _____

Unit 4
READER'S NOTEBOOK

About Time: A First Look
at Time and Clocks
Segment 4
Independent Reading

About Time: A First Look at Time and Clocks

Write Chapter Titles

Sometimes chapter titles use words that are not used in the text. These words are important but are inferred in the text. Suppose that the next chapter is pages 22–25. Most of this chapter is about more recent clock technology. The word *recent* is not used in the text, but it is inferred from the information. What are three other key words that you can infer from this chapter?

recent,
_____

Think about the key words you found. Using these key words, write a title for this chapter. The title should give the reader a good idea about what the chapter is mostly about.

_____

_____

Suppose that the next chapter will be pages 26–27. What are some key words from this chapter?

_____

_____

Think about the key words you found. Using these key words, write a title for this chapter.

_____

_____

Name _____ Date _____

Unit 4
READER'S NOTEBOOK

About Time: A First Look
at Time and Clocks
Segment 4
Independent Reading

Write an Advertisement

Answer the questions below. Then you will write an advertisement.

Read pages 23–24 and look carefully at the diagrams. What were the advantages of Huygens' balance spring versus using weights to drive a clock?

_____

_____

_____

_____

Look at the diagram on page 23. What problems can you infer about the use of the balance spring?

_____

_____

_____

_____

Read the first paragraph on page 25. Think about how the quartz watch was different from the spring-driven watches that came before it. What are some of the advantages of the quartz watch?

_____

_____

_____

_____

Name _____ Date _____

Unit 4
READER'S NOTEBOOK

About Time: A First Look at Time and Clocks
Segment 4
Independent Reading

An advertisement is written to persuade readers to buy a product. The Electro Watch Company manufactured its first quartz crystal watch in 1970, called *Quartzonic One*. Write a newspaper ad for this watch. Use vivid and persuasive language to sell your watch. Include an illustration to make your ad more exciting.

Unit 4
READER'S NOTEBOOK

**About Time: A First Look
at Time and Clocks**
Segment 4
Independent Reading

Plan an Airline Trip

Airline ticket agents help busy passengers
at airports check their bags and process
their tickets before passengers board their flights.
Ticket agents must have a good understanding
of time zones so that they can advise passengers
of exactly when they can expect to arrive at
their destinations.

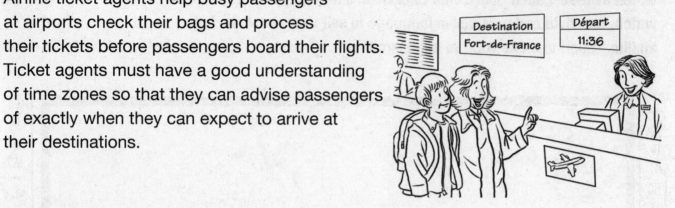

Look at the diagram on page 26. If it is 11:00 AM in Chicago,
what time is it in Cairo, Egypt? Explain your answer.

_____

_____

What is the time difference between Chicago and Cairo?

_____

If it is 12:00 PM in Chicago, what time is it in Cairo?

_____

Look at the diagram on page 27 and read the caption. If it is July 4
in the United States, what day is it in China? Explain why.

_____

_____

_____

Name _____ Date _____

Unit 4
READER'S NOTEBOOK

About Time: A First Look
at Time and Clocks
Segment 4
Independent Reading

Airline ticket agents at airports must be able to explain to confused passengers the time differences at their destinations. You are a ticket agent for Northeast Airlines. Help explain the arrival times for these passengers.

Northeast Airlines

Passenger: Thomas, Gary

Date of Travel: June 1, 2013

Flight: 392

Depart: Los Angeles, CA (LAX)   6:30 PM, June 1, 2013

Arrive: Denver, CO (DEN)   10:00 PM, June 1, 2013

Length of Flight: 2.5 hours

A snack will be served.

Why is Mr. Thomas arriving in Denver at 10:00 PM, even though the flight is only 2.5 hours long?

_____

_____

Northeast Airlines

Passenger: Jackson, Paula

Date of Travel: June 1, 2013

Flight: 52

Depart: Los Angeles, CA (LAX)   11:45 AM, August 5, 2013

Arrive: Tokyo, Japan (HND)   5:00 PM, August 6, 2013

Length of Flight: 12 hours, 15 minutes

Two meals will be served.

Why does Ms. Jackson's flight to Japan arrive the next day, although the flight is only 12 hours and 15 minutes long?

_____

_____

_____

Name _____ Date _____

Unit 4
READER'S NOTEBOOK

About Time: A First Look
at Time and Clocks
Segment 4
Independent Reading

Make a Table of Contents

A table of contents is like a map of a book. It gives the reader a list of the chapter titles and the beginning page number of each chapter. Using the chapter titles you wrote for each chapter, complete the table of contents for the book. Be sure to write the correct page number for the start of each chapter.

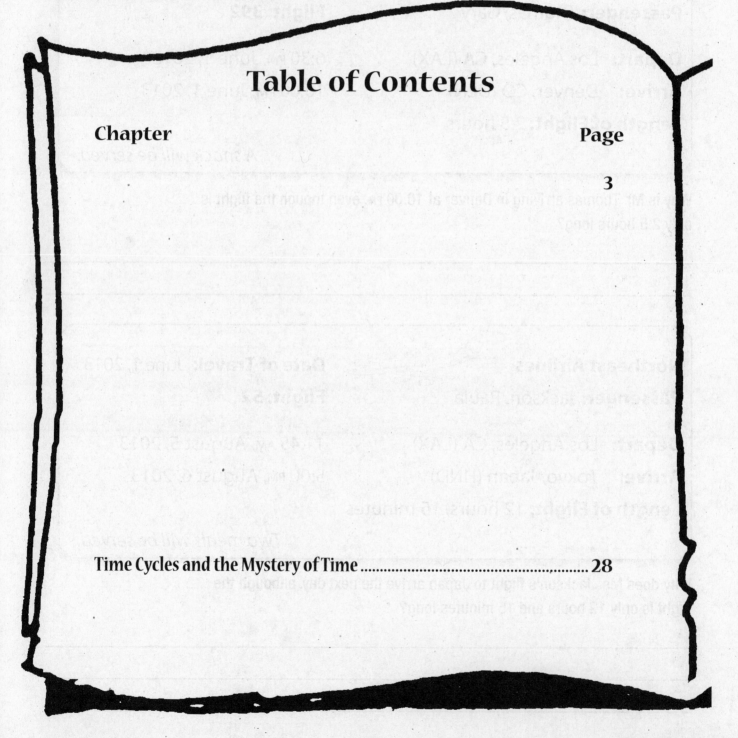

Table of Contents

Chapter   **Page**

3

Time Cycles and the Mystery of Time 28

Reader's Guide

Tucket's Travels

Make a Travel Timeline

Flashbacks are descriptions of events that happened before the events in the story. By telling about what happened before, flashbacks help the reader understand the story.

Reread page 636. Summarize the events in the order that the page names them.

_____

_____

_____

_____

_____

Now use what you understand about the writer's use of flashbacks. Rewrite the same events in the order that they actually happened.

_____

_____

_____

_____

_____

Because this story includes flashbacks, it can be difficult to remember the actual sequence of events as they occur. A timeline can help you visualize exactly when all of these events happened. Complete the sentences at each point on the timeline to show the actual sequence of events.

The Pawnees kidnapped ... _____

_____

Jason Grimes rescued ... _____

_____

Francis found ... _____

_____

Grimes helped ... _____

_____

Lottie saw ... _____

_____

The children reached ... _____

_____

Finally, ... _____

_____

Name _____ Date _____

Lesson 21
READER'S NOTEBOOK

Tucket's Travels
Vocabulary Strategies:
Shades of Meaning

Shades of Meaning

Circle the word in parentheses that matches the precise meaning of each underlined word.

1. In the <u>arid</u> soil, not one tree would grow. (dusty, scorched)

2. The task of sorting papers was so <u>tedious</u> that she fell asleep. (boring, repetitive)

3. There was a horrifying <u>gouge</u> in the surface of the antique table. (mark, gash)

4. We <u>meandered</u> down the street, just taking our time. (marched, strolled)

5. She decided not to make a <u>hasty</u> decision but to think about it. (quick, brief)

6. The old horse <u>shambled</u> along, hardly able to lift its feet up. (moved, shuffled)

7. The flood waters <u>receded</u> hour by hour. (decreased, subsided)

8. The boy felt <u>abandoned</u> when his friends ran off without him. (deserted, left)

Final /n/ or /ən/, /chər/, /zhər/

Basic Write the Basic Word that is the best synonym for the underlined word or words in each sentence.

1. Mom hung a new <u>window dressing</u> in the kitchen.
   _____

2. A short <u>film</u> about penguins is showing at the theater.
   _____

3. The <u>feel</u> of this wool sweater is scratchy. _____

4. A <u>doctor</u> performs operations. _____

5. Lori is the <u>leader</u> of our soccer team. _____

6. Trail mix is a <u>blend</u> of ingredients. _____

7. It is a <u>joy</u> to see my old friend. _____

8. The officer used a <u>hand motion</u> to signal traffic.
   _____

9. The <u>scoundrel</u> in the cowboy movie robbed a bank.
   _____

10. Dad is <u>sure</u> that his vacation is in June. _____

11. I made my <u>exit</u> from the meeting quietly. _____

12. Let's <u>calculate</u> the distance in miles. _____

Challenge 13–15. Write a short paragraph about a trip your class took to an art museum. Use three of the Challenge Words. Write on a separate sheet of paper.

Spelling Words

1. nature
2. certain
3. future
4. villain
5. mountain
6. mixture
7. pleasure
8. captain
9. departure
10. surgeon
11. texture
12. curtain
13. creature
14. treasure
15. gesture
16. fountain
17. furniture
18. measure
19. feature
20. adventure

Challenge
leisure
sculpture
architecture
chieftain
enclosure

Spelling Word Sort

Write each Basic Word beside the correct heading.

Final /n/ or /ən/ sounds	Basic Words: Challenge Words: Possible Selection Words:
Final /chər/ sounds	Basic Words: Challenge Words:
Final /zhər/ sounds	Basic Words: Challenge Words:

Challenge Add the Challenge Words to your Word Sort.

Connect to Reading Look through *Tucket's Travels.* Find words that have final /n/ or /ən/, /chər/, /zhər/ spelling patterns. Add them to your Word Sort.

Spelling Words

1. nature
2. certain
3. future
4. villain
5. mountain
6. mixture
7. pleasure
8. captain
9. departure
10. surgeon
11. texture
12. curtain
13. creature
14. treasure
15. gesture
16. fountain
17. furniture
18. measure
19. feature
20. adventure

Challenge
leisure
sculpture
architecture
chieftain
enclosure

Proofreading for Spelling

Find the misspelled words and circle them. Write them correctly on the lines below.

Dear Grandma,

   It is a real plezure being out here in nachure. A major feacher in the landscape is a mountin up ahead, and we see a new wild creeture almost every day. Our kaptain puts our wagon train into a big circle every afternoon, and then we cook supper. We seem to meazure out our long days in meals. The nights are becoming colder. There is so much furnitur in our wagon that I have little room to sit. Sometimes I walk alongside the wagon. It has been five weeks since our deparchur from St. Louis, and we have many weeks to go. I keep my eyes open for natural springs that spout water like a fountin. I am certin I'll find one in the near futur. Water from natural springs is a trezure. What an adventur it has been! I miss you.

                                  Yours truly,
                                  Molly

Spelling Words

1. nature
2. certain
3. future
4. villain
5. mountain
6. mixture
7. pleasure
8. captain
9. departure
10. surgeon
11. texture
12. curtain
13. creature
14. treasure
15. gesture
16. fountain
17. furniture
18. measure
19. feature
20. adventure

Challenge
leisure
sculpture
architecture
chieftain
enclosure

1. _____   8. _____
2. _____   9. _____
3. _____   10. _____
4. _____   11. _____
5. _____   12. _____
6. _____   13. _____
7. _____   14. _____

Use of Verbs *be* and *have*

The verbs *be* and *have* are irregular verbs. They change forms when the subject changes. The subject and verb in a sentence must agree in number and tense.

singular subject and present tense helping verb
She is looking out the window.
The weather **forecast** has predicted rain.

plural subject and past tense helping verb
They were wearing raincoats.
Gary and I had brought umbrellas.

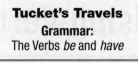

Thinking Questions
What tense is the verb? How many are in the subject?

Activity   Underline the correct helping verb in parentheses for each sentence.

1. My mom and I (has/had) gone out for a walk.

2. The sun (were/is) shining brightly in the blue sky.

3. The thick clouds (are/is) moving quickly.

4. Large droplets of rain (had/is) fallen.

5. We (am/are) running into the house for shelter.

6. The wind (were/was) blowing outside.

7. I (are/am) not going outside until it stops raining.

8. The drenched cat (has/have) returned to the house.

9. The cat (has/is) tried to shake off the water from his fur.

10. I (am/have) found a towel to dry the cat's fur.

Using Verb Phrases

A **verb phrase** contains more than one verb. The verbs *could*, *should*, *would*, or *must* are followed by another verb to form a verb phrase. The second verb in the verb phrase is often *be* or *have*.

verb phrase

It <u>could be</u> dangerous in the Wild West.

I <u>would have brought</u> some granola for a snack.

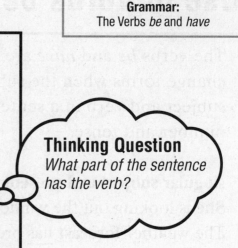

Thinking Question
What part of the sentence has the verb?

1–4. **Read each sentence. Write *be* or *have* on the line to complete each verb phrase.**

1. During the summer, the desert must _____ hot in the afternoon.

2. You should _____ plenty of water with you at all times.

3. If you feel dizzy, you could _____ suffering from the heat.

4. I would _____ worn a hat to protect myself from sunburn.

5–8. **Read each sentence. Choose the verb in parentheses that best fits the meaning of the sentence. Write the verb on the line.**

5. (must/could) The children _____ have been tired after the long walk.

6. (would/should) Don't worry. I _____ be home before the thunderstorm hits.

7. (must/would) It _____ be helpful to know what the weather will be like tomorrow.

8. (should/must) The sun _____ be out tomorrow, but you never know for sure!

Using Consistent Verb Tenses

When using the verbs *be* and *have*, remember to use verb tenses consistently. In order for your sentences to be correct, the verbs must be in the same tense.

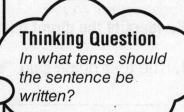

Thinking Question
In what tense should the sentence be written?

Not correct
The students <u>had gone</u> on a field trip before, and they <u>had remember</u> how much fun they had.

Correct
The students <u>had gone</u> on a field trip before, and they <u>had remembered</u> how much fun they had.

Activity   Rewrite each sentence so that the verbs are in the same tense as the underlined verb phrase.

1. A deer <u>had grazed</u> in the park before a noisy dog chase it away.

_____

2. Heavy rain <u>had fallen</u> a few days earlier and floods the streets.

_____

3. Mrs. Thomas <u>was looking</u> for a shady tree, and everyone is going to sit under it.

_____

_____

4. She <u>had supplied</u> snacks for everyone, and the students mix lemonade.

_____

_____

5. They <u>are going</u> to sing songs, and then they play games.

_____

6. The bus <u>is</u> here, but the students were not ready to leave.

_____

Direct Quotations and Interjections

1–6. Identify the direct quotation in the following sentences.

1. The tour guide said, "We will be leaving for the cavern shortly."

   _____

2. "I can't wait to see the glacier," said Miranda.

   _____

3. Marco talked a lot about his journey, saying, "I have seen many wonderful sights."

   _____

4. Kai had trouble explaining what he had seen: "The beauty of the rainforest is hard to describe."

   _____

5. Janet looked forward to the trip, saying, "I've always wanted to see the penguins."

   _____

6. "There are no words to describe it," said Erin, as she told her friends about plants and animals of the desert.

   _____

7–12. Identify the interjection in each direct quotation.

7. "Ouch!" cried Natasha, "Those rocks are sharp!" _____

8. Alex was stunned by the scenery: "Wow! That is amazing!" _____

9. "Goodness gracious," cried Tariq, "that is spectacular!" _____

10. "Oh! That elephant is huge!" said Nora. _____

11. "For goodness' sake," Martin smiled, "I'd be happy to come along."

   _____

12. "What an incredible sight!" declared Samantha. "Awesome!"

   _____

310

Connect to Writing

Sentence Without Helping Verb	Sentences with Helping Verb *have* or *be*
The lightning brightened the night sky.	The lightning **has brightened** the night sky. The lightning **had brightened** the night sky. The lightning **is brightening** the night sky. The lightning **was brightening** the night sky.

1–3. Rewrite each sentence using a form of the verb *have*.

1. We hear the sound of thunder.

_____

2. We buy flashlights in case of a blackout.

_____

3. My family ran out of batteries during the last storm.

_____

4–6. Rewrite the sentences below using a form of the verb *be*.

4. The thunder makes my dog nervous.

_____

5. I give my dog a treat to comfort him.

_____

6. Sheila hopes that the rain will be good for the lawn.

_____

Focus Trait: Purpose
Writing with Feeling and Personality

Writers of fiction and nonfiction want to convey their voice
to readers. *Voice* is the words and ideas that make clear the
personality of the writer or character.

Without Voice	With Voice
I have an opinion about the topic of outdoor adventure. My opinion is that people need to be prepared in order to enjoy outdoor adventure.	Enjoying the outdoors can be great fun—if you prepare yourself properly. Without the proper preparation, your plans for a great adventure may wind up in disaster.

**Revise these sentences. Add your voice to make each sentence
more interesting and to make your purpose clear.**

1. It is fun to hike in the woods.

   _____

   _____

2. Life out of doors carries some risks.

   _____

   _____

3. Nature can be harsh and unpleasant.

   _____

   _____

4. People should take care when heading into the wild.

   _____

   _____

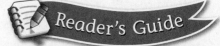Reader's Guide

The Birchbark House

Write a Thematic Poem

One of the important themes in "The Birchbark House" is honoring the traditions of ancestors. Omakayas refers to these traditions throughout the story. The concept map below will show how her words and actions connect to this theme.

Read page 672. How does the way Omakayas greets the bear cubs show her respect for traditions? Write your answer in one of the empty ovals on the concept map.

Read page 674. What tradition does Omakayas follow if she brings the bear cubs home? Write this detail in an empty oval.

Read page 677. How does Omakayas use a tradition to keep the mother bear from hurting her? Write it in the last oval on the map.

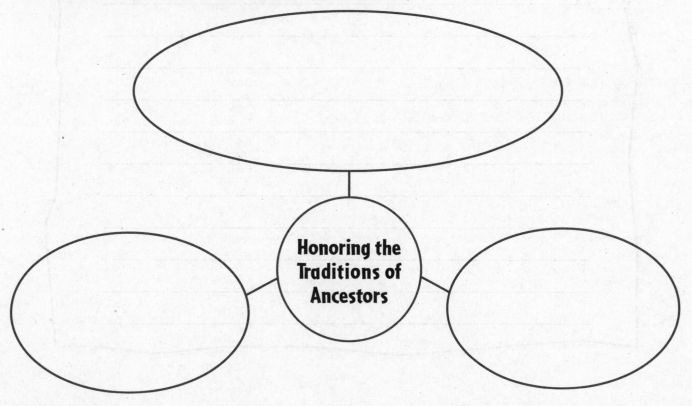

Honoring the Traditions of Ancestors

Write a poem about Omakayas' experience with the mother bear and her cubs. Use the information from the concept web to write your poem. It does not need to rhyme. Use words that express strong impressions about what Omakayas hears and sees and that show her respect for her people's traditions.

_____

_____

_____

_____

_____

_____

_____

_____

_____

_____

_____

_____

_____

_____

Name _____ Date _____

Lesson 22
READER'S NOTEBOOK

The Birchbark House
Vocabulary Strategies:
Reference Materials

Reference Materials

**1–8. Read each sentence carefully. Circle the choice that
is the most accurate synonym for the underlined word.
Use a dictionary and thesaurus as needed.**

1. Omakayas had to <u>stay</u> calm during her encounter with the bear.

   (support, remain, stick)

2. The <u>patter</u> of the hail hitting the roof was loud. (chatter, speech, tap)

3. The horse could be distinguished by the <u>blaze</u> on his nose. (light,

   stripe, proclaim)

4. They sewed a cloak from the <u>hide</u>. (conceal, shelter, pelt)

5. She will <u>bow</u> to her grandmother as an outward sign of respect.

   (bend, yield, arc)

6. The mother bear did not <u>desert</u> her cubs; they wandered off.

   (wilderness, leave, reward)

7. The baby bears were very <u>content</u> to play with Omakayas.

   (ingredients, subject, satisfied)

8. She decided to <u>bore</u> a hole through the shell and wear it on a string.

   (tire, drill, pest)

**9–10. Write an original sentence for both meanings of the word
below.**

9. **bluff**[1] *n.* The act of deceiving.

   _____

10. **bluff**[2] *n.* A steep cliff.

    _____

Final /ĭj/, /ĭv/, /ĭs/

Basic Complete the puzzle by writing the Basic Word for each clue.

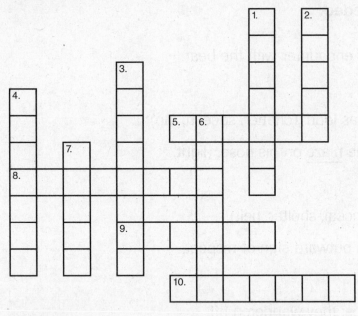

Across

5. growing in a certain place
8. family member
9. journey
10. satisfaction of customers' needs

Down

1. fairness
2. a picture or likeness
3. imaginative
4. space for keeping things
6. typical or normal
7. small black or green salad item

Challenge 11–14. Josie's grandfather is a plumber, and so is her mother. Write a paragraph about why Josie might or might not choose to become a plumber when she grows up. Use four of the Challenge Words. Write on a separate sheet of paper.

Spelling Words

1. storage
2. olive
3. service
4. relative
5. cabbage
6. courage
7. native
8. passage
9. voyage
10. knowledge
11. image
12. creative
13. average
14. justice
15. detective
16. postage
17. cowardice
18. adjective
19. village
20. language

Challenge

prejudice
cooperative
beverage
heritage
apprentice

Spelling Word Sort

Write each Basic Word beside the correct heading.

Final /ĭj/	**Basic Words:**
	Challenge Words:
	Possible Selection Words:
Final /ĭv/	**Basic Words:**
	Challenge Words:
	Possible Selection Words:
Final /ĭs/	**Basic Words:**
	Challenge Words:

Challenge   Add the Challenge Words to your Word Sort.

Connect to Reading   Look through *The Birchbark House*. Find words that have final /ĭj/, /ĭv/, /ĭs/ sounds in the singular or base form. Add them to your Word Sort.

Spelling Words

1. storage
2. olive
3. service
4. relative
5. cabbage
6. courage
7. native
8. passage
9. voyage
10. knowledge
11. image
12. creative
13. average
14. justice
15. detective
16. postage
17. cowardice
18. adjective
19. village
20. language

Challenge
prejudice
cooperative
beverage
heritage
apprentice

Name _____ Date _____

Proofreading for Spelling

The Birchbark House
Spelling: Final /ĭj/,/ĭv/,/ĭs/

Find the misspelled words and circle them. Write them correctly on the lines below.

My brother Ben, who was my only reletive, and I wanted to work together. A pasagge from a Pony Express newspaper ad read, "Willing to risk death daily." It left no room for cowerdice. The ad also said that a knowlege of riding was required. We had horses on our cabagge farm before we moved out West, so we could ride. Ben decided to play decktive and find out more about the Pony Express. He discovered that the pay was $100 a month, but the work was dangerous. It would take a lot of courrage to gallop along trails through strange, new lands in all kinds of weather. What if we came across an American Indian vilage? We wouldn't know the native langauge to communicate.

After our interview, Ben and I smiled at the adjetive the boss used: "You two are a 'perfect' fit for the job," he said. It certainly helped that we knew that the required postege for a letter was $5, and that the servis was fast—sometimes only 10 days!

Spelling Words

1. storage
2. olive
3. service
4. relative
5. cabbage
6. courage
7. native
8. passage
9. voyage
10. knowledge
11. image
12. creative
13. average
14. justice
15. detective
16. postage
17. cowardice
18. adjective
19. village
20. language

Challenge
prejudice
cooperative
beverage
heritage
apprentice

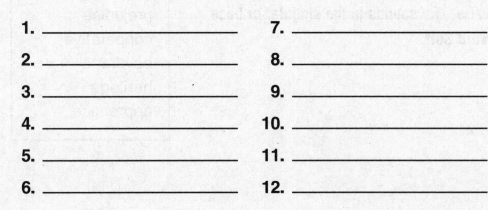

1. _____   7. _____

2. _____   8. _____

3. _____   9. _____

4. _____   10. _____

5. _____   11. _____

6. _____   12. _____

The Present Perfect Tense

The Birchbark House
Grammar: Perfect Tenses

The **present perfect tense** of a verb shows an action that began in the past and is still happening. To write the present perfect tense, use *has* or *have* as a helping verb. Then write the correct form of the main verb.

present perfect tense

She <u>has lived</u> in the village since she was born.

They <u>have taken</u> this road many times.

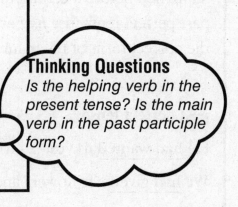

Thinking Questions
Is the helping verb in the present tense? Is the main verb in the past participle form?

Activity Write the present perfect tense of the verb in parentheses on the line.

1. Angel and I (know) _____ each other since third grade.

2. Chess (be) _____ a part of our culture for a long time.

3. We (play) _____ many games of chess together.

4. Jusef (learn) _____ to play chess, too.

5. A new family (move) _____ into town.

6. The new girl (tell) _____ us about traditions in her culture.

7. They (be) _____ busy unpacking their things.

8. I (finish) _____ all my extra chores.

The Past Perfect Tense

The **past perfect tense** of a verb shows an action that happened before a certain time in the past. To write the past perfect tense, use *had* as a helping verb. Then write the correct form of the main verb.

past perfect tense

He had wanted to visit his friend on her birthday.

We had given her flowers and a birthday cake before.

Thinking Questions
Is the helping verb had? *Is the main verb in the past participle form?*

Activity Write the past perfect tense of the verb in parentheses on the line.

1. We (stop) _____ fishing when the lake froze over.

2. I already (eat) _____ by the time the guests came.

3. Before we knew it, they (leave) _____ the building

   for the ceremony.

4. She (help) _____ gather fruits and nuts.

5. He (read) _____ the old book that belonged to his

   grandmother.

6. Rudy never (see) _____ a bear before.

7. She (make) _____ a special blanket for the baby.

8. You (promise) _____ to walk through the woods

   with me.

The Future Perfect Tense

The **future perfect tense** of a verb shows an action that will be finished by a certain time in the future. To form the future perfect tense, write *will have* before the correct form of the main verb.

Thinking Questions
Is the helping verb will have? *Is the main verb in the past participle form?*

future perfect tense

I <u>will have played</u> ten games by the end of the season.

They <u>will have driven</u> across the country by next week.

Activity Write the future perfect tense of the verb in parentheses on the line.

1. By custom, we (finish) _____ our breakfast long before nine o'clock.

2. We (clean) _____ up by the time you get home.

3. Tanya (have) _____ enough time to make the cake for the festival.

4. By next June, Jordan (complete) _____ her traditional dance lessons.

5. If she reads every book on her list, Carmen (read) _____ ten books about ancient cultures.

6. This horse (be) _____ groomed and ready to ride in the parade by noon.

7. Our class (earn) _____ enough for our trip by next week.

8. She (tell) _____ them the news about the festival before they read about it.

Using Commas and Semicolons

Commas (,) and **semicolons (;)** are punctuation marks
used within sentences. Commas set off words and phrases
and items in a series. Semicolons separate items in a
series that already contain commas.

Commas: Hugo, *Treasure Island* was the best book we've
ever read, wasn't it?

Semicolons: We have read books about New York City,
NY; San Francisco, CA; and Kansas City, MO.

1–8.   Rewrite each sentence with the correct punctuation.

1. Maria would you be able to start the fire by sundown?

   _____

2. We have been best friends for three years three months and three days.

   _____

3. Since there's no party Andy will have come for no reason.

   _____

4. In our culture a baby is given a naming ceremony after it turns one.

   _____

5. She found out her great aunts were born on January 25 1932
   February 11 1934 and May 6 1940.

   _____

   _____

6. Yes the horses have been eating grass quietly all morning.

   _____

7. By evening everyone had gathered around the fire for storytelling and music.

   _____

8. Bring more wood please the fire is about to go out.

   _____

Connect to Writing

The perfect tenses of verbs describe past and continuing action.

Present Perfect	Past Perfect	Future Perfect
I <u>have adopted</u> a dog.	I <u>had thought</u> about going to a pet store.	The dog <u>will have received</u> all his shots by tomorrow.

Activity Read each sentence. Rewrite the sentence using the correct perfect tense of the underlined verb.

1. (future perfect) I <u>finished</u> my packing in time for dinner.

   _____

2. (past perfect) We already <u>set</u> a time to meet for the festival of culture.

   _____

3. (present perfect) Jason <u>met</u> some new friends at school.

   _____

4. (future perfect) By tomorrow, Allison <u>will meet</u> all of them.

   _____

5. (present perfect) They <u>agreed</u> to meet at the park and wear costumes.

   _____

6. (past perfect) Remember, you <u>said</u> you would come!

   _____

Focus Trait: Organization
Presenting Evidence in a Logical Order

Good writers support their opinions with evidence, such as facts and details, written in a logical order. They use transition words and phrases, such as *for example* and *next,* to link reasons to their opinions.

> **Opinion:** Omakayas is a kind person.
>
> **Reasons:** Omakayas is gentle with the bear cubs and speaks to them sweetly. For example, she calls the cubs "little brothers" and offers them berries.

Read the opinion and supporting reasons below. Rewrite the reasons into a logically ordered set of facts and details. Use transition words as needed to link ideas. Circle the transition words and phrases you use.

Opinion: Omakayas is good with animals.

Reasons: She plays with the cubs. She knows about
animals. She offers them berries.

_____

_____

_____

Reasons: Mother bear tackles Omakayas. Omakayas
clips the mother bear's fur by mistake.
Omakayas talks to the mother bear.
Omakayas remains still when the bear
tackles her. Omakayas is smart.

_____

_____

_____

Name _____ Date _____

Lesson 23
READER'S NOTEBOOK

Vaqueros: America's
First Cowboys
Independent Reading

Vaqueros: America's First Cowboys

Write Captions for Graphics

In an informational text, graphic features such as maps and drawings help the reader understand the text. There is usually a close connection between the text and images appearing on the page.

Read page 698. Then look carefully at the picture on the page. How does this illustration help you understand the discoveries made by Columbus?

_____

_____

Read page 700. Then look carefully at the map on the page. How does this map help you understand the information in the text about New Spain?

_____

_____

Read page 701. Then look carefully at the image of the *vaquero* on the page. How does this picture help you understand the work of the *vaquero*?

_____

_____

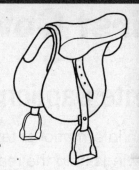

A caption is a brief statement that accompanies an image.
The caption should help link the image with the text on the page.

The author of "Vaqueros: Americas First Cowboys" has asked you
to write new captions for some of the graphic features in the story.

**Read page 703. Write a new caption for the picture on that page.
Give information that helps the reader connect the picture to the text.**

_____

_____

_____

_____

**Read page 704. Write a caption for the picture of the cowboy at the top
of the page. Give information that helps the reader connect the picture
to the text.**

_____

_____

_____

_____

Name _____ Date _____

Lesson 23
READER'S NOTEBOOK

Vaqueros: America's
First Cowboys
Vocabulary Strategies:
Adages and Proverbs

Adages and Proverbs

> You can lead a horse to water, but you can't make it drink.
> A watched pot never boils.
> All that glitters is not gold.
> Don't make mountains out of molehills.
> You can't make an omelet without breaking some eggs.
> A stitch in time saves nine.
> People who live in glass houses shouldn't throw stones.
> Make hay while the sun shines.
> Two wrongs do not make a right.

Read each sentence below. Write the expression from the box that has the same or nearly the same meaning.

1. Take advantage of opportunities while they are available.

   _____

2. Taking care of a small problem now will prevent a bigger one later.

   _____

3. Even if something is attractive, it is not necessarily valuable.

   _____

4. It doesn't help to be impatient. _____

5. Don't imagine that things are worse than they really are.

   _____

6. To achieve something better, sometimes you have to give up what you already have.

   _____

7. You can't force someone to take advantage of a good opportunity.

   _____

8. Getting revenge on someone for doing something bad to you does not solve any

   problems. _____

9. Unless you are perfect, it is not wise to criticize others.

   _____

Unstressed Syllables

Basic Write the Basic Word that best completes each analogy.

1. *Person* is to *house* as *soldier* is to _____:

2. *Uninformed* is to *ignorance* as *knowledgeable* is to

   _____.

3. *Dryer* is to *laundry room* as *stove* is to _____.

4. *Robber* is to *house* as _____ is to *boat*.

5. *Two* is to *pair* as *twelve* is to _____.

6. *Soothe* is to *calm* as *scare* is to _____.

7. *Orange* is to *carrot* as *green* is to _____.

8. *Some* is to *partial* as *all* is to _____.

9. *Out* is to *in* as *exit* is to _____.

10. *Allow* is to *permit* as *prevent* is to _____.

Challenge 11–14. Suppose there is only one newspaper in your city.
Write a paragraph for your school bulletin persuading people that a
second newspaper would be a good idea. Use four Challenge Words.
Write on a separate sheet of paper.

Spelling Words

1. entry
2. limit
3. talent
4. disturb
5. entire
6. wisdom
7. dozen
8. impress
9. respond
10. fortress
11. neglect
12. patrol
13. kitchen
14. forbid
15. pirate
16. spinach
17. adopt
18. frighten
19. surround
20. challenge

Challenge
adapt
refuge
distribute
industry
somber

Spelling Word Sort

Write each Basic Word beside the correct heading.

Spelling Words

Unstressed syllables with VCCV spelling pattern	**Basic Words:**
	Challenge Words:
	Possible Selection Words:
Unstressed syllables with VCCCV spelling pattern	**Basic Words:**
	Challenge Words:
	Possible Selection Words:
Unstressed syllables with VCV spelling pattern	**Basic Words:**
	Challenge Words:
	Possible Selection Words:

Challenge Add the Challenge Words to your Word Sort.

Challenge Look through *Vaqueros: America's First Cowboys*. Find words that have unstressed syllables. Add them to your Word Sort.

Spelling Words

1. entry
2. limit
3. talent
4. disturb
5. entire
6. wisdom
7. dozen
8. impress
9. respond
10. fortress
11. neglect
12. patrol
13. kitchen
14. forbid
15. pirate
16. spinach
17. adopt
18. frighten
19. surround
20. challenge

Challenge
adapt
refuge
distribute
industry
somber

Proofreading for Spelling

Find the misspelled words and circle them. Write them correctly on the lines below.

Cowboys in the Wild West welcomed the opportunity to patroll a landscape that never failed to inpress them. They would regularly rispond to the chalenge of shepherding intire herds of cattle through wild spaces that might frigten lesser men. They would not let the difficult terrain disterb them or limmit their efforts. They learned to adopd a can-do attitude and suround themselves with reliable partners. They had the wisdom to recognize the tallent a young cowboy might bring to the group. They could spot signs of nuglect that told them an animal was in trouble. They knew at least a douzen ways to help the animal. Being a cowboy was a difficult job, but for those special men who were up to it, there was much satisfaction.

1. _____   8. _____

2. _____   9. _____

3. _____   10. _____

4. _____   11. _____

5. _____   12. _____

6. _____   13. _____

7. _____   14. _____

Spelling Words

1. entry
2. limit
3. talent
4. disturb
5. entire
6. wisdom
7. dozen
8. impress
9. respond
10. fortress
11. neglect
12. patrol
13. kitchen
14. forbid
15. pirate
16. spinach
17. adopt
18. frighten
19. surround
20. challenge

Challenge
adapt
refuge
distribute
industry
somber

Easily Confused Verbs

Some verbs are easily confused because their meanings are closely related. Study the meanings of these easily confused verbs to avoid using the wrong one.
I'm going to **sit** in the shade under a tree.
She **set** the diary down on the bed.

sit to lower yourself onto a seat
set to place an item

can able to do
may allowed to do

teach to give instruction to someone
learn to receive instruction from someone

lie to recline on something
lay to put an item on top of something

rise to get up or to stand up
raise to lift something up

Thinking Questions
What definition fits the sentence? How does the sentence sound if you say it aloud?

1–6.   Underline the correct verb in each sentence below.

1. Natalie is (teaching/learning) how to use a lasso.

2. The smoke was (rising/raising) from the valley below.

3. The cowboy was ready to (lie/lay) down his rope at the end of
   the day.

4. She (sit/set) her poncho on the ground.

5. Vaqueros often had to (lie/lay) on the cold, hard ground.

6. You (may/can) still see barbed wire fences marking the
   boundaries of ranches.

Other Easily Confused Words

Vaqueros: America's First Cowboys
Grammar: Easily Confused Verbs

Study the meanings of each of these words to avoid using the wrong one. Pay attention to the part of speech of each.

good (adj.) favorable, useful
well (adj.) healthy
well (adv.) with skill, properly
their (pron.) possessive of *they*
there (adj.) location
they're contraction of *they* are
Conditions are **good** for riding outdoors.
The soldier fought **well** after eating a good meal.

Thinking Questions
What definition fits the sentence? What part of speech is needed?

Activity   Write the word in parentheses that correctly completes each sentence.

1. You had to be a (good, well) horseback rider to be a vaquero.

   _____

2. It was difficult to hear (good, well) because of the howling

   coyotes. _____

3. He didn't feel (good, well) after eating his breakfast.

   _____

4. Luckily, (there, their, they're) ranch was not in the path of the

   wild fire. _____

5. The ranch was the largest in the area, and many cowboys

   worked (there, their, they're). _____

6. (There, Their, They're) reading a book about the Mexican War of

   Independence. _____

Choosing the Right Word

Vaqueros: America's First Cowboys
Grammar: Easily Confused Verbs

To help you choose the correct word for a situation, try saying the sentence aloud. Memorize the meanings of easily confused words that sound alike. You can also check definitions in a dictionary.

affect (v.) to influence or cause a change

effect (n.) a result

few (adj.) small in number

less (adj.) small in amount

The fog will **affect** their ability to see the enemy.

The fog had no **effect** on their spirits, however.

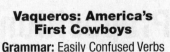

Thinking Questions
What definition fits the sentence? What part of speech is needed?

Activity   Write the word in parentheses that best completes each sentence.

1. (There, Their, They're) are a lot of books in the library about the

   Mexican-American War. _____

2. I found a book about the famous battles and (sit, set) it on the

   counter. _____

3. I'm going to (sit, set) down on the chair and read about how Texas

   became a state. _____

4. The librarian told us that each student (may, can) take out two books

   about the Gold Rush. _____

5. This rule will (affect, effect) which books I decide to take home.

   _____

6. This library has (few, less) biographies of cowboys. _____

Prepositions

Prepositions are words that relate a noun or pronoun, called the **object of the preposition**, to the other words in a sentence. Most prepositions tell where things are in time and space.

The book was <u>below</u> the table.
John showed up <u>after</u> the horses were fed.

Prepositional phrases are phrases that begin with a preposition and end with the noun or pronoun that is the object of the preposition.

The book was below the table.
John showed up after the horses were fed.

Activity Underline all the prepositions in each sentence. Circle the prepositional phrases.

1. Luke rode his horse across the prairie with his friend Maria.

2. The weather is beautiful in New Mexico at this time of year.

3. He left the saddle on the ground and threw the bridle over it.

4. Robert fell asleep after dinner.

5. She climbed on the saddle and looked toward the horizon.

6. The young men cleaned the house before noon.

7. Luis left the campfire without his poncho.

8. The rattlesnake slithered through the grass.

Connect to Writing

Incorrect Word Choice	Correct Word Choice
Since there are **less** of us, we can **sit** our coats on the counter.	Since there are **few** of us, we can **set** our coats on the counter.

Activity   Read the first paragraph of a persuasive essay. Circle the word in parentheses that best completes each sentence.

Rodeos are entertainment for millions of people. But (they're/there/their) also a (good/well) way to keep the traditions of the vaqueros and cowboys alive. (They're/There/Their) are many sports in a rodeo, and each of them reflects the jobs that cowboys performed (good/well) for generations. For example, in a steer roping event, a cowboy (sitting/setting) on a horse, (rises/raises) a lasso and throws it at just the right moment to rope the steer. Many years ago, cowboys on the range used the same skills to round up cattle. Now, there are (fewer/less) cowboys than there once were. But rodeos carry on (they're/there/their) traditions. The (affect/effect) is that cowboy culture lives on.

Focus Trait: Organization
Using Supporting Details

**Effective writers use precise details to support their statements. They
also present those details in ways that are easy for readers to follow.**

Without Details or Corrections	With Details and Corrections
The Aztecs were conquered by Cortez. Frank was studying the Aztec people. He read about their culture. They lived in Mexico and had power.	Because the subject interested him, Frank began studying the Aztec people of Mexico, who rose to great power. First, he read about their architecture and astronomy. Then he researched their conquest by Cortez of Spain in the sixteenth century.

A. **Answer the following questions based on the passages above.**

1. What supporting details does passage 2 use that passage 1 does not?

_____

_____

2. What important change has been made to the beginning of the passage?

_____

_____

B. **Rewrite the following sentences to add details.**

Pair/Share   **Work with a partner to brainstorm details.**

3. Andrea had played the trumpet for four years. However, she didn't like it. By
contrast, Olivia had played the tuba for two years and loved it.

_____

_____

_____

4. The weather has been strange. It has been cold but has not damaged the crops.

_____

_____

Name _____ Date _____

Lesson 24
READER'S NOTEBOOK

Rachel's Journal: The
Story of a Pioneer Girl
Independent Reading

Reader's Guide

Rachel's Journal: The Story of a Pioneer Girl

Write a Trail Journal

Some stories are written like a chain of causes and effects, like a trail of events. One event causes the next one to happen, up until the end of the trail.

Read page 728. After Rachel and the children finally find the camp, what is the effect of their mother's scolding them?

_____

_____

Read page 729. What was the effect of taking a cut-off on this day? What did they learn from this experience?

_____

_____

Read page 731. What caused the Platte River to become swollen?

_____

What was the effect of the swollen river on the wagon train?

_____

_____

Read page 734. What caused the families to pull the wagons close together?

_____

Name _____ Date _____

Lesson 24
READER'S NOTEBOOK

Rachel's Journal: The
Story of a Pioneer Girl
Independent Reading

Below is a page from Rachel's journal. Help her finish her journal entry
for that day. Write about the effect of the broken wagon wheel on
Rachel's family.

June 25, 1850

Today was another hot day on the parched and dusty
trail. As I walked behind our wagon, I noticed one of the
rear wheels begin to wobble. Suddenly, the wheel hit a
rock and came off its axle with a loud crash. The wagon
lurched to a stop, and ...

_____

_____

_____

_____

_____

_____

_____

_____

Using Context

Each item below contains two sentences. Choose a word from the box to fill in the blank so the second sentence restates the idea of the first sentence. Use a dictionary if you need help.

beacon	mishap	pioneer	lectured
treacherous	parcel	journal	challenge

1. Historians shine light on life in the past. Their work is like a

   _____.

2. She accidentally dropped food on her shirt. She had a

   _____ at lunch.

3. A personal diary recorded the journey. The _____

   became a historic record.

4. He explained why we were wrong. He _____ us on

   staying safe.

5. They had to overcome the dust and heat. The harsh climate was a

   _____.

6. A doctor named Jenner led the way in vaccinations. He was a

   _____ in his field.

7. A disloyal trail guide ran away. His cowardice was

   _____.

8. We put in a claim for a large section of land in the valley. Our new

   _____ was going to be so much bigger than our old

   farm!

Prefixes *in-*, *un-*, *dis-*, and *mis-*

Rachel's Journal: The Story of a Pioneer Girl

Spelling: Prefixes *in-*, *un-*, *dis-*, and *mis-*

Basic Write the Basic Word that best fits each clue.

1. If people purposely harm a living thing, they do this.

   _____

2. If you're not sure someone is telling you the truth, you might describe that person like this.

   _____

3. To find something new, you do this.

   _____

4. If you and a friend argue, you do this.

   _____

5. You might describe a very wobbly chair like this.

   _____

6. If you leave a letter out of a word, you do this.

   _____

7. If your brother gets $10 for a job and you get $5 for the same job, payment is this.

   _____

8. A hurricane or tornado would be called this.

   _____

9. This is what you would call a casual way of dressing.

   _____

10. A person showing bad judgment is called this.

    _____

Challenge 11–14. Write an e-mail message to a friend that tells about an embarrassing moment. Use four of the Challenge Words. Write on a separate sheet of paper.

Spelling Words

1. mislead
2. dismiss
3. insincere
4. unable
5. indirect
6. mistreat
7. disaster
8. dishonest
9. insecure
10. unknown
11. incomplete
12. unequal
13. unstable
14. misspell
15. disagree
16. informal
17. discover
18. unwise
19. mislaid
20. disgrace

Challenge

invisible
mishap
unfortunate
discourage
unnecessary

Spelling Word Sort

Write each Basic Word beside the correct heading.

un-	**Basic Words:** **Challenge Words:**
dis-	**Basic Words:** **Challenge Words:** **Possible Selection Words:**
in-	**Basic Words:** **Challenge Words:** **Possible Selection Words:**
mis-	**Basic Words:** **Challenge Words:**

Challenge   Add the Challenge Words to your Word Sort.

Connect to Reading   Look through *Rachel's Journal: The Story of a Pioneer Girl.* Find words that have the prefixes and spelling patterns on this page. Add them to your Word Sort.

Spelling Words

1. mislead
2. dismiss
3. insincere
4. unable
5. indirect
6. mistreat
7. disaster
8. dishonest
9. insecure
10. unknown
11. incomplete
12. unequal
13. unstable
14. misspell
15. disagree
16. informal
17. discover
18. unwise
19. mislaid
20. disgrace

Challenge
invisible
mishap
unfortunate
discourage
unnecessary

Proofreading for Spelling

Find the misspelled words and circle them. Write them correctly on the lines below.

Last night I was unabil to sleep. I heard a sound from an unknone source. I woke my sister, but she had heard nothing. Still, I could not dismis the sound.

The day before, Pa had mislade his saw, so the roof was still incompleet and the house was unstabell. Ma's smile was insinceer as she told us not to worry. We knew she felt it was a disgrase that we didn't have a proper home here in Oklahoma. She didn't want to misleed us, but we knew our future was unsecure. Pa was sure everything would be fine. He always took an undirect path to solve any problem. Usually we would descover that his methods worked. We hoped they would this time.

1. _____	7. _____
2. _____	8. _____
3. _____	9. _____
4. _____	10. _____
5. _____	11. _____
6. _____	12. _____

Spelling Words

1. mislead
2. dismiss
3. insincere
4. unable
5. indirect
6. mistreat
7. disaster
8. dishonest
9. insecure
10. unknown
11. incomplete
12. unequal
13. unstable
14. misspell
15. disagree
16. informal
17. discover
18. unwise
19. mislaid
20. disgrace

Challenge
invisible
mishap
unfortunate
discourage
unnecessary

Comparative and Superlative Adjectives

Use a **comparative adjective** to compare two things and a **superlative adjective** to compare more than two things. To form a comparative adjective, add *-er* to a short adjective and use the word *more* before a long adjective. To form a superlative adjective, add *-est* or use the word *most*.

Thinking Question
How many things are being compared in the sentence?

| **comparative adjective** | **superlative adjective** |

Jan is stronger than Mike, but Anna is the strongest of the three.
Troy was more worried than Chung, but Tonya was the most worried of all.

Read each sentence. Write the correct form of the adjective in parentheses on the line.

1. (fast) Sometimes it was _____ to go around a mountain than to hike over it.

2. (old) The _____ child in a family usually had more responsibilities than the younger children.

3. (dark) At night, the wilderness was _____ than the towns people had left behind.

4. (beautiful) The Rocky Mountains were the _____ thing I saw throughout the trip.

5. (snowy) In the winter, the trails would be _____ than at other times.

6. (hot) Summer is the _____ season, so you should drink more water.

Comparing with *Good* and *Bad*

The adjectives *good* and *bad* are irregular adjectives. To form their comparative and superlative forms, do not add *-er* or *-est* endings or use the word *more* or *most*. The chart below shows which form of *good* and *bad* to use.

adjective	comparative	superlative
good	better	best
bad	worse	worst

Wild strawberries are <u>good</u>, but wild blackberries are <u>better</u> and wild raspberries are the <u>best</u>!

Thinking Question
How many things are being compared in the sentence?

1–4. Look at the underlined word in each sentence. If it is correct, write C on the line. If it is incorrect, write the correct form of *good* or *bad*.

1. Many people traveled west because they wanted a <u>best</u> life.

   _____

2. Which is <u>worst</u>, keeping a small farm or working hard to start a new farm? _____

3. A pioneer needed to be <u>good</u> at hunting and farming. _____

4. Some people had <u>best</u> reasons for moving than others.

   _____

5–8. Circle the word that correctly completes the sentence.

5. Schoolchildren tried to earn (good, best) scores on their tests.

6. The farmer's (worse, worst) fear was that there would be a drought.

7. Is a drought (worse, worst) than locusts?

8. Hannah plays the banjo much (better, worst) than Joe does.

Comparing with Adverbs

You can compare the way that actions are done. To compare two actions, form a **comparative adverb** by using the word *more* before an adverb ending in *–ly*. To compare three or more actions, form a **superlative adverb** by using the word *most*.

Karina's calf ran <u>more gracefully</u> than she had run yesterday.
Maddy's horse ran the <u>most gracefully</u> of all the horses on the field.

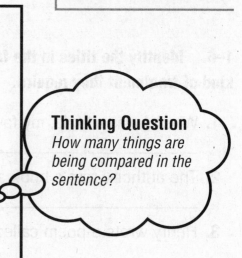

Thinking Question
How many things are being compared in the sentence?

1–4.   Circle the adverb in each sentence. Write C on the line if it is a comparative adverb. Write S if it is a superlative adverb.

1. People traveled more carefully along the trails than they did on the flat prairies. _____

2. Pioneers looked for water most eagerly when they were near a desert. _____

3. Pioneers traveled most carefully when they were crossing a river. _____

4. Thunder seemed to crash more powerfully out on the open plain. _____

5–8.   Write the correct form of the adverb in parentheses.

5. (superlative, *happily*) Children played _____ when they felt safe.

6. (comparative, *restfully*) The adults slept _____ in a cabin.

7. (superlative, *forcefully*) The rivers ran _____ after a strong rain.

8. (comparative, *slowly*) The older cattle moved _____ than the young calves.

Writing Titles

1–6.   Identify the titles in the following examples and indicate what kind of treatment they require.

1. When I was a child, my favorite TV show was Prairie Days.

_____

2. The author wrote a book about the state's early settlers called Hearty Folk.

_____

3. Henry wrote a poem called The Mountain Pass.

_____

4. The magazine article was titled Tales from the Trail.

_____

5. In the movie Finding the Frontier, the young girl learned to gather wild berries.

_____

6. Old copies of the Territory Reporter have many news stories about pioneer days.

_____

7–12.   Provide for the proper capitalization of the sample titles given.

7. my life in the wilderness _____

8. the life and times of a mountain man

_____

9. of mountain high and river wide

_____

10. life, liberty, and the pursuit of happiness

_____

11. the elephant who tried to swim in the ocean

_____

12. if at first you don't succeed, try, try, again

_____

Connect to Writing

You can use comparisons with adjectives and adverbs to add
details to your writing.

Without Comparisons	With Comparisons
For most pioneers, setting out toward a new or unexplored land must have been an adventure.	For most pioneers, setting out toward a new or unexplored land must have been the greatest adventure of their lives.

**Read each sentence and the adjective or adverb in parentheses. Rewrite
the sentence using the adjective or adverb to make a comparison.**

1. The farmers knew how to care for the animals and fields.
   (successful)

   _____

   _____

2. A plow was one of the items on a farm. (expensive)

   _____

   _____

3. The mother would use sugar during hard times. (sparingly)

   _____

   _____

4. Children would be taught to read at home. (young)

   _____

   _____

5. Once a town was set up, the community would build a school.
   (small)

   _____

   _____

Focus Trait: Evidence
Main Ideas and Supporting Details

In a response essay, each paragraph has a main idea that relates to the topic of the essay. The other sentences provide supporting details, or evidence.

A. Read the main ideas and the supporting details below. Decide which supporting details belong with each main idea. Write A or B next to each detail.

Main Ideas

A. Traveling the Oregon Trail was a challenging experience.

B. The Oregon Trail became less popular when trains could cross the country.

Supporting Details

____ The trip that once took six months took just days by train.

____ The trip usually took between five and six months.

____ The train was not only faster, it was also much safer.

____ The first transcontinental railroad was completed in 1869.

____ Travelers faced many dangers, including extreme heat or cold.

____ Supplies were scarce along the way.

____ The dust on the trail was often blinding.

____ Soon, the railroad replaced the Oregon Trail for long-distance travel.

B. Read the supporting details. Write a sentence that tells the main idea.

Supporting Details

The Oregon Trail starts near the Missouri River. Then it goes along the

Platte River. It crosses through the Green River Valley and the Snake

River area. Finally, it travels down the Columbia River to end in the

Willamette Valley.

Main Idea _____

Name _____ Date _____

Reader's Guide

Lewis and Clark

Create a Museum Map

Museums often use maps to help visitors better understand a time and place in history. These maps show brief summaries, or the main idea, of what happened at each location.

For each location in the story of Lewis and Clark, write two important details that support the main idea of the paragraph.

Great Falls

Read the second paragraph on page 755.

Two Details: _____

_____

Cameahwait's Village

Read the first paragraph on page 758.

Two Details: _____

_____

Clearwater Valley

Read the second paragraph on page 759.

Two Details: _____

_____

Mouth of the Columbia River

Read the second paragraph on page 760.

Two Details: _____

_____

A history museum in Oregon is making an exhibit about the Lewis and Clark expedition. You are helping them make a map that shows important events along the route. For each point on the map, tell what happened there. Write the main idea. The main idea should be based on the details from the text.

❶ Great Falls	❷ Cameahwait's Village	❸ Clearwater Valley	❹ Mouth of the Columbia River
_____	_____	_____	_____
_____	_____	_____	_____
_____	_____	_____	_____
_____	_____	_____	_____
_____	_____	_____	_____
_____	_____	_____	_____
_____	_____	_____	_____

Name _____ Date _____

Analogies

Each sentence contains an analogy that features two pairs of words. The words in each pair may be related as synonyms, antonyms, by degree, or as part of a whole. For each sentence, choose a word from the box to fill in the blank and complete the analogy. Then state how the words in each pairing are related.

cascading	swarm	canoe	approach	thaw
civil	depart	width	plentiful	document

1. *Rock* is to *stone* as *pouring* is to _____ .

Relationship: _____

2. *Cold* is to *freeze* as *heat* is to _____ .

Relationship: _____

3. *Pedal* is to *bicycle* as *paddle* is to _____ .

Relationship: _____

4. *Attack* is to *defend* as _____ is to *avoid*.

Relationship: _____

5. *Shirt* is to *fabric* as _____ is to *paper*.

Relationship: _____

6. *Discourteous* is to *rude* as _____ is to *polite*.

Relationship: _____

7. *Overcast* is to *sunny* as *scarce* is to _____ .

Relationship: _____

8. *Heavy* is to *weight* as *diameter* is to _____ .

Relationship: _____

Suffix *-ion*

Basic Read the paragraph. Write the Basic Word that best replaces the underlined word or words in the sentences.

Dear Senator:

    I would first like to say that I chose to **(1)** <u>vote for</u> you in the 2004 race, and I made a **(2)** <u>donation</u> to your campaign earlier this month. It was a **(3)** <u>suspenseful</u> race, but I really thought you had a **(4)** <u>bond</u> with the people. I must **(5)** <u>admit</u>, however, that I am disappointed in how you are handling the issue of pollution. I feel the need to **(6)** <u>state</u> my concerns. I think this matter requires a strong and immediate **(7)** <u>response</u> from you. Other than that, I **(8)** <u>like</u> your brave positions on difficult issues. I hope that you are able to **(9)** <u>give</u> your talents to the public, and that you will win the next **(10)** <u>contest</u>.

Sincerely,

Jane Rodriguez

Spelling Words

1. elect
2. election
3. tense
4. tension
5. react
6. reaction
7. confess
8. confession
9. decorate
10. decoration
11. contribute
12. contribution
13. express
14. expression
15. imitate
16. imitation
17. connect
18. connection
19. admire
20. admiration

Challenge
fascinate
fascination
construct
construction

1. _____   6. _____

2. _____   7. _____

3. _____   8. _____

4. _____   9. _____

5. _____   10. _____

Challenge 11–14. Write a paragraph about a city that you enjoyed visiting. Use four of the Challenge Words. Write on a separate sheet of paper.

Spelling Word Sort

Write each Basic Word pair beside the correct heading.

No Spelling Change When Adding Suffix –ion	**Basic Words:** **Challenge Words:** **Possible Selection Words:**
Final e Dropped When Adding Suffix –ion	**Basic Words:** **Challenge Words:** **Possible Selection Words:**

Challenge Add the Challenge Words to your Word Sort.

Connect to Reading Look through *Lewis and Clark.* Find words with the suffix *-ion*. Add them to your Word Sort.

Spelling Words

1. elect
2. election
3. tense
4. tension
5. react
6. reaction
7. confess
8. confession
9. decorate
10. decoration
11. contribute
12. contribution
13. express
14. expression
15. imitate
16. imitation
17. connect
18. connection
19. admire
20. admiration

Challenge
fascinate
fascination
construct
construction

Proofreading for Spelling

Lewis and Clark
Spelling: Suffix -ion

Find the misspelled words and circle them. Write them correctly on the lines below.

When Jacques Marquette started his expedition down the Mississippi, his eyes were wide and he wore a curious expresion. He knew the New World was not just an immitashun of the old. He was ready to conect to new experiences and hoped to contribewte to history. Marquette tried not to reackt too strongly to the sight of strange animals such as bison, but he made a confesion that one of the things he saw made him tennse. He called it a "monster with the nose of a wildcat." The tenshun eased when he realized it was just an ugly fish—a catfish! He laughed when his men started to immitate his reacktion. Marquette also knew he needed to educate himself about squash, melons, and other native American foods. Although some were pretty enough for dekorashun, he did not use them to dekorate. He needed to eat these foods to survive!

1. _____   7. _____
2. _____   8. _____
3. _____   9. _____
4. _____   10. _____
5. _____   11. _____
6. _____   12. _____

Spelling Words

1. elect
2. election
3. tense
4. tension
5. react
6. reaction
7. confess
8. confession
9. decorate
10. decoration
11. contribute
12. contribution
13. express
14. expression
15. imitate
16. imitation
17. connect
18. connection
19. admire
20. admiration

Challenge
fascinate
fascination
construct
construction

Forming Contractions with *Not*

A **contraction** is a word formed by joining two words into one shorter word. An **apostrophe** (') takes the place of the letter or letters dropped in making the shorter word. You can combine some verbs with the word **not** to make contractions.

Thinking Question
Which contraction is made with the word not?

contractions

do + not = don't   are + not = aren't

have + not = haven't   will + not = won't

1–5. On the line, write a contraction for the underlined words.

1. We hope they <u>will not</u> get lost when they hike through the national park.

_____

2. Nasser knows there <u>are not</u> many different paths to take. _____

3. Paula <u>does not</u> think they need a map for the hike. _____

4. After all, Lewis and Clark <u>did not</u> have a map. _____

5. Would Lewis and Clark have succeeded if they <u>had not</u> had a guide?

_____

6–8. Rewrite the sentence using a contraction with the verb and *not.*

6. The explorers did not stop traveling for many months.

_____

7. They could not wait to explore the lands west of the Rocky Mountains.

_____

8. I think they would not have made it very far without horses.

_____

Contractions with Pronouns

You can make contractions with pronouns and some
helping verbs. Use an apostrophe (') to take the
place of the letter or letters dropped.

I + am = I'm	he + is = he's
they + are = they're	she + has = she's
you + have = you've	he + had = he'd

Thinking Question
*Which word is made
up of a pronoun and a
verb?*

1–4. Write a contraction for the underlined words.

1. You will like the article about the Grand Canyon.

   _____

2. He is planning to go with us. _____

3. She walked the Appalachian Trail, but he said he would

   never do it. _____

4. We have been to the Rocky Mountains. _____

**5–8. Rewrite each sentence to use a contraction for each pronoun
and helping verb.**

5. I am reading a book about Lewis and Clark.

   _____

6. Thomas Jefferson knew he would be expanding U.S. territory.

   _____

7. He has found a map of the Louisiana Territory.

   _____

8. If you would only listen to this story about the Oregon Trail.

   _____

Pronoun Contractions and Homophones

Some pronoun contractions have **homophones.**
Homophones are words that sound the same, but are
spelled differently and have different meanings.

contraction	homophones	
it's	its	belongs to *or* of it
they're	there	in or at that place
you're	your	belongs to *or* of you
who's	whose	belongs to *or* of who/whom

Activity Circle the errors in this story. Look for pronoun contractions and
their homophones.

"Whose ready to see the Grand Canyon?" Rosa's dad cried
out.

"Not me," Rosa huffed from the back seat of the car. " Its not
fair," she thought, "that there making me come on this trip. Still, its
better than babysitting," she concluded.

Rosa's father stopped the car and the family tumbled out.
Everyone stretched and Rosa shaded her eyes against the bright
sunlight as the family made they're way toward the canyon.

"Your in luck," a guide said as he took their tickets. "We're
only taking one more group today."

The tour guide led them on a hike around the South Rim
of the canyon. He spoke about the geology of the area and the
native plants and animals. But Rosa could not take her eyes off the
canyon and it's colored streaks of rock.

As they neared the end of the hike, Rosa's dad leaned in and
whispered, "So, what's you're opinion of the Grand Canyon now?

"Awesome," Rosa whispered back.

Perfect Tenses

The present perfect tense expresses action that ends in the present. The past perfect tense expresses action that was completed in the past before another action. The future perfect tense expresses action that will be completed by a specific time in the future.

Present perfect verbs are formed by adding *has/have* to the past participle of the verb.

Cole has gone to the museum.

Past perfect verbs are formed by adding *had* to the past participle of the verb.

Marco had found the trail by the time the others arrived.

Future perfect verbs are formed by adding *will have* or *shall have* to the past participle of the verb.

They will have finished setting up the tent by noon.

Activity Rewrite each sentence using the present perfect, past perfect, or future perfect tense of the underlined verb.

1. John Muir <u>wanted</u> to protect some of America's natural treasures.

   _____

2. Congress already <u>created</u> Yellowstone National Park in 1872 by the time Yosemite was created in 1890.

   _____

   _____

3. She <u>will go</u> on a camping trip by the end of the year.

   _____

4. He <u>explores</u> new trails each time he's visited the park.

   _____

Name _____ Date _____

Lesson 25
READER'S NOTEBOOK

Lewis and Clark
Grammar:
Connect to Writing

Connect to Writing

> Good writers avoid double negatives. When you use
> a contraction with **not**, do not include another "no"
> word, such as **no**, **neither**, **none**, or **never**. Avoid
> using the contraction **ain't**.
>
> Good word choice: He doesn't have any maps.
>   He has no maps.
> Poor word choice: He doesn't have no maps.
>   He ain't got none.
>   He doesn't have none.

Activity   If the sentence is incorrect, rewrite it correctly. If it is
correct, write *correct* on the line.

1. Sacagawea couldn't never have known how famous she would become.

   _____

2. We don't have no information on her early childhood.

   _____

3. But there is no doubt that when she was about 12 years old,

   Sacagawea was kidnapped. _____

4. Haven't you never heard about how she was sold to a fur trader?

   _____

5. When Lewis and Clark met Sacagawea, they didn't want her for a guide.

   _____

6. The explorers hadn't wanted the young woman to do nothing more

   than act as a translator with Indians.

   _____

   _____

7. Sacagawea never went nowhere without her baby.

   _____

Focus Trait: Conventions
Using Descriptive Language

A. Adding strong verbs and adjectives to opinions can make writing stronger.

Weak Writing	Strong Writing
Canoeing up the river was difficult.	We strained against the powerful current of the river, using oars to pull our canoes upstream.

B. Read each weak sentence. Rewrite it by adding descriptive words and phrases. Pay attention to writing conventions, such as correct spelling and use of punctuation marks.

Weak Writing	Strong Writing
1. The Rocky Mountains are beautiful.	
2. The hike through the woods was tiring.	
3. Building a campfire is hard.	
4. The lake water was too cold to swim in.	

Reader's Guide

Animals on the Move

Illustrate a Science Book

Science books usually include graphic features such as diagrams to help the reader understand what the text describes. Diagrams show parts and details of an object.

Read page 8. How do bats find food and other objects? Explain, in your own words, how this process works.

_____

_____

_____

Draw a diagram to describe how bats find objects in the dark. Use arrows and labels to identify the parts of your diagram. Write a caption that summarizes what the diagram shows.

[diagram box]

Caption: _____

Choose two animals from "Animals on the Move." For each animal, create a diagram showing how the animal uses its senses to find its way, locate objects, or communicate with others. Use arrows and labels to identify the parts of your diagrams. Give each diagram a caption.

Caption: _____

Caption: _____

Word Parts: *com-, con-, pre-, pro-*

Animals on the Move
Spelling: Word Parts: *com-, con-, pre-, pro-*

Basic: Write the Basic Word that could go in each group.

1. expectation, possibility
2. competition, tournament
3. verify, uphold
4. assemble, manufacture
5. affix, suffix
6. business, corporation
7. shield, defend
8. confusion, disturbance
9. improvement, development
10. disclose, reveal
11. offer, recommend
12. fight, resist

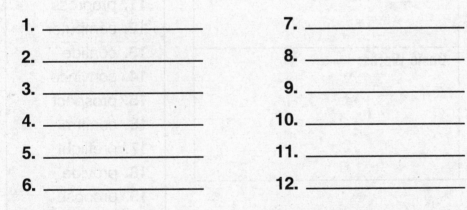

1. _____
2. _____
3. _____
4. _____
5. _____
6. _____

7. _____
8. _____
9. _____
10. _____
11. _____
12. _____

Spelling Words

Basic
1. produce
2. company
3. protect
4. preview
5. contain
6. combat
7. prejudge
8. commotion
9. contest
10. prefix
11. progress
12. computer
13. confide
14. convince
15. prospect
16. confirm
17. preflight
18. provide
19. propose
20. promotion

Challenge
concurrent
conscious
commercial
complete
conversation

Challenge 13-15: Read the headline in the box below. On a separate sheet of paper, write a paragraph about it, using three of the Challenge Words.

Habitats are Important to Animal Populations!

Spelling Word Sort

Write each Basic Word next to the correct word part.

com-	**Basic Words:** **Challenge Words:**
con-	**Basic Words:** **Challenge Words:**
pre-	**Basic Words:**
pro-	**Basic Words:**

Challenge: Add the Challenge Words to your Word Sort.

Spelling Words

Basic
1. produce
2. company
3. protect
4. preview
5. contain
6. combat
7. prejudge
8. commotion
9. contest
10. prefix
11. progress
12. computer
13. confide
14. convince
15. prospect
16. confirm
17. preflight
18. provide
19. propose
20. promotion

Challenge
concurrent
conscious
commercial
complete
conversation

Proofreading for Spelling

Animals on the Move
Spelling: Word Parts: *com-,
con-, pre-, pro-*

**Find the misspelled words and circle them. Write them
correctly on the lines below.**

> The scientist family Reed was terrified. There had
> been no prevue in the preflite plan that showed the huge
> waterfall and river which their vehicle needed to cross. The
> navigational komputer no longer could proevide guidance.
> Sarah, the youngest, cowered behind her father's chair. She
> didn't want to prejuge her father's knowledge but hoped he
> could guide them out of the comotion and protekt them.
> Her mother sat next to her father, shouting out instructions
> and trying to convinse them to all be calm as they tried to
> kombat the crisis.
>
> As they started through the water, there was a loud
> crash and the vehicle tipped left. Sarah could not contane
> her terror. Just as she was about to scream, her mother
> and father laughed. The river was actually very shallow
> and they were able to continue on their journey to see
> interesting animals.

1. _____   6. _____

2. _____   7. _____

3. _____   8. _____

4. _____   9. _____

5. _____   10. _____

Spelling Words

Basic
1. produce
2. company
3. protect
4. preview
5. contain
6. combat
7. prejudge
8. commotion
9. contest
10. prefix
11. progress
12. computer
13. confide
14. convince
15. prospect
16. confirm
17. preflight
18. provide
19. propose
20. promotion

Challenge
concurrent
conscious
commercial
complete
conversation

Singular Possessive Nouns

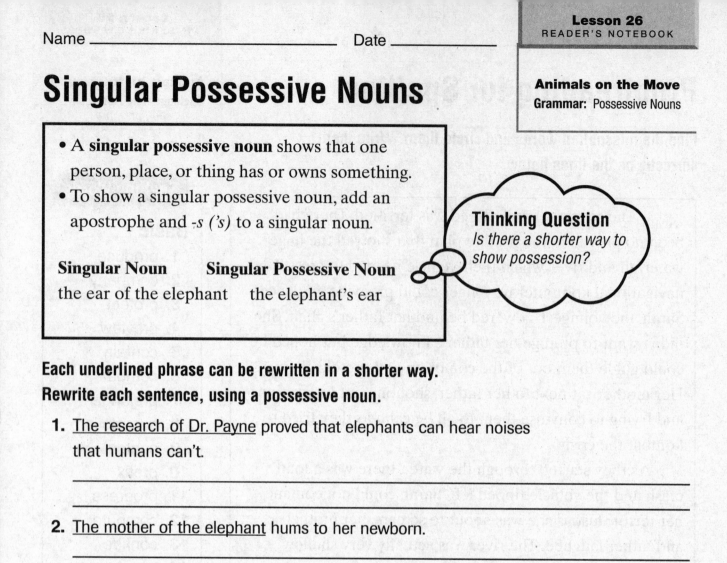

- A **singular possessive noun** shows that one person, place, or thing has or owns something.
- To show a singular possessive noun, add an apostrophe and -s ('s) to a singular noun.

Singular Noun   **Singular Possessive Noun**
the ear of the elephant   the elephant's ear

Thinking Question
Is there a shorter way to show possession?

Each underlined phrase can be rewritten in a shorter way.
Rewrite each sentence, using a possessive noun.

1. <u>The research of Dr. Payne</u> proved that elephants can hear noises that humans can't.

   _____

   _____

2. <u>The mother of the elephant</u> hums to her newborn.

   _____

3. The insect will become <u>the dinner of the hungry bat</u>.

   _____

4. <u>The dance the bee does</u> shows the other honeybees where to find pollen.

   _____

   _____

5. In order to track its movements, the scientist put a band around <u>the leg of the bird</u>.

   _____

   _____

6. Many animals use <u>the magnetic field of Earth</u> to navigate over long distances.

   _____

   _____

Plural Possessive Nouns

- A **plural possessive noun** shows that more than one person, place, or thing has or owns something.
- When a plural noun ends in -*s*, add only an apostrophe after the -*s (s')*.
- When a plural noun does not end in -*s*, add (*'s*) to form the plural possessive noun

Plural Noun	Plural Possessive Noun
the hive of the bees	the bees' hive
the den of the mice	the mice's den

Thinking Question
Is there a shorter way to show possession?

Each underlined phrase can be rewritten in a shorter way. Rewrite each sentence, adding plural possessive nouns.

1. Scientists continue to study <u>senses of animals</u>.

_____

2. We could hear <u>the trumpeting calls of the elephants</u> from a long distance.

_____

3. <u>The squeaking sounds the bats make</u> are part of echolocation.

_____

4. Bats use echoes to find the <u>location of their prey</u>.

_____

5. I read about how bees dance in <u>a science article for children</u>.

_____

_____

6. <u>The sounds of the bees</u> give information to the rest of the hive.

_____

_____

Possessive Nouns

- A **singular possessive noun** shows ownership for one person, place, or thing. To show a singular possessive noun, add an apostrophe and -*s* to a singular noun.
- A **plural possessive noun** shows ownership for more than one person, place, or thing. When a plural noun ends in -*s*, add only an apostrophe after the -*s* (*s'*). When a plural noun does not end in -*s*, add an apostrophe and an -*s* (*'s*).

Noun	Possessive Noun
fur of the dog	dog's fur
dishes of the dogs	dogs' dishes
the club of women	the women's club

Each underlined phrase can be written in a shorter way. Rewrite each sentence, adding plural possessive nouns.

1. The constant eating of the hungry mice ruined the wheat crop.

_____

2. The hunter woke up to the thunder of the hooves of the stampeding deer.

_____

3. Depending on the strength of the oxen to pull the heavy load, the farmer filled his wagon with cotton bales.

_____

_____

4. The offspring of snow geese spend their first months on the Arctic tundra.

_____

5. Migrating zebras aroused the interest of the children.

_____

The Verbs *be* and *have*

The chart below shows the present and past tense forms of *be* and *have*.

	Form of *be* Present	Form of *be* Past	Form of *have* Present	Form of *have* Past
Singular subjects: I	am	was	have	had
You	are	were	have	had
He, She, It (or noun)	is	was	has	had
Plural subjects: You	are	were	have	had
We, They, (or noun)	are	were	have	had

Write the form of *be* or *have* in parentheses that best completes each sentence.

1. Polar bears (is, are) patient hunters. _____

2. Polar bear cubs (is, are) about the size of a rat when they
   are born. _____

3. The polar bear cub (has, have) been with its mother for
   nearly a year. _____

4. You should (have, of) seen how big the bear was! _____

5. Its sense of smell (is, are) very powerful. _____

6. The polar bear (has, have) eaten all of the meat. _____

7. They (is, are) protected from the cold by layers of blubber. _____

Name _____   Date _____

Lesson 26
READER'S NOTEBOOK

Sentence Fluency

Animals on the Move
Grammar: Connect to Writing

Instead of writing two sentences to tell about one noun, you can often use a possessive noun to combine the two sentences into one smooth sentence.

Two sentences	One sentence using a possessive noun
A bat has a special ability to hunt and capture prey. It is called echolocation.	A bat's ability to hunt and capture prey is called echolocation.

Combine each pair of sentences using a possessive noun.

1. My uncle has a cabin. It is near the place where the river meets the sea.

   _____

   _____

2. The salmon have a breeding ground. It is near the first bend in the river.

   _____

   _____

3. Uncle Steven has a boat. We will use it to catch fish.

   _____

   _____

4. My brother has a favorite fishing lure. The lure is red and silver.

   _____

   _____

5. A huge bird flew over the river. We saw its red tail.

   _____

   _____

6. Amanda caught a fish. We will cook it for dinner tonight.

   _____

   _____

Focus Trait: Word Choice

Good writing helps readers understand the topic they are reading about. Good writers include definitions of unfamiliar words within their writing. Definitions provide simple explanations of the meaning of unfamiliar terms.

Read each sentence. Identify the word that might require definition.

Pair/Share Work with a partner to rewrite the sentences in a way that helps provide the reader with the definition of a word.

Unclear Sentence	Sentence with a Definition
1. The fish know how to navigate.	
2. The bees are able to communicate with the other bees.	
3. The birds complete this migration every year.	
4. The bats find insects using echolocation.	

Name _____ Date _____

Lesson 27
READER'S NOTEBOOK

Mysteries at
Cliff Palace
Independent Reading

Reader's Guide

Mysteries at Cliff Palace

Write a Job Description

A company writes a job description when the company is looking for a new worker for a job. The job description tells what qualities or characteristics the company is looking for in a person.

From reading the dialogue between Ranger Jenkins and the family, you can find out:

- what kind of characteristics a park ranger needs to have, and
- what a park ranger needs to know to do his or her job.

Reread page 21. What characteristics can you tell about Ranger Jenkins? What information does she seem to know much about?

_____

_____

_____

Reread page 22. In what other subjects is Ranger Jenkins an expert?

_____

_____

_____

Reread page 27. Think about how Ranger Jenkins responds to Ruben's interest. What else does this say about Ranger Jenkins's character?

_____

_____

_____

Name _____ Date _____

Lesson 27
READER'S NOTEBOOK

Mysteries at
Cliff Palace
Independent Reading

Because of the increase in tourists visiting Mesa Verde National Park, the National Park Service needs to hire another ranger to guide them through the cliff dwellings. They have asked you to write a job description for the position of Park Ranger. Use the characteristics of a park ranger that you found in "Mysteries at Cliff Palace" to write the job description.

National Park Service Job Opening

Position: Park Ranger
Location: Mesa Verde National Park

Qualifications: Must be friendly and courteous to national park guests.

_____

_____

_____

_____

_____

_____

_____

_____

Name _____ Date _____

Suffixes: *-ant, -ent, -able, -ible, -ism, -ist*

Basic: Write the Basic Word that completes each sentence.

Because the entire staff wanted our school newspaper to be the best it could be, we held (1) meetings to discuss improvements. Usually we met in a (2) classroom, where we could spread out and be (3). At last week's meeting, our editor was (4) that we needed to "spice up" our paper. She felt it was (5) that we start a new feature called "Our School's Globe Trotters." (She took the idea from a (6) seminar she attended online.) She showed a lot of (7) that this column would be popular among readers. We decided to introduce it with a contest to see which of our students had traveled to the most exotic place. Each (8) would submit a short essay about his or her adventure. The staff would pick the winner. This (9) would receive a (10) coin as a prize and have an entire article devoted to him or her.

1. _____   6. _____

2. _____   7. _____

3. _____   8. _____

4. _____   9. _____

5. _____   10. _____

Challenge 11–14: Read the headline below. On a separate sheet of paper, write a sentence about it using four of the Challenge Words.

| **Picnic Lunch Disappears!** |

Spelling Words

Basic
1. vacant
2. insistent
3. reversible
4. patriotism
5. finalist
6. honorable
7. contestant
8. observant
9. urgent
10. pessimist
11. comfortable
12. absorbent
13. optimism
14. journalism
15. novelist
16. terrible
17. frequent
18. laughable
19. radiant
20. collectible

Challenge
evident
triumphant
occupant
digestible
curable

Spelling Word Sort

Write each Basic Word next to the correct suffix.

Suffix *-ent*	**Basic Words:**
	Challenge Words:
Suffix *-ant*	**Basic Words:**
	Challenge Words:
Suffix *-able*	**Basic Words:**
	Challenge Words:
Suffix *-ible*	**Basic Words:**
	Challenge Words:
Suffixes *-ism, -ist*	**Basic Words:**
	Challenge Words:

Challenge: Add the Challenge Words to your Word Sort.

Spelling Words

Basic
1. vacant
2. insistent
3. reversible
4. patriotism
5. finalist
6. honorable
7. contestant
8. observant
9. urgent
10. pessimist
11. comfortable
12. absorbent
13. optimism
14. journalism
15. novelist
16. terrible
17. frequent
18. laughable
19. radiant
20. collectible

Challenge
evident
triumphant
occupant
digestible
curable

Spelling: Suffixes: *-ant, -ent, -able, -ible, -ism, -ist*

Find the misspelled words and circle them. Write them correctly on the lines below.

Do you like travel adventure stories? If so, then *Around the World in Eighty Days,* by Jules Verne is a book for you. Verne was a 19th-century French writer and novalist who also wrote some of the earliest science fiction stories. In this book, Englishman Phineas Fogg and his servant Passepartout must race around the world in eighty days. (Remember, this was before air travel, so it wasn't easy.) As you can imagine, the two are not always in the most confortible of situations! The two find their plans blocked at nearly every turn, but their urgint need to keep moving drives the story along. Obviously, neither is really a pessimst. In addition, *Around The World in Eighty Days* offers many details about other lands for observent readers to enjoy.

Verne's radient works have been the source of movies, other books, and countless adaptations. One reason for this is that he showed optimizm about the future. In his stories, people are able to solve problems, even in the most terible circumstances.

Spelling Words

Basic
1. vacant
2. insistent
3. reversible
4. patriotism
5. finalist
6. honorable
7. contestant
8. observant
9. urgent
10. pessimist
11. comfortable
12. absorbent
13. optimism
14. journalism
15. novelist
16. terrible
17. frequent
18. laughable
19. radiant
20. collectible

Challenge
evident
triumphant
occupant
digestible
curable

1. _____   5. _____
2. _____   6. _____
3. _____   7. _____
4. _____   8. _____

Writing Abbreviations

An **abbreviation** is a shortened form of a word.

Some abbreviations have capital letters and periods. Others use only capital letters.

Places	
U.S.A.	United States of America
D.C.	District of Columbia
NM	New Mexico
CA	California
TX	Texas

Rewrite the sentences below using the correct abbreviations.

1. The address on the letter read, "San Antonio, Texas."

_____

2. We boarded the train in Santa Fe, New Mexico.

_____

3. We traveled all the way to San Francisco, California.

_____

4. After weeks of traveling abroad, I was glad to be back in the United States of America.

_____

5. The White House is in our capital, Washington, District of Columbia.

_____

Writing Abbreviations

Common Abbreviations					
Addresses		**Businesses**		**States**	
St.	Street	Co.	Company	MS	Mississippi
Ave.	Avenue	Corp.	Corporation	AL	Alabama
Blvd.	Boulevard	Inc.	Incorporated	FL	Florida
Dr.	Drive			NM	New Mexico
Apt.	Apartment			SC	South Carolina

Rewrite each address using correct abbreviations.

1. James Johnson

1342 Almond Street

Patterson, Florida

_____

_____

_____

2. Mrs. Carole Barber

Acme Bolts Company, Incorporated

961 Moreno Drive

Montgomery, Alabama

_____

_____

_____

3. Emily Burke

35 Lockwood Avenue

Santa Fe, New Mexico

_____

_____

_____

4. Lewis Parker

17 Amber Boulevard, Apartment 3

Jackson, Mississippi

_____

_____

_____

Writing Abbreviations

An **abbreviation** is a shortened form of a word. Abbreviations for days of the week and months begin with a capital letter and end with a period. Abbreviations for units of measurement do not require capital letters and many do not require a period.

Common Abbreviations					
Days of the Week		**Months**		**Units of Measurement**	
Sun.	Sunday	Jan.	January	in.	inch
Mon.	Monday	Feb.	February	ft.	foot
Tues.	Tuesday	Mar.	March	mi	mile
Wed.	Wednesday	Aug.	August	m	meter
Thurs.	Thursday	Sept.	September	km	kilometer
Fri.	Friday	Oct.	October	lb	pound
Sat.	Saturday	Dec.	December	oz	ounce

Rewrite the sentences below using the correct abbreviations.

1. I left on Saturday, the third of March, after dinner.

_____

2. The alcove opening is 8 feet 7 inches wide.

_____

3. One mile equals 1.6 kilometers, rounded to the nearest tenth.

_____

4. The urn weighed 8 pounds 14 ounces, or about 4 kilograms.

_____

5. Ruben climbed the 100 meter ladder without looking down.

_____

Perfect Tenses

- Add *has, have,* or *had* to the past tense form of the verb to make the **perfect tense**.
- Irregular verbs have special forms to show the past.

Verb	Past Tense	Perfect Tense
have	had	(has, have, had) had
think	thought	(has, have, had) thought
say	said	(has, have, had) said

Rewrite each sentence, changing the underlined verb to a form of the perfect tense.

1. Rosa <u>bring</u> her camera to the cliff.

_____

2. Ruben always <u>say</u> he could solve any mystery.

_____

3. They <u>go</u> on this museum tour earlier in the year.

_____

4. Ruben <u>looked</u> closely at all of the exhibits.

_____

5. We <u>investigated</u> other mysteries.

_____

Connect to Writing

Proofreading

Capitalize the first, last, and all other important words in **titles**. Titles of books are underlined and shorter works are set off by quotation marks.

An **abbreviation** is a shortened form of a word. An abbreviation usually begins with a capital letter and ends with a period.

<u>Charlie and the Chocolate Factory</u> (book)
"Head, Shoulders, Knees, and Toes" (song)

Monday	Mon.
Avenue	Ave.
January	Jan.

Use proofreading marks to correct errors in the letter below.

1882 Rosewood Aven.
Omaha, NEB.
Nove. 16, 2024

Dear Mrs Sanchez,

Thank you so much for the wonderful books. My favorite was "wind over The Andes," but I also enjoyed A Long Journey home. Your suggestion that I read the article The Cliffs Of Dover was also very helpful.

Sincerely,
Hazel Roger

Focus Trait: Voice

A strong voice gives your writing personality and lets your reader
know how you feel about your subject.

Ineffective Opening	Opening with Strong Voice
Cliff Palace in Mesa Verde National Park reminds visitors of the past.	No one knows where the Native Americans who lived in Cliff Palace went, but visitors can almost hear the voices of ancient warriors when visiting Mesa Verde National Park.

Read each paragraph opening. Revise the opening, adding details to give a stronger voice.

Ineffective Opening	Opening with Strong Voice
1. You might not know how the alcoves of the Cliff Palace were formed.	_____ _____ _____ _____
2. We don't know what happened in the kivas.	_____ _____ _____
3. A drought may have caused problems at the Cliff Palace.	_____ _____ _____ _____

Fossils: A Peek Into the Past

Create a Museum Exhibit

It is important to distinguish between facts and opinions in informational texts. Facts can be proven by observation. Opinions are statements that are not based on facts or knowledge.

Reread page 36. Write two opinions that are given on that page.

_____

_____

Write two **facts** that are given on page 36.

_____

_____

Reread page 38. Write two **opinions** that are given on that page.

_____

_____

Write two **facts** that are given on page 38.

_____

_____

Name _____ Date _____

Lesson 28
READER'S NOTEBOOK

Fossils: A Peek
Into the Past
Independent Reading

A natural history museum is building an exhibit on the discoveries of Mary Anning. You have been asked to create signs for each fossil.

Reread pages 39–40. Then write the signs. Tell when each dinosaur fossil was discovered. Then write facts about each fossil.

Specimen: *ichthyosaurus*

Discovered: _____

Facts: _____

_____

_____

_____

_____

Specimen: *plesiosaur*

Discovered: _____

Facts: _____

_____

_____

_____

_____

The museum also wants to include a display about Miss Anning's work. Reread page 41. Then write facts about her work.

The Work of Mary Anning (1799–1847)

_____

_____

_____

_____

Name _____ Date _____

Lesson 28
READER'S NOTEBOOK

Fossils: A Peek
Into the Past
Spelling: Greek Word Parts

Greek Word Parts

Basic: Read the paragraph. Write the Basic Words that best complete the sentences.

A few weeks ago, a (1) _____ in a newspaper article described an upcoming performance. The (2) _____ would be playing a concert featuring both jazz and world music. The local TV station planned to (3) _____ the event. My mother picked up the (4) _____ and called the box office to buy tickets. Before we went to the theater, I read about the conductor's life in a short (5) _____. He studied archaeology before he decided on a career in music. Between songs, the conductor spoke into a (6) _____ to tell us about the music. I enjoyed watching a woman playing the metal bars of a (7) _____ with two mallets. My favorite part of the jazz program was a solo on the (8) _____. Cameras weren't allowed inside, so I was unable to take even one (9) _____. But, after the show, I asked the conductor to (10) _____ my program, and he did!

Challenge 11–13: Write a paragraph using three of the Challenge Words. Write on a separate sheet of paper.

Spelling Words

Basic
1. telephone
2. autograph
3. microscope
4. photograph
5. televise
6. biology
7. microphone
8. paragraph
9. symphony
10. telegraph
11. megaphone
12. microwave
13. photocopy
14. biography
15. saxophone
16. telescope
17. calligraphy
18. xylophone
19. homophone
20. homograph

Challenge
telecommute
bibliography
phonetic
microbe
autobiography

Spelling Word Sort

Write each Basic Word next to the correct word part.

graph ("something written")	**Basic Words:** **Challenge Words:**
phone ("sound")	**Basic Words:** **Challenge Word:**
micro ("small")	**Basic Words:** **Challenge Words:**
other Greek word parts	**Basic Words:** **Challenge Words:**

Challenge: Add the Challenge Words to your Word Sort.

Spelling Words

Basic
1. telephone
2. autograph
3. microscope
4. photograph
5. televise
6. biology
7. microphone
8. paragraph
9. symphony
10. telegraph
11. megaphone
12. microwave
13. photocopy
14. biography
15. saxophone
16. telescope
17. calligraphy
18. xylophone
19. homophone
20. homograph

Challenge
telecommute
bibliography
phonetic
microbe
autobiography

Name _____ Date _____

Proofreading for Spelling

**Find the misspelled words and circle them. Write them
correctly on the lines below.**

As a grade-school teacher, I was tired from educating
students about what a homofone and a honograph were,
how biologie played a part in everyday life, and how to use a
mickroscope. When I got a telegraf from my cousin inviting
me to Alaska, I was ready to use a megafone to announce my
departure! Instead, I relied on the telefone. Since I look at every
trip as a learning adventure, I packed my telascope, made a
photocoppy of some information about fossils in Alaska, and
set off.

Once I got to Alaska, I discovered that my cousin lived in a
remote cabin. Other than a mikrowave, a radio, and a computer,
he had few modern conveniences. He even had the time to write
letters using caligraphy. I couldn't wait to get outside and look for
fossils—and, of course, to report back everything to my students!

1. _____   7. _____

2. _____   8. _____

3. _____   9. _____

4. _____   10. _____

5. _____   11. _____

6. _____

Spelling Words

Basic

1. telephone
2. autograph
3. microscope
4. photograph
5. televise
6. biology
7. microphone
8. paragraph
9. symphony
10. telegraph
11. megaphone
12. microwave
13. photocopy
14. biography
15. saxophone
16. telescope
17. calligraphy
18. xylophone
19. homophone
20. homograph

Challenge

telecommute
bibliography
phonetic
microbe
autobiography

Commas with Introductory Words and Phrases

- An **introductory word,** such as *meanwhile, well, yes,* or *no,* that begins a sentence is usually followed by a comma.
- An **introductory phrase,** such as *a short while later,* is also usually followed by a comma.

Yes, I'll go with you.

Earlier today, he was not in the room.

Thinking Questions
Is there a word or phrase that begins the sentence? Is there a place in the sentence where I would naturally pause?

Write each sentence correctly, adding commas where they are needed.

1. Yes Dr. Winston will tell the story of his first fossil find.

_____

_____

2. Well the scientist thought he was extremely lucky to find the fossil.

_____

_____

3. After some time the museum hoped he would donate the fossil.

_____

_____

4. In the morning will you tell us about the new fossil exhibit?

_____

_____

5. No I have not seen the fossil of a dinosaur leg.

_____

_____

Commas with Names

- When a person is spoken to directly by name, the name is set apart from the rest of the sentence by **commas.**
- **Names** can appear at the beginning, in the middle, or at the end of sentences.

Finding fossils is important work, Jake, because fossils teach us about life long ago.

Thinking Questions
Is the person who is being spoken to addressed by name in the sentence? Where in the sentence do I naturally pause?

Rewrite each sentence. Add commas where they are needed.

1. Lauren how did it feel to find such an unusual fossil?

_____

_____

2. Well Luis I thought I was just digging up an interesting rock.

_____

_____

3. So many people Lauren are going to want to see what you found.

_____

_____

4. Do you think Lauren that you'll find more fossils?

_____

_____

5. I sure hope so Luis.

_____

6. What most people don't understand Philip is how hard it is to discover anything worthwhile.

_____

_____

Name _____ Date _____

Lesson 28
READER'S NOTEBOOK

Fossils: A Peek
Into the Past
Grammar: Commas in Sentences

Commas in Sentences

Rewrite each sentence correctly. Add commas where they are needed.

1. About 10,000 years ago woolly mammoths became extinct.

_____

2. After finding a fossil the scientist recorded his discovery in a notebook.

_____

_____

3. Finally Dr. Winston found the remains of a giant sea creature.

_____

_____

4. Hoping to improve their collection museum officials asked
Dr. Winston to donate the fossil.

_____

_____

5. If you could give us the fossil Dr. Winston our collection would be
complete.

_____

_____

Name _____ Date _____

Lesson 28
READER'S NOTEBOOK

**Fossils: A Peek
Into the Past**
Grammar: Spiral Review

Correct Adjectives

- *A*, *an*, and *the* are special adjectives called **articles**.
  A and *an* refer to any noun. *The* refers to a specific noun.
- A **demonstrative adjective** tells which one. *This* and
  these refer to nouns close by. *That* and *those* refer to
  nouns farther away. *This* and *that* are used with singular
  nouns. *These* and *those* are used with plural nouns.
- A **proper adjective** is formed from a proper noun. It is
  capitalized.

**1–5. Write the correct article or demonstrative adjective in parentheses to complete
each sentence.**

1. (Those, That) fossils are the oldest in the museum. _____

2. Jorge visited (the, a) National History Museum. _____

3. (These, That) fossils need to be cleaned. _____

4. I wrote a book about (a, an) great fossil discovery. _____

5. Scientists believe that climate change was one reason (these, this)

mammoths disappeared. _____

6–8. Rewrite the sentences, using adjectives to combine them.

6. After discovering the dinosaur fossil, the boy appeared on the evening
news. The boy was from Canada.

_____

_____

7. The boy said the fossil looked like a rock. It was rough and jagged.

_____

_____

8. They found the fossil buried in the ground. The ground was frozen.

_____

_____

Name _____ Date _____

Lesson 28
READER'S NOTEBOOK

Fossils: A Peek
Into the Past
Grammar: Connect to Writing

Sentence Fluency

Use **introductory phrases** to combine sentences when
you want to vary sentence length. A comma sets
off all introductory phrases.

Short, Choppy Sentences	Combined Sentence with an Introductory Phrase
Jared was walking home from school. He found a fossil of a mammoth tooth.	Walking home from school, Jared found a fossil of a mammoth tooth.

Combine each pair of sentences by changing one sentence to an introductory phrase.

1. We were visiting the museum. We saw the fossil collection.

_____

2. The fossilized tooth weighed seven pounds. It was almost as big as my whole head!

_____

_____

3. Scientists discovered the bones of an 18,000-year-old man. The discovery was made during a trip to Indonesia.

_____

_____

4. Over 100 dinosaur eggs were discovered in India. Three explorers discovered them while hunting.

_____

_____

5. The hunter investigated what he thought was a reindeer. The Russian hunter discovered it was the remains of a 40,000-year-old baby mammoth.

_____

_____

Name _____ Date _____

Lesson 28
READER'S NOTEBOOK

Fossils: A Peek
Into the Past
Writing: Ideas

Focus Trait: Ideas

Main idea statements need strong support, such as examples and details.
Read the statement and the weak example. Then notice how this example
was made stronger by adding details.

Statement: Fossils give scientists important information.	
Weak Example	**Strong Example**
They show where they came from.	Scientists can learn the age and size of an animal from fossil remains.

Read each statement and the weak example that follows it. Then rewrite the weak
example by adding more details.

1. *Statement:* Below-average temperatures preserve animal remains.

Weak Example	**Strong Example**
In the Arctic the weather is freezing.	

2. *Statement:* Some animal species have been found in different geographical zones.

The mammoth has been found in a few places.	

3. *Statement:* Mammoths were huge animals.

Some were bigger than an adult person.	

4. *Statement:* You can hunt for fossils at any age.

Even little children find them.	

Name _____ Date _____

Lesson 29
READER'S NOTEBOOK

The Case of the
Missing Deer
Independent Reading

Reader's Guide

The Case of the Missing Deer

Write an Advice Column

In *The Case of the Missing Deer*, Blake uses inferences to crack this case. By making inferences, he is able to draw a conclusion about the deer by his family's cabin.

Reread pages 54–56. In Blake's investigator notebook, write four clues that lead him to infer what was keeping the deer away.

1. _____

_____

_____

2. _____

_____

_____

3. _____

_____

_____

4. _____

_____

_____

Name _____ Date _____

An advice column is written to help readers solve everyday problems.
The *North Woods Gazette* is a local newsletter that is read by the
families in Pinewood Park, where Blake's family has their cabin.
Blake has been chosen by the *North Woods Gazette* to give advice
about how to attract deer. Help Blake finish his column, using both
inferences and conclusions drawn from his investigation
of the missing deer.

Life in the North Woods
by Blake Davis

It's deer season! But are deer staying clear of your backwoods pad?
Are you jealous of the herds of white tails flocking to your
neighbor's hutch? Well, you, too, can have plenty of does and bucks
rushing to your humble home by following this advice:

_____

_____

_____

_____

_____

_____

_____

_____

_____

_____

_____

Name _____ Date _____

Latin Word Parts

Basic: Write the basic word that could go with each group.

1. witness, observer, _____

2. explode, blow up, _____

3. look over, examine, _____

4. move, carry, _____

5. disturb, interrupt, _____

6. admiration, praise, _____

7. show, display, _____

8. movable, transportable, _____

9. forecast, guess, _____

10. ruler, leader, _____

11. decision, judgment, _____

Challenge 12–14: Write two or three sentences about an encounter with nature. Use at least three of the Challenge Words. Write on a separate sheet of paper.

Spelling Words

Basic

1. inspect
2. export
3. erupt
4. predict
5. respect
6. bankrupt
7. dictate
8. porter
9. report
10. spectacle
11. deport
12. interrupt
13. dictator
14. import
15. disrupt
16. portable
17. transport
18. spectator
19. verdict
20. dictionary

Challenge

spectacular
contradict
corrupt
retrospect
rupture

Spelling Word Sort

Write each Basic Word next to the correct word part.

Word Part: *spect*	**Basic words:** **Challenge words:**
Word Part: *port*	**Basic words:**
Word Part: *dict*	**Basic words:** **Challenge word:**
Word Part: *rupt*	**Basic words:** **Challenge words:**

Challenge: Add the Challenge Words to your Word Sort.

Spelling Words

Basic
1. inspect
2. export
3. erupt
4. predict
5. respect
6. bankrupt
7. dictate
8. porter
9. report
10. spectacle
11. deport
12. interrupt
13. dictator
14. import
15. disrupt
16. portable
17. transport
18. spectator
19. verdict
20. dictionary

Challenge
spectacular
contradict
corrupt
retrospect
rupture

Proofreading for Spelling

Name _____ Date _____

Find the misspelled words and circle them. Write them correctly on the lines below.

Are you ready to write your reeport on the La Brea Tar Pits in Los Angeles, California? Here's what you need to do: Look up this historical specticle in your online dictionery. Then inport the facts about these tar pits where prehistoric animals were trapped, and exxport what you learn into a separate document. You may want to interupt your research to imagine the pits as they looked thousands of years ago when prehistoric animals roamed the earth.

If you don't want to write the final report yourself, perhaps you can dictat it to one of your parents. They may decide to take you on a trip to La Brea by train, where a portter will load your bags and the cost of a ticket will not cause your family to go bancrupt. Everyone will give the same vurdict on the tar pits: They're amazing!

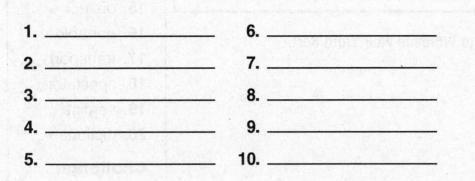

1. _____   6. _____
2. _____   7. _____
3. _____   8. _____
4. _____   9. _____
5. _____   10. _____

Spelling Words

1. inspect
2. export
3. erupt
4. predict
5. respect
6. bankrupt
7. dictate
8. porter
9. report
10. spectacle
11. deport
12. interrupt
13. dictator
14. import
15. disrupt
16. portable
17. transport
18. spectator
19. verdict
20. dictionary

Challenge

spectacular
contradict
corrupt
retrospect
rupture

Commas with Appositives

- An **appositive** is a noun or pronoun, often with adjectives and other words, placed after a noun to identify or explain it. Commas are usually used to set off an appositive from the rest of the sentence.

The red deer, a large and impressive looking animal, has a slender body and long legs.

Thinking Questions
Is there a phrase that follows a noun? Does the phrase identify or explain the noun?

Rewrite each sentence. Add commas where they are needed.

1. The caribou of North America animals famous for long migrations often travel in herds numbering in the tens of thousands.

   _____

   _____

   _____

2. The elk the largest species of deer has a humped back and long, thin legs.

   _____

   _____

   _____

3. Elk creatures active during the early morning rest during the middle part of the day.

   _____

   _____

   _____

4. The elk's coat fur that is thick and coarse in texture is short except for the shoulders, where it forms a distinctive mane.

   _____

   _____

   _____

Name _____ Date _____

Lesson 29
READER'S NOTEBOOK

The Case of the
Missing Deer
Grammar: More Commas

Other Uses for Commas

Use a comma to separate items in a series of three or more items, elements of dates, and elements of an address when they appear in a sentence.

Deer, elk, and caribou are all herbivores.

The deer was seen on October 6, 2011, in St. Paul, Minnesota.

Thinking Question
Are there three or more items in a series?

Rewrite the sentences below, using commas where they are needed.

1. White-tailed deer eat a variety of foods, including hay acorns grasses and wildflowers.

_____

_____

2. The herd started their migration south on November 3 2011.

_____

_____

3. Elk are the prey of mountain lions bears wolves and coyotes.

_____

_____

4. Deer can be found near Helena Montana.

_____

_____

5. Deer live in grassland forest and tundra habitats.

_____

_____

Commas in Sentences

Rewrite each sentence. Add commas where they are needed.

1. The tundra a treeless plain of the arctic region has a permanently frozen layer below the surface soil.

   _____

   _____

2. Common colors for a white-tailed deer's hide include light brown tan or deep red.

   _____

   _____

3. Caribou are able to smell lichens a favorite food lying beneath the snow.

   _____

   _____

4. My dad first saw an elk on October 17 1998.

   _____

   _____

5. Woodland caribou have been sighted in the mountains north of Spokane Washington.

   _____

   _____

Making Comparisons

Use superlative adjectives to compare three or more items.

Adjective	Comparing Three or More Items
One syllable (small, weak)	Add -*est* (smallest, weakest)
Ending with *e* (safe, white)	Drop *e*, add -*est* (safest, whitest)
Ending with *y* (easy, hairy)	Drop *y*, add *iest* (easiest, hairiest)
Long adjectives (interesting, puzzled)	Use *most* before long adjectives (most interesting, most puzzled)

Write the correct choice on the line provided.

1. The elk is the (most large, largest) member of the deer family.

   _____

2. The fallow deer is the (most common, commonest) deer species in

   Europe. _____

3. Elderly caribou are vulnerable to wolves and suffer the (most great,

   greatest) losses. _____

4. Of the deer's many predators, the wolf is the (most deadly,

   deadliest). _____

5. The bucks compete to see who is the (most strong, strongest).

   _____

Name _____ Date _____

Lesson 29
·READER'S NOTEBOOK

The Case of the
Missing Deer
Grammar: Connect to Writing

Sentence Fluency

Instead of writing two or more short sentences, you can often write
one longer sentence that combines similar items. Separate the items
with commas when there are more than two. Be sure to use the word
and before the last item.

Choppy Sentences	Combined Sentence: Items in a Series
A male turkey is called a tom or a gobbler. A female is called a hen. A baby turkey is called a poult.	A male turkey is called a tom or a gobbler, a female is called a hen, and a baby turkey is called a poult.

Combine each set of sentences by using commas and the word *and*.
Write your sentence on the lines provided.

1. Elephants can run 25 miles per hour. Deer can race at 40 miles per
   hour. Cheetahs can sprint at 70 miles per hour.

   _____

   _____

2. Deer shed their antlers each winter. They grow new ones from
   spring until fall. In the fall the antlers harden and can be used as
   weapons.

   _____

   _____

3. A young male turkey is called a jake. A young female is called a
   jenny. A group of turkeys is called a flock.

   _____

   _____

4. Turkeys enjoy the company of other creatures. They love having
   their feathers stroked.

   _____

   _____

Focus Trait: Organization

Good writers think about the best way to present information in an essay. In a short essay or single paragraph, writers begin with an opening statement which identifies the topic, a body which explains or expands on the topic with facts and details, and a conclusion which summarizes the information.

Think about how you might write an informational essay on animals that are or were native to your area. Complete the following chart to plan the essay, including possible sources of information for the body of the essay. For this exercise, imagine that you learned that some animals no longer live in the area because of human development.

Informational Essay	
Essay part	**Information**
Opening	
Body	Possible sources of facts, details – at least 2 Facts/details
Conclusion	

Name _____ Date _____

Lesson 30
READER'S NOTEBOOK

Get Lost! The Puzzle
of Mazes
Independent Reading

Reader's Guide

Get Lost! The Puzzle of Mazes

Write a Travel Guide

A travel guide is written as a short, handy source of information for travelers on the go. Because they are meant to be small and light, travel guides only give the most important information about popular landmarks and locations.

Reread page 67. What are three interesting details about the Silver Jubilee maze?

1. _____

2. _____

3. _____

What is the most important idea you can infer from these details that travelers would want to know about this maze?

_____

_____

Reread page 72. What are three details that visitors would want to know about cornstalk mazes in the United States?

1. _____

2. _____

What is one big idea you can infer about these details that you should tell visitors about this maze?

_____

_____

Name _____ Date _____

Lesson 30
READER'S NOTEBOOK

Get Lost! The Puzzle
of Mazes
Independent Reading

You are writing a travel guide to the mazes of England. Write the entries for the Longleat Hedge maze on page 68 and the Leeds Castle Maze on pages 69–70. Provide tourists with one important reason for visiting the maze, along with two or three highlights, or details about the maze.

Longleat Hedge Maze
Location: Wiltshire, England

Why you should visit: _____
_____

Highlights:

1. _____

2. _____

Leeds Castle Maze
Location: Kent, England

Why you should visit: _____
_____

Highlights:

1. _____

2. _____

3. _____

Lesson 30
READER'S NOTEBOOK

Get Lost! The Puzzle of Mazes
Spelling: Words from Other Languages

Words from Other Languages

Basic: Complete the puzzle by writing the Basic Word for each clue.

Spelling Words

Basic

1. ballet
2. echo
3. bouquet
4. cassette
5. coupon
6. safari
7. portrait
8. barrette
9. depot
10. courtesy
11. petite
12. denim
13. brunette
14. buffet
15. garage
16. khaki
17. crochet
18. chorus
19. essay
20. alphabet

Challenge

encore
collage
matinee
premiere
embarrass

Across

4. a painting of a person

7. a hair clip

8. a repeated sound

10. a trip for observing or hunting animals

Down

1. a person with brown or black hair

2. a small case that holds tape

3. small and slim

5. yellowish brown, heavy cloth

6. consideration

9. a large group of people who sing together

Challenge 11–12: Write a sentence that is about a play or musical at your school that you are curious to attend. Use two of the Challenge Words. Write on a separate sheet of paper.

Spelling Word Sort

Write each Basic Word next to the correct heading. Use a
dictionary to help you.

Words from French	**Basic Words:** **Challenge Words:**
Words from other languages	**Basic Words:**

Challenge: Add the Challenge Words to your Word Sort.

Spelling Words

Basic
1. ballet
2. echo
3. bouquet
4. cassette
5. coupon
6. safari
7. portrait
8. barrette
9. depot
10. courtesy
11. petite
12. denim
13. brunette
14. buffet
15. garage
16. khaki
17. crochet
18. chorus
19. essay
20. alphabet

Challenge
encore
collage
matinee
premiere
embarrass

Proofreading for Spelling

Find the misspelled words and circle them. Write them correctly on the lines below.

The girl was intensely curious about the world of balet. She asked her parents to enroll her in ballet school and traded her denum skirt for a tutu. Every week she went to the train depo to take the train to the city. One day she received a cupon for free admission to *Swan Lake*. Before the show, the coupon promised, she would enjoy a vast buffay meal, where food represented by every letter of the alphabette would await. Her mother had time to croche a shawl for her so she wouldn't get cold during the ballet. The girl was also able to buy a bouquay of roses to give to the dancers. Both of her parents drove her to the garrage next to the theater. The girl thanked them and decided she would write an informative essey about the world of ballet.

1. _____   6. _____
2. _____   7. _____
3. _____   8. _____
4. _____   9. _____
5. _____   10. _____

Spelling Words

Basic
1. ballet
2. echo
3. bouquet
4. cassette
5. coupon
6. safari
7. portrait
8. barrette
9. depot
10. courtesy
11. petite
12. denim
13. brunette
14. buffet
15. garage
16. khaki
17. crochet
18. chorus
19. essay
20. alphabet

Challenge
encore
collage
matinee
premiere
embarrass

Name _____ Date _____

Lesson 30
READER'S NOTEBOOK

Get Lost! The Puzzle
of Mazes
Grammar: Other Punctuation

Using Colons

Colons are used to	
set off a list that is formally introduced.	The following people will create a maze: Ellen, Sonja, and Devin.
separate hours and minutes.	We will have a planning meeting today at 2:45 p.m.
follow the greeting in a business letter.	Dear Ms. Garcia:

Thinking Question
Does the sentence include a list, hours and minutes, or the greeting in a business letter?

Add colons where they are needed in the sentences.

1. Ms. Liakos will give a talk on ancient mazes at 730 p.m.

2. She will need the following equipment a projector, a table, and a screen.

3. Dear Ms. Liakos
   We are interested in mazes and would like to invite you to give a talk to Jefferson School's Art Club.

4. Explain the meaning of the following terms *maze, riddle,* and *quiz.*

5. The A-Mazing Adventure maze opens at 800 a.m. and closes at 700 p.m.

6. Dear Editor
   Students at Arborside Junior High School are curious to know if there are any people in town who could teach them about challenging games and puzzles.

Lesson 30
READER'S NOTEBOOK

Get Lost! The Puzzle of Mazes
Grammar: Other Punctuation

Using Parentheses

Use **parentheses ( )** to set off information that interrupts a sentence and is not of major importance to the sentence.

*A labyrinth (**sometimes called a unicursal maze**) has a single path that winds in toward the center.*

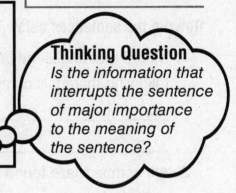

Thinking Question
Is the information that interrupts the sentence of major importance to the meaning of the sentence?

Rewrite each sentence. Add parentheses where they are needed.

1. Creating a hedge maze they are very popular requires careful measurement and planning.

   _____

   _____

2. Yew trees make good maze borders borders are important for outdoor mazes because they grow slowly and keep their shape.

   _____

   _____

   _____

3. Some outdoor mazes the better designed ones have tunnels and bridges to keep people interested as they go through.

   _____

   _____

4. A weave maze the kind Marsha is most curious about has pathways that go under and over each other.

   _____

   _____

Name _____ Date _____

Lesson 30
READER'S NOTEBOOK

Get Lost! The Puzzle
of Mazes
Grammar: Other Punctuation

Other Punctuation

Rewrite the sentences below, using correct punctuation where needed.

1. Mazes that challenge people to solve them can be made from the
   following materials corn yew or stone.

   _____

   _____

2. Ashcombe Maze found near Melbourne is the oldest and largest
   maze in Australia.

   _____

   _____

3. You can find any of the following mazes in England multicursal
   mazes weave mazes and logic mazes.

   _____

   _____

4. According to myth, King Minos who was from Crete asked Daedalus
   to build the Labyrinth to hide the Minotaur.

   _____

   _____

5. A well-known circular maze a challenging type of maze can be found
   in Touraine, France.

   _____

   _____

Name _____ Date _____

Lesson 30
READER'S NOTEBOOK

Get Lost! The Puzzle
of Mazes
Grammar: Spiral Review

Proper Mechanics

Titles require proper capitalization. In handwritten work, titles of longer works such as books, movies, and plays, should be underlined. In papers written on the computer, these types of titles should be in italics.

> My favorite book of puzzles is <u>Amazing Mazes</u> because it helps me learn how to solve problems.
>
> My favorite book of puzzles is *Amazing Mazes* because it helps me learn how to solve problems.

Titles of shorter works, such as stories, poems, and songs, should appear inside quotation marks in both written and typed work.

> Anya's poem, "A Turning Path," was published in the school paper.

1–4 Rewrite the sentences to correctly represent the titles.

1. She won the lead role in Shakespeare's Romeo and juliet.

_____

_____

2. The nature trail reminded me of the yellow brick road from the movie, The wizard of Oz.

_____

_____

3. We finished all of the mazes in The Big book of Puzzles and mazes.

_____

_____

4. The concertmaster led everyone in singing The Long and winding Road.

_____

_____

Name _____ Date _____

Lesson 30
READER'S NOTEBOOK

Get Lost! The Puzzle of Mazes
Grammar: Connect to Writing

Conventions

Confusing Sentence with Punctuation Errors	Clear Sentence with Correct Punctuation
Kara studied the following subjects science the one she was most curious about, art, and history.	Kara studied the following subjects: science (the one she was most curious about), art, and history.

Using proofreading marks, correct the errors in each sentence. Then write the sentence correctly.

1. Roman labyrinths have been found in the following countries Italy, Egypt, Syria, and England.

   _____

   _____

2. The following rulers built complex mazes Amenemhat III of Egypt, King Minos of Crete, and King Louis XIV of France.

   _____

   _____

3. Challenging trivia games Tim's favorite type of puzzle are difficult to find.

   _____

   _____

4. Kim studied for nearly three months the history of ancient games to learn about techniques people used to solve puzzles in the past.

   _____

   _____

Lesson 30
READER'S NOTEBOOK

**Get Lost! The Puzzle
of Mazes**
Writing: Ideas

Focus Trait: Ideas

When writing to inform, good writers begin with a topic, or an interesting focus. They use main ideas to expand upon the topic.

Review "Get Lost! The Puzzle of Mazes" to identify main ideas. Record ideas from selected pages in the the chart below.

"Get Lost! The Puzzle of Mazes"	
Focus:	
Page Number	**Idea**
67	
68	
69	
71	
72	

Pair/Share Work with a partner to compare your lists of main ideas from the chart. Write a sentence below about how the ideas you listed connect to the topic of "Get Lost! A Puzzle of Mazes."

_____

_____

_____

Reading and Writing Glossary

Use this glossary to help you remember and use words that you are learning about reading and writing.

A

abbreviation A shortened form of a word.

account A report of something that happened.

acronym A name made from initials that can be read as a word.

action verb A verb that tells what the subject does, did, or will do.

adage A traditional expression that has proven to be true over time.

adjective A word that describes a noun.

adventure story A story that includes exciting action that may take place in an unusual setting.

adverb A word that describes a verb, adjective, or other adverb.

affix A prefix or a suffix attached to a base word, stem, or root that changes the word's meaning.

alliteration Repeating consonant sounds at the beginning of words.

analogy A kind of comparison in which one pair of words is compared to another.

analyze To look at or study something carefully.

animal characters Animals that have human traits and characteristics.

antecedent The noun or nouns that the pronoun replaces and refers back to.

antonym A word that has the opposite, or very different, meaning as another word.

apostrophe Mark of punctuation.

appositive A noun, noun phrase, or series of nouns placed next to another word or phrase to identify or rename it, which is set off by commas.

attitude A point of view or feeling about something.

author's purpose An author's reasons for writing.

autobiography An account of a person's life told by that person.

B

base word A word to which prefixes and suffixes are added.

behavior The way a character acts.

biography An account of a person's life told by someone else.

body The part of an extended piece of writing that contains most of the details and content; it falls between the beginning and ending of a text.

C

....

caption Information that explains more about a photograph or illustration.

cause An event that makes another event happen.

cause-and-effect relationship Related events in which one event causes another to occur, sometimes setting off a chain of events.

character A person or animal in a story.

characterization How a character is described by an author.

chart Drawing that organizes information in a simple, clear way.

claim A statement or declaration.

closing The ending part of a letter, just before the signature.

collective noun Names a group of people, animals, or things that act as a unit.

colon A punctuation mark that introduces a list, separates hours and minutes, or follows the greeting in a business letter.

comma Mark of punctuation used to separate elements in a sentence.

common noun A general person, place, or thing.

common saying A well-known expression, such as a motto.

comparative adjective An adjective used in a comparison of two people, places, or things.

comparative adverb Formed by putting *more* in front of an adverb and used to compare two people, places, or things.

compare and contrast To find similarities and differences.

complete predicate All the words telling what the subject is or does.

complete subject All the words telling whom or what a sentence is about.

complex sentence A sentence containing a dependent and an independent clause joined by a subordinating conjunction.

compound direct object The words that receive the action of the same verb.

compound sentence Two sentences joined by a comma and a conjunction such as *and, or,* or *but.*

concluding statement The final paragraph of an essay, in which the writer sums up his or her main points.

conclusion A reasonable guess about ideas that are not stated in the text, based on text details and the reader's own experiences.

concrete words Words that name things you can see, hear, touch, taste, or feel.

conflict The struggle or problem that a character tries to solve.

conjunction A word such as *and, or,* or *but* that connects other words in a sentence.

context Words and sentences around a word that give readers clues to its meaning.

contraction Joins two small words.

contradictory Expresses opposite ideas.

coordinating conjunction A conjunction that joins two words, groups of words, or sentences.

correlative conjunctions A pair of conjunctions that joins parallel words or phrases.

D

declarative sentence A sentence that tells something and ends with a period.

definition The meaning of a word or phrase.

descriptions Impressions of people, places, or events.

diagram Drawing that shows how something works.

dialect A variety of language spoken in a particular place or time period by a particular group of people.

dialogue Conversation between characters in a story.

dictionary A source that contains information on the pronunciations and meanings of words.

dictionary entry The definitions, part of speech, origin, pronunciation, and spelling of the entry word.

digital dictionary A dictionary that can be accessed on a computer or other electronic device.

direct object The word that receives the action of the verb.

distinguish To tell one thing apart from another.

document A piece of writing that gives information.

domain-specific words Vocabulary commonly used in a particular subject area.

E

editorial Writing that conveys the writer's opinion about a current issue or news story.

effect What happens as a result of a cause.

evidence Facts or examples that support an opinion.

exclamatory sentence A sentence that expresses strong feeling and ends with an exclamation point.

explanation A statement that uses details to make information clear.

eyewitness Someone who saw an event happen.

F

fact A statement that can be proved true.

fairy tale A story with magical elements and characters.

fictional narrative An imaginative story in which characters solve a problem.

figurative language Words that express ideas that are not literally, or actually, true.

first-person point of view One person tells the story as "I."

flashback A description of past events that interrupts the story's main action.

follow-up question A question that builds on a question or answer that has already been presented.

formal language Includes precise language and complete sentences; does not include slang expressions.

fragment A group of words that does not express a complete thought; not a sentence.

frequency Tells how often.

future perfect tense Includes *will have* as a helping verb.

future tense Verb form that describes an action that will happen in the future.

G

generalization A broad statement that is usually true.

genre A type of writing, such as poetry, fiction, nonfiction, or drama.

glossary An appendix that includes meanings or words found in a text.

glossary entry Information on the words in a specific text, such as a school book, including the definition, pronunciation, and location in the text.

graph A visual representation of numerical information.

graphic features Photographs or drawings, such as maps or charts, that stand for ideas or add to details in a text.

Greek root A word part that comes from Greek and has meaning but cannot stand alone.

H

helping verb A verb that adds details to the main verb.

historical events Important events from the past.

historical fiction A story set in the past that contains characters, places, and events that may or may not have existed or happened in real life.

homograph A word that is spelled the same as another word but has a different origin and meaning and may have a different pronunciation.

homophone A word that is pronounced the same as another word but that has a different spelling and meaning.

humorous fiction A story that is written to entertain and has funny or unusual characters and events.

hyperbole An exaggeration used for dramatic effect.

I

idiom An expression that has a meaning different from the literal meaning of the words.

imagery The use of sensory words and vivid details to create images in readers' minds.

imperative sentence A sentence that gives an order and ends with a period.

implied Suggested rather than stated directly.

indefinite pronoun Pronoun that refers to a person or thing that is not identified.

indirect object Word that tells to or for whom or what the action is done.

infer To figure out something that is not stated directly.

inference Things figured out from indirect evidence.

informal language A more relaxed form of speaking and writing that includes slang expressions and incomplete sentences.

informational essay An essay that informs readers about a particular topic.

informational text Text that gives facts and examples about a topic.

informative writing Writing that gives facts about a topic.

initials The first letter of each important word.

intensity Tells how much.

interjection A word or words used to express a feeling or emotion.

interrogative pronoun Pronoun that begins a question.

interrogative sentence A sentence that asks something and ends with a question mark.

interview Text that uses a question-and-answer format to give information in a person's own words.

introductory word/phrase A word or phrase that comes before the comma in a sentence.

irony An outcome that is the opposite of what is expected.

irregular verb Verb that forms the past tense by changing a vowel; some forms need to be memorized.

italic A type style in which words slant to the right.

J

journal Type of writing in which a person regularly records his or her thoughts, feelings, and observations.

L

Latin root A word part that comes from Latin and has meaning but cannot stand alone.

linking verb A verb that connects the subject of a sentence to information about it.

logical order A way of arranging ideas so that they make sense.

M

main character The most important person, animal, or imaginary creature taking part in a story's action.

main idea The major point an author wants readers to understand.

main verb The verb in a sentence that tells the most important action, state, or condition in a sentence.

map Drawing of an area, such as a city or a state.

metaphor A comparison between two unlike things that does not use *like* or *as*.

misleading Intends to deceive the reader.

moral A lesson that teaches people how they should behave.

motivation Reason why a character acts a certain way.

multiple-meaning word A word that has more than one possible meaning.

myth A story that tells what a group of people believes about the world or an aspect of the world.

N

narrative A story.

narrative nonfiction Text that tells about real people, things, events, or places.

narrative writing Writing that tells a story. A narrative tells about something that happened to a person or a character.

negative A word that means "no."

O

object pronoun A word that takes the place of a noun that is used after a verb or preposition.

off-stage A stage direction referring to something happening off the stage, where the audience cannot see.

onomatopoeia Words that sound like their meaning.

opening statement Identifies the subject of an essay.

opinion A person's position or belief about a topic.

opinion writing Writing that tells what the writer believes and gives reasons.

P

....

pacing The rhythm or speed of a narrative.

paraphrase To restate an idea in one's own words.

parentheses Punctuation marks that come before and after a word or phrase that is inserted into a sentence but is not essential to the meaning of the sentence.

part of speech The way a word is used in a sentence.

past perfect tense Includes *had* as a helping verb.

past tense Verb form that describes an action that happened in the past.

perfect tense A group of verb tenses with *has, have,* or *had* as a helping verb.

personal narrative A story in which the writer expresses his or her own experiences, thoughts, or feelings.

persuade To convince a person or organization to think or act in a certain way.

persuasive techniques Techniques used by an author to try to convince readers to think or act in a certain way; may include strong wording, catch phrases, promises, or emotional appeals.

persuasive text Text that seeks to convince the reader to think or act in a certain way.

plagiarism Passing off someone else's work or ideas as one's own.

play A story that can be performed for an audience.

plot The events in a story, including a problem and a solution.

plural noun Names more than one person, place, or thing.

plural possessive noun Noun that shows ownership by more than one person or thing.

poetry Uses the sound and rhythm of words to suggest images and express feelings in a variety of forms.

point of view The perspective or view from which a story is told.

political document An informational text about a nation's history or laws, such as the Constitution or Bill of Rights.

position A point of view or belief about something.

possessive pronoun Pronoun that shows ownership.

predict To figure out what might happen in the future.

prefix An affix attached to the beginning of a base word or word root that changes the word's meaning.

preposition A word that shows relationships of location, time, or direction.

prepositional phrase Begins with a preposition and ends with a noun or pronoun; adds detail.

present perfect tense Includes *has* or *have* as a helping verb.

present tense Verb form that describes an action happening now or that happens over and over.

primary source An original document, photograph, or artifact.

procedural composition Text that describes a process or a series of events or steps.

pronoun A word that takes the place of a noun.

pronunciation The way a word is said aloud.

proper noun A particular person, place, or thing.

proverb A saying that expresses common-sense wisdom in simple language.

purpose A goal, intent, or reason for doing something.

Q

question To ask oneself questions about a selection before, during, and after reading.

quotation The exact words spoken or written by someone.

quotation marks Punctuation marks at the beginning and end of a quotation.

R

realistic fiction A type of story that includes characters and events that are like people and events in real life.

reasons The explanation for why readers should think or act in a certain way.

reference materials Sources, either print or digital, that contain facts and information on a wide range of subjects.

regular verb Verb that adds *-ed* or *-d* to its present tense to show action that happened in the past; may use helping verbs *has, have, had*.

repetition Repeating of a sound, word, phrase, line, or stanza.

research report Writing that tells what a writer learned from doing research about a topic.

resolution The solution to a problem.

response essay Writing that involves stating an opinion about a topic.

rhyme scheme The pattern created by rhyming words.

rhythm The pattern or beat created by the number and syllables in a line.

root The base, or building block, of a word.

S

....

salutation A word of greeting to begin a letter.

scene A section of a play.

science fiction A story based on scientific ideas and that is often set in the future.

scientific ideas Concepts or principles that relate to science.

semicolon Mark of punctuation used to link or separate parts of a sentence.

sensory details Details that appeal to the five senses and create a picture through writing.

sensory language Words and phrases that appeal to the five senses.

sentence A group of words expressing a complete thought.

sequence The order in which events happen.

series A list of three or more items written in the same form.

setting The time and place in which a story occurs.

simile A comparison between two unlike things using *like* or *as*.

simple predicate The main word that tells what the subject is or does.

simple subject The main word that tells whom or what the sentence is about.

singular noun Names one person, place, or thing.

singular possessive noun Noun that shows ownership by one person or thing.

source Anything that supplies information.

source list The names of all the resources from which information is taken for a report.

stage directions Text in a play that tells actors how to act and helps readers picture the action.

story structure The basic parts of a story's plot.

subject pronoun A word that takes the place of a noun and is used as the subject of a sentence.

subject-verb agreement A rule stating that subjects and verbs must be both singular or both plural.

subjective Based on personal thoughts or beliefs.

subordinating conjunction A conjunction that combines two clauses into a complex sentence.

suffix An affix that is added to the end of a word and that changes the meaning of the word.

summarize To retell the main ideas of a text.

summary The main ideas of a text, retold in one's own words.

superlative adjective An adjective used in a comparison of more than two people, places, or things.

superlative adverb Formed by putting *most* in front of an adverb and used to compare more than two people, places, or things.

supporting details Facts, examples, descriptions, and other evidence used to develop and expand on a main idea.

synonym A word that has a similar meaning as another word.

T

technical text Text that includes facts and domain-specific words and phrases that provide readers with a deeper understanding of a topic.

text and graphic features Elements, such as headings and illustrations, that organize and support or add information to a text.

text evidence Details in the selection that support an inference.

text features Parts of the text, such as titles, headings, or special type.

text structure The way an author organizes ideas and information in a text.

theme The central message or idea.

thesaurus A reference source that lists related words, usually in the form of synonyms and antonyms.

third-person limited point of view A narrator tells the story using "he," "she," or "they."

timeline A line that shows the sequence of important events in a specific time span.

title The name of a book or other creative work.

tone A writer's particular attitude toward a subject.

topic The subject of a text.

topic sentence The sentence that clearly states the main idea of a paragraph.

traits Ways of speaking and acting that show what a character is like.

transition A word, phrase, or clause that shows readers how one idea is linked to another.

V

variable Something that changes.

verb tense A verb form that shows time, sequence, state, or condition.

visuals Illustrations, charts, and other graphics that enhance a text.

voice An author's style, which reveals his or her personality and feelings.

W

word origin The language or region in which a word originated.

word root A part of a word that has meaning but cannot always stand alone and to which prefixes and suffixes are added.

X

x-axis Horizontal line that charts one of the variables in a graph.

Y

y-axis Vertical line that charts one of the variables in a graph.